MW01093523

On Interrogation, Introspection, Dialectic and the Ineluctable Polarity of Being and Knowing

READING AUGUSTINE

Series Editor
Miles Hollingworth

In collaboration with the Wessel-Hollingworth Foundation
Reading Augustine presents books that offer personal, nuanced
and oftentimes literary readings of Saint Augustine of Hippo. Each
time, the idea is to treat Augustine as a spiritual and intellectual
icon of the Western tradition, and to read through him to some
or other pressing concern of our current day, or to some enduring
issue or theme. In this way, the writers follow the model of
Augustine himself, who produced his famous output of words and
ideas in active tussle with the world in which he lived. When the
series launched, this approach could raise eyebrows, but now that
technology and pandemics have brought us into the world and
society like never before, and when scholarship is expected to live
the same way and responsibly, the series is well-set and thriving.

Recent volumes in the series
*On Distance, Belonging, Isolation and the Quarantined
Church of Today*, Pablo Irizar
On Images, Visual Culture, Memory and the Play without a Script,
Matthias Smalbrugge
On Signs, Christ, Truth and the Interpretation of Scripture,
Susannah Ticciati
*On Christology, Anthropology, Cognitive Science and \)e
Human Body*, Martin Claes
On The Confessions as 'confessio', Barry \. David
*On Regular Life, Freedom, Modernity, \u Augustinian
Communitarianism*, Guille\\\o M. Jodra
*On Hellenism, Judaism, Individ\\\sm, and Early Christian
Theories of the Subi*, Guillermo M. Jodra
On the Nature, Lin\\\, Meaning, and End of Work,
Z\\\ary Thomas Settle

On Interrogation, Introspection, Dialectic and the Ineluctable Polarity of Being and Knowing

Matthew W. Knotts

BLOOMSBURY ACADEMIC
LONDON • NEW YORK • OXFORD • NEW DELHI • SYDNEY

BLOOMSBURY ACADEMIC
Bloomsbury Publishing Plc
50 Bedford Square, London, WC1B 3DP, UK
1385 Broadway, New York, NY 10018, USA
29 Earlsfort Terrace, Dublin 2, Ireland

BLOOMSBURY, BLOOMSBURY ACADEMIC and the Diana logo are
trademarks of Bloomsbury Publishing Plc

First published in Great Britain 2024

A catalogue record for this book is available from the British Library.

A catalog record for this book is available from the Library of Congress.

ISBN: HB: 978-1-3502-6302-4
        PB: 978-1-3502-6303-1
        ePDF: 978-1-3502-6301-7
        eBook: 978-1-3502-6305-5

Series: Reading Augustine

Typeset by Integra Software Services Pvt. Ltd.
Printed and bound in Great Britain

To find out more about our authors and books visit www.bloomsbury.com
and sign up for our newsletters.

To my father, Harold Lee Knotts, Jr (1961–2021)
Requiescat in pace cum sanctis.

CONTENTS

ACKNOWLEDGEMENTS

I would like to thank my parents, Harold and Patricia, for their unwavering and essential assistance. I also thank Miles Hollingworth, the Editor of this fine series, for his support and patience.

Gratitude is also due to Christoph Müller and Christian Tornau, who helped me extensively in the framing and development of this project.

I also thank my colleagues and the students at Loyola Academy for their encouragement and support.

I am very grateful to Rev Dr hab Marcin Wysocki and *Vox Patrum* for permission to republish portions of the following article:

'God and Self in *Confessiones* IV and Beyond: *Therapeia*, Self-Presence, and Ontological Contingency in Augustine, Seneca, and Heidegger'. *Vox Patrum* 82 (15 June 2022): 113–44.

https://doi.org/10.31743/vp.12725.

I am also very grateful to Rev Dr Jonathan Farrugia for allowing me to republish portions of the following contribution:

'In Search of the Augustinian *Imago Dei*: The "Nothingness" of the Human Person'. In Non Laborat Qui Amat, edited by A. P. DeBattista, J. Farrugia and H. Scerri, 159–71. Valletta, Malta: Maltese Augustinian Province, 2020.

ABBREVIATIONS

Works by Augustine

Ciu.	*De Ciuitate Dei*
Conf.	*Confessiones*
Doctr. Chr.	*De Doctrina Christiana*
En. Ps.	*Enarrationes in Psalmos*
Ep./Epp.	*Epistola/Epistolae*
Gn. Litt.	*De Genesi ad Litteram*
Io. Eu. Tr.	*In Ioannem Euangelium Tractatus*
Lib. Arb.	*De Libero Arbitrio*
Mag.	*De Magistro*
S./Ss.	*Sermo/Sermones*
Sol.	*Soliloquia*
Trin.	*De Trinitate*

Editions of Augustine's Works

CCL	Corpus Christianorum Series Latina
CSEL	Corpus Scriptorum Ecclesiasticorum Latinorum
PL	Patrologia Latina

Seneca

Ep./Epp.	*Epistola/Epistolae*
Quaest. Nat.	*Quaestiones Naturales*

Marcus Aurelius

Med.	*Meditations*

General Introduction

In a sense, this book arises from a remark in a magisterial article by Lope Cilleruelo, in which Augustine is described as a 'Christian Heraclitus' ('un Heráclito cristiano').[1] When I first read this several years ago, I thought little of it, viewing it as related to the fact that both sources were attentive to the constant flow of time. Since then, however, it has occurred to me that Cilleruelo's curious sobriquet may contain a richer significance. After further research, this intuition has been confirmed. In the following pages, I discuss the continuities between these figures and establish an initial dialogue between them.

However, this work is oriented towards a distinct question, albeit one which was fundamental to the thought of both Heraclitus and Augustine. It concerns what it means to be human in the anthropological sense and what it means to be oneself in a deeply personal sense. One often speaks for instance of finding oneself, deciphering one's identity, becoming one's best self. A more careful consideration of these quotidian locutions leads to puzzling questions. How is it possible for one not to be (with) oneself? Where could one go to find oneself? Would this self be identical with the searcher? If so, how to distinguish between the searcher and the sought? If not, then how can one say that that which is discovered is truly one's self?

With the advances of the empirical sciences, one can articulate this challenge in biochemical terms. Commenting on the work of Steven Grand, Richard Dawkins states that humans are better described as 'waves' than determinate objects.[2] One thinks of oneself as a continuously existing entity, yet from a biological perspective, this apparently self-evident intuition is far from obvious.[3] He notes how one's current body contains none of the material constituents from one's childhood. One both is and is not oneself.[4] Grand illustrates this point in the following way:

> [Think of] an experience from your childhood. Something you remember clearly, something you can see, feel, maybe even smell, as if you were really there. After all, you really were there at the time, weren't you? How else would you remember it? But here is the bombshell: you *weren't* there. Not a single atom that is in your body today was there when that event took place. ... Matter flows from place to place and momentarily comes together to be you. Whatever you are, therefore, you are not the stuff of which you are made. If that doesn't make the hair stand up on the back of your neck, read it again until it does, because it is important.[5]

Grand's example would be music to the ears of David Hume, who observed that when he looked within, he did not find a particular self, but rather a series of impressions.[6] Something as apparently self-evident as one's continuous identity, when analysed from a critical perspective, seems to vanish.

The perplexing observations just described were anticipated millennia ago by Heraclitus of Ephesus, who famously said that we are and are not, compared human beings to rivers, recognized the constant flux of the world and claimed that he went in search of himself, yet also boldly declared that one will never find the limits of the soul. Heraclitus' method is remarkably simple: He calls upon his audience to think more carefully about common experience and realize in it something truly paradoxical. Then one interrogates it further, allowing the mystery to unfold. These reasons – Heraclitus' recognition of the conundrum of human identity, his philosophical treatment of this topic and the accessibility of his methodology – motivate the investigation of Heraclitus with respect to philosophical anthropology.

This research can also intervene in the broader controversies related to the major philosophical and historical dispensations. The literature is replete with trenchant criticisms of the Cartesian subject. Nonetheless, as Bernard Williams observes, the subject versus object distinction seems to be an unavoidable part of our experience and is perhaps even required to make sense of a significant portion of it.[7] However, as Grand's example demonstrates, one must take seriously the seeming impermanence of the human being. This psychological and philosophical insight has been radicalized in our contemporary world. Jeffrey Pugh looks to Proteus, who frequently changed forms, as an image for our society, in which one has the ability to construct multiple identities, especially through social media.[8] Furthermore, one is constantly bombarded by multifarious life options and cultural ideas, leading to a sense of fragmentation, or what Kenneth Gergen has called the 'multiphrenic self'.[9] As Pugh writes, the result is that 'we lose all sense of what an authentic self might look like, indeed whether such a thing even exists'.[10]

The importance of this question also extends to ethics. As Ingolf Dalferth indicates, there is no contemporary consensus on what it means to be human. However, this lack of agreement extends to the earliest days of philosophy. Nonetheless, it remains a pressing question, as we cannot know how to live if we do not know what (or who) we are.[11] As Alasdair MacIntyre observes in *After Virtue*, any ethical theory is situated within a broader theoretical context, which includes a conception of the human person.[12]

One reason for researching Heraclitus and Augustine is that they and their respective cultures had no fundamental problem accepting some of the oppositions that have troubled us in the aftermath of Enlightenment, such as the division between the interior human being and the exterior world. Nevertheless, they could respect the tensions and paradoxes raised by such contrary realities. Thus it seems to me that the task that lies before us is simultaneously easy and difficult. On the one hand, classical sources provide a wealth of insight into how to think about human selfhood in the midst of otherness. On the other hand, we cannot and must not ignore the monumental advances in knowledge which have occurred since antiquity. Negotiating this challenge is a key theme implicit in this research.

Despite the deficiencies of a Modern anthropology, no clear alternative has yet emerged. This book is a step towards articulating such an alternative. This research is also intended to contribute specifically to scholarship on Augustine's theological anthropology. Although this literature is extensive, many open questions remain. Some recent research has called greater attention to the enigmatic and abyssal quality of Augustinian interiority. 'It is time,' writes David Tracy, 'to rethink the complete Augustinian overdetermined portrait of the self'.[13] My research makes a contribution to this pressing task.

Furthermore, I concur with Tina Beattie's response to Grand's example. She claims that if theology *qua* theology can give a compelling account of this paradoxical fact of human existence, it should be permitted to do so.[14] As Beattie writes, 'this vision of a continuity of memory and experience which transcends the body's flux and impermanence might legitimately look to theology for an explanation'.[15] In a 2017 article in *Philosophy & Theology*, I have argued for the possibility of a similar methodology. That is, one should take into consideration the explanatory capacity of a variety of theories and, if a theological perspective provides a compelling account, it should not be excluded simply because it is theological.

My argument proceeds in the following way. In the first chapter, I consider Heraclitus and his understanding of the oppositional – that is, dialectical – structure of the cosmos. The universe is like a harmony generated by oppositions in relationship with one another. He draws upon various examples taken from ordinary life to support his position. One result of Heraclitus' philosophy is the understanding that, given one's essential relationship to the ineffable *logos*, the search for oneself will never be complete. Heraclitus calls his audience to continuous self-enquiry, which is inseparable from knowledge of the divine. In the next chapter, I discuss how Augustine can be reasonably connected with Heraclitus. In addition to various historical and theoretical commonalities, I note that both of them committed themselves to obedience to the Delphic imperative to know oneself.

The next two chapters focus on Augustine. Chapter 3 concerns Augustine's understanding of the dialectical constitution of the human person in the first sense. Created according to God's image, one cannot understand oneself apart from the constitutive presence of God. Yet God is beyond all comprehension and understanding. How, therefore, can one meaningfully pursue knowledge of oneself? The next chapter addresses this question, which simultaneously addresses the second sense of dialectical constitution, how one seeks to construct one's identity through dialogue. We shall see that Augustine builds upon the classical dialogue genre while innovating to fit the needs of his own introspective programme. He ultimately arrives at *confessio*, the dialogue with God, as the normative means for pursuing self-integration.

The consideration of the self's identity reveals at least as much obscurity as it does clarity. As one searches for God and the soul, one is confronted with ever greater uncertainty. This exploration opens one to the *abyss*, the nothingness and groundlessness implicit in human life, most clearly seen in the reality of death, which lies at the periphery of the conditions of human understanding. The introspective endeavour leads one inexorably into this dark valley. However, it is precisely in and through the methods of introspection that one can address the unsettling reality of one's nothingness. This aspect of self-enquiry pertains to the conception of classical philosophy as a form of therapy which, in some respects, anticipates contemporary psychology. Thus this work concludes with some thoughts on how the philosophical-theological investigation of the dialectically constituted self could contribute to a dialogue with psychology.

The title of this work – *On Interrogation, Introspection, Dialectic and the Ineluctable Polarity of Being and Knowing* – represents, I contend, a synopsis of the thought of both Heraclitus and Augustine on what it means to be human. One begins from the *interrogation* of one's experience of the world. Heraclitus urged one to be attentive to the puzzles of being hidden in plain sight, such as the existence of fire or the nature of rivers. For Augustine, his interrogation of creation forced him back on himself. Through *introspection*, he arrived at the realization of how otherness – especially divine Otherness – is constitutive of his being, hence his *dialectical* constitution. This insight resulted from his use of dialogical methods and was continuously supported by them. As for Heraclitus, his interest lay not in the external world but in the internal. His introspective programme was informed by his understanding of the cosmos as a unity produced from opposing forces in perpetual tension. To do justice to reality, both opposites – both poles – had to be maintained together, not collapsed into each other. According to Augustine, the paradox of opposition is revealed most clearly in God, who is present everywhere yet confined to no place, who remains ever above yet is more interior to one than one is to oneself. Both of these figures in their own ways conclude that *polarity* is fundamental to the world, and thus reflected in *human being and knowing*.

These ideas also flout what appears to be common sense and the rules of rational thought, not least of all the principle of non-contradiction. However, I argue that Heraclitus and Augustine are challenging our perspective, calling us beyond the apparent opposition. These are not primarily esoteric philosophical theories but positions demanded by a careful reflection on universally available human experience. When we begin from this level, we are inexorably led along a vertiginous ascent beyond binary categories. It seems that we must say that we are both one and many, that we both are and are not ourselves. We are compelled to contradict ourselves. Heraclitus shows us how this is possible.

'Dialectical' is a word one often encounters in psychology, philosophy and even theology. Given its centrality to my argument, I should clarify the two distinct if related senses in which I use it. The first sense of dialectic pertains to how apparent oppositions can be brought together in unity. One finds this sense of 'dialectical' in psychology – as in dialectical behaviour therapy (DBT) – as well as in Continental philosophy (notably Hegel).[16] The second sense focuses on the methodological aspect of dialectic. This concerns how two contrary positions are brought together and resolved into a single point, which can then be confronted by another counterpoint.[17] This exchange can be extended indefinitely.[18] Furthermore, this sense of dialectic relates to dialogue, insofar as a verbal exchange is the vehicle for this process.

I argue that human being is best conceived as *dialectically constituted* in these two senses. First, one is composed essentially of that which one is *not*. Put differently, otherness is a *constitutive* aspect of the human person. Secondly, to appropriate and more fully realize one's identity, one must engage in a method which can be broadly described as dialogical. As we shall see, dialogue can take a variety of forms, some of which were Augustine's own unique invention for the purposes of self-enquiry. Indeed, in antiquity, one envisioned an essential connection between introspection and dialogue.[19] Moreover, the dialectical method becomes especially important in light of Heraclitus and Augustine's understandings of human being not merely as dialectical, but as somehow constituted by the ultimate, divine Other, the *logos* for Heraclitus and the *imago Dei* for Augustine. Therefore, I speak of their respective conceptions of the constitution of the human person as 'log-ical' and 'theo-log-ical'.

A further qualification is in order concerning terminology. I employ a plethora of words – for example, self, soul, subject, human being, human person, *psyche* – more or less interchangeably. Such imprecision can certainly be problematic, as will become clear for example when we see the difficulties raised by the uncritical use of the phrase 'the self' in Augustinian scholarship, as Cavadini has noted. An even more complicated challenge concerns the various senses of such words in their original contexts and the concepts they encapsulate. One may also worry about the correspondence between certain terms across time, cultures, languages, etc. That being said, I have followed other scholars in using this range of terms. Perhaps such questions of terminology would be an excellent topic of further research, but this is not the place to undertake it.

1

Ephesian Resonances

Background

Heraclitus' biographical information

Heraclitus, acknowledged as one of the earliest Greek philosophers, came from Ephesus, located on the west coast of present-day Turkey.[1] The main source for his biography is Diogenes Laërtius (fl. third century CE), who in turn relied on Heraclitus' own work, which was a customary practise in the former's time.[2] According to contemporary scholarship, Heraclitus' dates are rather precise. By the time of the sixty-ninth Olympiad, Heraclitus had reached his *acmê*, or fortieth birthday, which would fall between 504/503 BCE and 501/500 BCE.[3] Heraclitus died at the age of sixty-three, which would place his dates from *c.* 544/541 BCE to 484/481 BCE. Thus he was active from the late sixth century to the early fifth century BCE.[4]

Heraclitus was born into an aristocratic (if not royal) family.[5] According to A. Finkelberg, Heraclitus' family lineage can be traced to Androclus, son of the Athenian king Codrus, who founded Ephesus and administered the colony of Ionia.[6] Heraclitus' corpus displays similarities with elements of the mystery religions (Eleusinian and Orphic) and the style of Apollo's oracle at Delphi.[7] Given his lineage, Heraclitus was heir to the priesthood at Eleusis. He visited Athens annually, and during these travels likely visited Delphi as well.[8] As we shall see presently, the relationship between Heraclitus and religion is important for the evaluation of both the style and the content of his texts.

Questions of reception and interpretation

Laërtius informs us that Heraclitus composed a book, entitled *On Nature*, which he dedicated to the Temple of Artemis, where it was available for public consultation.[9] Beginning in the early fifth century, this work was widely circulated throughout the Greek world.[10] Both the style and the content of Heraclitus' writing appear in authors of the fifth century and subsequently in Plato.[11] The knowledge and reception of Heraclitus remained prominent throughout antiquity, even into the early centuries of the Common Era.[12] For example, Plutarch (*c*. 46 CE–119 CE) owned a copy of Heraclitus' book.[13] Finkelberg suggests further evidence for Heraclitus' profound influence in antiquity, considering that the latter's book was the *only* prose work subjected to critical exegetical study in the ancient world.[14]

Despite the extensive knowledge of Heraclitus, the correct interpretation of his philosophy was and remains a vexed question.[15] Already in antiquity, Heraclitus had acquired a reputation for esotericism. Cicero (106 BCE to 43 BCE) for example claimed that Heraclitus was deliberately obscure.[16] Laërtius writes that Heraclitus opted to express his ideas in an arcane style so that the less worthy could not attain to the secrets of being without moral and intellectual purification.[17] Other ancient commentators, such as Timon (*c*. 320 BCE to 230 BCE) and Lucretius (fl. first century BCE), rather than identifying in Heraclitus' style a sense of nobility, criticized and dismissed his writing for its obscurity, even associating it with the Ephesian's apparent hubris.[18]

Though the correct interpretation of Heraclitus remains a pressing challenge in the literature,[19] one may question the extent to which Heraclitus' work is hopelessly enigmatic.[20] (Indeed, the wide reception of Heraclitus' work belies its supposed impenetrability.[21]) According to Finkelberg, one of the reasons for the attribution of obscurity to Heraclitus has to do with the changing nature of philosophical discourse beginning in the fourth century. This led to Heraclitus being interpreted as a natural philosopher.[22] However, even in antiquity, Diodotus had noted that Heraclitus' interest did not lie in nature as such, but rather the extent to which examples drawn from one's experience of the world illustrated deeper philosophical truths.[23] Heraclitus' work did not conform to the expectations associated with natural philosophy, thus leading to incomprehension.[24] This apparent lack of clarity fuelled the image of Heraclitus as arrogant and hiding his message from the unworthy.[25] Despite the opinions mentioned *supra*, not all ancient commentators agreed with the appraisal of Heraclitus as *skoteinos*.[26] Either they did not interpret him through the categories of later Greek philosophy or they did not read him as a natural philosopher.[27]

On a related note, Heraclitus lived at a liminal time in terms of the evolution of literature itself, in particular the movement from an emphasis on the spoken to the written word.[28] The assumption of intentional systematic ambiguity on the part of Heraclitus leads to the idea that Heraclitus' book was only meant to be read and not spoken aloud.[29] However, evidence indicates that Heraclitus did in fact lecture on his work.[30] According to C. Vieira, the Ephesian sought to harness the advantages of both oral and written discourse.[31] Heraclitus seems to exploit the phonetic possibilities of his words to create an influence on his listeners and to imitate what he sees as the oppositional structure of reality.[32]

Finkelberg notes a further reason why some have interpreted Heraclitus as a philosopher steeped in obscurity. Scholars have generally assumed that Heraclitus composed his book in concise, pithy statements. As a result, one reads the fragments as discrete units, each of which is intended to express one specific idea. When a reader does not identify such an idea in a particular fragment, one concludes either that the fragment is corrupted or incomplete or that it was *purposefully* obscure.[33] 'This way of reading the fragments,' writes Finkelberg, 'combined with ignoring the context in which they are quoted, is responsible for the image of Heraclitus as a thinker who buried his thought in equivocation'.[34] However, textual evidence indicates that the content of Heraclitus' book was not exclusively aphoristic.[35] *On Style*, attributed to Demetrius of Phaleron (*c.* 350 BCE to 280 BCE), suggests that Heraclitus wrote in continuous prose.[36] Generally, the shorter fragments seem more obscure, but that is only natural.[37]

Reconsidering Heraclitus' reputation

If the foregoing observations are correct, then what explains Heraclitus' reputation, both in antiquity and in the recent past? Above all, it is imperative to recognize that the form and style of Heraclitus' texts are composed so as to reflect the truth they describe.[38] As we shall see, Heraclitus understands the cosmos as a unity constituted by opposing forces in continuous conflict. Recalling Grand's image from before, one can say for example that one both is and is not oneself.[39] Therefore, the language of paradox and apparent contradiction will be the only way to capture the mystery of the world one inhabits.[40] Heraclitus' writing bespeaks a deliberate compositional choice, not for the purpose of obfuscation *per se*, but rather to reflect in his text a truth transcending the bounds of language.[41] For Heraclitus, Sassi writes, enigma is 'the paradigmatic form in which reality presents itself'.[42] Therefore, more important than Heraclitus' style itself is the reality it is intended to reflect, namely that the cosmos at its core represents an 'irreducible duplicity',[43] in light of which the human capacity for comprehension and expression reaches its limits.[44] In this situation, perhaps the best that one can do is merely to gesture towards this mystifying truth through one's words.[45] While it may be frustrating to the reader, Heraclitus would see himself as beholden to the reality he encounters in experience and which he interrogates in his philosophy.[46] Heraclitus' *logos*, like the world it attempts to describe, strives to remain hidden (B123).[47] As Miller explains, '[Heraclitus'] logos must remain forever ambiguous in order to report faithfully the logos of a world whose own ambiguity never ends.'[48]

A key facet of Heraclitus' style is to exploit both semantic and syntactical ambiguity, thus allowing for multiple possible meanings.[49] For example, B54 reads 'The invisible structure is greater than the visible.'[50] Miller explains how two words of this fragment – *harmoniê* and *kreittôn* – provide as many as six valid English translations.[51] For our purposes, the details of these varying meanings are less important than the methodological principle they illustrate. According to Miller, Heraclitus was inspired by Apollo's oracle at Delphi, in particular the ambiguous and mysterious style of the utterances.[52] (However, Finkelberg questions this assessment.) In the oracular tradition, one ignored alternative interpretations at great risk.[53] Herodotus refers to Croesus, who received an oracle which admitted of two possible meanings. One was that he would destroy a great empire (the one he accepted), while the other valid meaning was that a great empire would destroy him (the version that came to pass).[54] The same principle applies, *mutatis mutandis*, to Heraclitus' sayings.[55] His texts both conceal and reveal, like those of Apollo, who gives signs (B93).[56] Let us take the example of B50, which Graham translates as 'Having harkened not to me but to the Word, you should agree that wisdom is knowing that all things are one.'[57] Miller notes that this text seems to express a robust monism.[58] However, the latter part of the fragment, which consists of an indirect statement, could also be translated as 'one is all things'.[59] Heraclitus always maintains the togetherness of unity and diversity, and that the hidden harmony is greater than the unity which is apparent.[60] Whenever one focuses on the unity of the *logos*, one must not leave behind its inseparable multiplicity.[61] Those who fail to account for all possible interpretations (or for us, translations) of Heraclitus' texts put themselves at great risk of missing truth and failing to understand the *logos*.[62] Correct understanding of his words is especially crucial because, as Heraclitus understands it, what is at stake is nothing less than the soul's immortality.[63]

Heraclitus' texts also include an essentially *formative* aspect. Heraclitus deliberately constructs his text so as to mimic the mysterious *logos* and provide an example for others to follow and imitate as they become attuned to the log-ical structure of reality.[64] By carefully reading or listening to his words, one engages in a pedagogical exercise which transforms one's thinking and perception. Certain aphorisms are designed to surprise the audience or frustrate their expectations, thus inviting them into a deeper investigation.[65] Heraclitus believes in the oppositional, paradoxical disposition of the universe. His texts imitate this so that one can come to see how the human *logos* can accommodate such a counterintuitive truth. Then, once attuned to this, one can alter one's perception so as to perceive the same pattern elsewhere, thus uncovering the true nature of the cosmos.[66] The *logos* in the form of the text – written or spoken – instantiates, demonstrates, reveals the cosmic *logos*.[67] One can consider the example of B48: 'The name of the bow [*biós*] is Life [*bíos*], but its work is death.'[68] The word *bíos* means 'life', while *biós* means 'bow' (note the location of the acute accents). Heraclitus plays on the near identity of these two words to demonstrate that human *logos* can include contradiction, and thus an example drawn from the level of human experience can illustrate the cosmic *logos*.[69] Furthermore, the transformation engendered by such engagement with the texts extends to one's entire being. If the universe is a harmony arising from competing forces, one can best know it by conforming oneself to such harmony.[70] As Miller writes, 'Heraclitean aphorisms share the logos of the world; their goal is to help us share it as well.'[71] In the following pages, we shall see how the various dialogical methods Augustine employs are designed to have a similar formative effect. The reader is instructed on how to appropriate and internalize the exercises Augustine models in his writings.

If the foregoing observations about Heraclitus' work are correct, writes Finkelberg, then they make a difference to the interpretation of the former's corpus.[72] On his view, the proper approach to Heraclitus is to read him carefully under the guidance of an expert, just as one would be initiated into a mystery religion.[73] Sassi seems to agree with Finkelberg's assessment, stating that Heraclitus' audience would have read his work multiple times, interpreting and parsing it carefully to extract its true meaning.[74] To be sure, this still leaves room for the interpretation of Heraclitus as veiling his message and protecting it from the 'unworthy'.[75] However, despite the enigmatic nature of his discourse, Heraclitus' objective is not to confuse but to challenge one to move to a deeper understanding.[76] In principle, Heraclitus' message is accessible to all of those who are willing to make an effort, but it is addressed *de facto* to a small audience capable of understanding the complexity of the message.[77] One must work consistently and with determination to understand the nature of things.[78] Understanding requires great effort, which only a few are willing to undertake.[79]

Heraclitus' cosmology: The doctrine of opposites

Do I contradict myself?
Very well then I contradict myself,
(I am large, I contain multitudes.)

WALT WHITMAN

Heraclitus and flux

Traditionally, both in antiquity as well as in some contemporary scholarship (such as Barnes), Heraclitus has been read as the champion of the idea of pure flux, namely that all things are in perpetual motion and that nothing is truly stable or whole.[80] (Indeed, Cherniss claims that Parmenides' version of monism represents a reaction against what the latter saw as the intolerable idea, implied in Heraclitus' writing, that one can speak of non-being.[81]) However, recent scholarship has rejected as incorrect this reading of Heraclitus as the philosopher of flux over and against any stability.[82] Both P. Adamson and D. Graham attribute the mistaken reading of Heraclitus to the caricature of him by Plato (428/427 BCE to 348/347 BCE) (for instance, the latter's treatment of him in the *Theaetetus* and his interpretation of B125, which follows that of Cratylus).[83] An accurate interpretation of Heraclitus' understanding of flux is crucial because, according to C. Kahn, it provides a synopsis of the former's entire philosophy.[84] Furthermore, as we shall see, Heraclitus' understanding of change is pertinent to his doctrine of opposites, which informs his understanding of the essence of the human being and the cosmos.

Heraclitus is certainly a philosopher of flux, but this flux is paradoxically essential to stability. In the following pages I shall discuss several fragments which illustrate this doctrine, as well as its connection to Heraclitus' anthropology and theology. The key to understanding Heraclitus' philosophy is to notice that he begins from using a tangible example – that is, an example drawn directly from human experience – to illustrate a paradigmatic, universal, abstract truth.[85] Fragment B125 attests to this principle. Graham translates the text as follows: 'The barley drink stands still by moving.'[86] To update the example, Adamson describes a vinaigrette. This dressing requires motion and interaction to realize its identity. Without agitation, the ingredients separate, and the vinaigrette ceases to be. Heraclitus indicates that stability is located precisely in change and motion.[87] As we shall see, Heraclitus wishes to maintain the tensile nature of things without collapsing them into one pole or the other.

B61: Salt water

In B61 (cf. B10), Heraclitus writes that salt water possesses two opposing properties, namely the property of being life-giving (e.g. for certain kinds of aquatic life) and also of being life-destroying (as for human beings).[88] This seems to be one of Heraclitus' less obscure and paradoxical pronouncements on opposition; in fact, far from philosophically interesting, it may seem, *prima facie*, rather trivial. However, not only does this fragment provide a paradigmatic example of the doctrine of opposites itself, but it also reveals the ultimate purpose of this doctrine for Heraclitus' disciples.

As Kahn notes, this fragment differs in significant ways from others dealing with opposites.[89] Whereas the latter include poles confined to the totality of human experience (such as health versus sickness in B111), this fragment assimilates human experience to only *one* of the poles in this opposition.[90] The precise kinds of opposites in this fragment are crucial: All of them include a positive term – something favourable to or necessary for human life – and a negative term – something hostile to human life, which is nonetheless essential to other kinds of life.[91] Heraclitus' treatment of a particular reality exceeds the evaluation of it as 'negative' from a purely human perspective.[92]

As in other fragments, Heraclitus begins from a truth so obvious as to escape notice: Although one of the most basic human needs is water, the most immediate source thereof – at least for coastal populations – is non-potable salt water, which can in fact be dangerous for humans in multifarious ways.[93] Moreover, one can say that salt water *itself* both is and is not water. Certainly it is water in what one may now call 'chemical' terms, but it is not water with respect to its function *for humans* (although this is no 'fault' of the salt water itself).[94]

While it may be tempting to interpret Heraclitus here as endorsing a radical form of Protagorean subjectivism – according to which the human being is the measure of all things –[95] the upshot of this fragment is rather the reverse.[96] Ultimately, Heraclitus' message constitutes a challenge to acknowledge and reflect critically on one's (all too) human perspective and its limitations.[97] The problem with human perception is that one only focuses on one property at a time; thinking according to the cosmic *logos* teaches one to see both together.[98]

In my estimation, in this fragment, especially because he uses a more familiar and accessible example, it seems that Heraclitus' discussion of opposition, while certainly gesturing towards the paradoxical nature of the cosmos, is also about the *transformative effect* it is intended to have on the thoughtful listener or reader.

According to Kahn, 'the doctrine of opposites is, among other things, [1] an attempt to attain a larger vision by recognizing the life-enhancing function of the negative term, and hence [2] comprehending the positive value of the antithesis itself'.[99] In other words, one comes to appreciate the opposite, that which one reflexively considers 'negative', and one sees the value for the dynamic relationship of both poles. As one begins to appreciate the complexity of cosmic being one enters more deeply into its oppositional structure, and thereby gains a new perspective on how one is always already implicated in this arrangement.

B51: Bow and lyre

Heraclitus' text about the bow and lyre (B51) is a paradigmatic illustration for his theory of opposites.[100] Here I use Kahn's translation since it includes what is merely implicit in Graham's: 'They do not comprehend how a thing agrees at variance with itself: <it is> an attunement (or "fitting together," harmoniê) turning back <on itself>, like that of the bow and the lyre.'[101] One could say that both the bow and the lyre, despite their differences, are each characterized by 'harmony'.[102]

When Heraclitus uses the term harmoniê, it could invoke as many as three distinct senses, namely (1) the structure or composition of something, (2) harmony in music and (3) peace brokered between enemies.[103] One can easily see how the lyre could relate to at least the first two senses of 'harmony'. Interestingly, these three distinct senses can generate a unity which provides a richer illustration of the truth Heraclitus is attempting to express.[104] Concerning the first sense, the lyre realizes its nature in virtue of its tensile construction.[105] Even this sense is relevant to Heraclitus' understanding of human identity and knowledge.[106] However, Kahn stresses the *musical* nature of the lyre image.[107] Indeed, Heraclitus had a great interest in music, which comes to the foreground in this fragment. Aside from his aristocratic background, Heraclitus may have been interested in music because of its association with unity and cosmic order, both at the popular level and among the Pythagoreans.[108] The specifically musical aspect of the lyre's harmony reveals the essential connection of unity and diversity. The specific structure of the instrument, disposition of the strings and the musician's

skilful use of them are required for the realization of the lyre's full
being, the production of music.[109] Due to the lyre's structure, it can
produce not simply individual notes, but these can be arranged in a
'harmonious conflict'.[110] A singer can accompany the music of the
lyre, and a singer a chorus.[111] Overall, the example of the music
produced from the lyre is a clear instance of how an individual
reality arises from ordered multiplicity.[112]

It is fairly straightforward how harmony can be predicated of
the lyre, but it is less clear for the bow, as well as the way in which
the latter is 'back-turning' (palintropos).[113] Certainly one can say
that in the case of the bow, a single directed flight of an arrow
results from opposing forces and tensions, such as the archer's hands
moving in opposite directions.[114] However, Heraclitus' terminology
points to a deeper meaning. Kahn notes that Heraclitus' use of
palintropos (back-turning) here to describe the bow rather than
palintonos (back-stretching) seems odd; the former adjective has
a wider meaning which includes the latter.[115] His solution is that
this fragment, through the use of – tropos, indicates that it should
be read in relation to the fragments on fire and the seasonal cycles
of the sun (B31, B94). This juxtaposition reveals that the harmony
described in B51 governs and structures the cosmic system of unity
and opposition.[116] Thus B51 reflects two key ideas. First, it links
the doctrine of opposites to Heraclitus' cosmology, and secondly it
links human existence with the cosmic order.[117]

The central message of this fragment is that the universe exists
in virtue of the tensions within it. These conflicts are ordered; they
are not random but harmonious.[118] Oppositions are essential to
the unity they produce, namely harmony, which refers to opposites
in nature unified by an underlying structure.[119] Indeed, one could
consider 'harmony' synonymous with logos, as both refer to the
fundamental disposition of the world.[120] This fragment refers to
the logos as that which governs all things through a system of
tension and opposition.[121] The concept expressed in this fragment
provides a comprehensive overview of the Ephesian's philosophy.[122]
True wisdom consists in perceiving this principle at the foundation
of all things.[123]

One must once again recall that the unity and the multiplicity
belong together. In the bow and lyre fragment, 'Heraclitus is
highlighting a principle according to which every unity is a tension
of warring opposites, while every battle of opposites hides a deeper

unity.'[124] For Heraclitus, the constitutive tension of things holds constantly, without disintegrating into a synthetic unity.[125] This text denounces the error of identifying opposites yet failing to discern their underlying unity.[126] This principle is interestingly exemplified by Apollo. This deity is depicted with bow and lyre, one a symbol of war, the other of peace, and thus embodies the cosmic *logos*.[127]

On a final note concerning B51, the text discloses further meanings through its resonance with other parts of Heraclitus' corpus. As Kahn explains, the opening phrase of this fragment, 'They do not comprehend', includes a reference to three major themes throughout Heraclitus' work. First, it evokes the proem's statement that many fail to heed the logos (cf. B34).[128] The Greek verb Heraclitus uses (*xyniasin*) reflects the adjective *xunos* (shared, common), thereby emphasizing his idea that one errs by treating one's own thought as private rather than a participation in the common *logos*.[129] Heraclitus believes that to speak with understanding is to speak according to what is shared by all (B114).[130]

B10: Graspings

The fragment B10 is a key text for Heraclitus' doctrine of opposites, but it is also of special importance for his respective understandings of the human being, knowledge and god.[131] Along with B67 – the fragment explicitly about 'the god' – this fragment is fundamental to Heraclitus' theology.[132] Indeed, according to Kahn, these two fragments summarize Heraclitus.[133]

Graham's translation reads thus: 'Collections: wholes and not wholes; brought together, pulled apart; sung in unison, sung in conflict; and from all things one and from one all things.'[134] The first word of the fragment, *syllapsies*, presents various difficulties for translation and interpretation. In Kahn, 'graspings' translates *syllapsies*, placing the emphasis on the act of seizing.[135] In contrast, Miller stresses the importance of preserving the idea of tension implied by the concept.[136] He therefore appropriates the term 'syllapsis', and this concept will become crucial for understanding human being and knowing.

However one translates *syllapsies*, this term refers to various examples which illustrate the formal structure of the pattern of unity.[137] According to Kahn, the term *syllapsis* itself admits – in typically Heraclitean fashion – of several senses, all of which are legitimate interpretations.[138] Two of these include (1) the intellectual gathering of ideas to achieve understanding and (2) what Kahn calls the 'pairwise structure of reality' fundamental to Heraclitus' thought.[139] Moreover, B10's discussion of wholes and not-wholes refers to the most comprehensive framework according to which to conceptualize reality.[140] Whereas fragments such as B67 include actual instances of opposites (namely day versus night, summer versus winter, peace versus war and satiety versus famine), the opposition between wholes and not wholes refers to a logically higher kind of combination.[141] The abstract character of this form of opposition implies that it can be predicated of any particular entity within the cosmos – including human beings.[142] The universality of this arrangement implies that there is an integral connection among self, cosmos and even god.[143]

This selection from Heraclitus indicates something about the specific sense of opposition he wishes to convey. Heraclitus' conception of a 'whole' suggests internal diversity. He believes that there is dynamism inherent in unity, and hence his conception of the whole is more nuanced than a mere binary opposition between one and many.[144] A figurative sense of 'convergent divergent', Kahn writes, is the idea that there is a 'dynamic tension between totality and partiality, unity and diversity that runs through all cases of opposition'.[145] Another sense refers to harmony and conflict, and can be connected to B51, the fragment on the bow and the lyre. This idea of the tensile relationship between unity and multiplicity is particularly evident in the final portion of this fragment ('from all things one and from one all things').[146] While this phrase certainly refers to the pattern of cosmic cycles indicated elsewhere in Heraclitus' oeuvre, it cannot be limited to this sense. Heraclitus presents this relation in abstract terms, thereby indicating that the foregoing pattern represents 'a paradigm of unity-in-opposition manifested by every system of rational structure',[147] a structure which applies especially to the human being.[148]

If the foregoing pattern of oppositional unity is universal, then this will also be reflected at the *epistemic* level.[149] In other words, to know reality, one must be able to think according to its tensile, oppositional structure.[150] This conclusion can be drawn in particular from the second major part of the fragment, which addresses wholes and not-wholes. We have seen how Heraclitus understands the structure of opposition as universal. True knowledge of being will require one to maintain the tension between the unity and the diversity.[151] As Miller explains, 'The object of our understanding is thus neither the one nor the other – neither the unity nor the opposition, neither the whole nor the not-whole – *but both at once.*'[152] One can achieve this by learning to think according to what Miller calls syllapsis. This consists in the *simultaneous* performance of two opposing activities, namely analysis, whereby one discerns differences and opposition, and synthesis, whereby one perceives the deeper unity.[153] Viewing reality exclusively according to either analysis or synthesis hides its true nature. Heeding the *logos* means seeing and thinking according to both simultaneously.[154] Just as a particular being exists in combination with its opposition, so too must one's thought integrate both processes at the same time.[155]

With his emphasis on the unity of opposites, Heraclitus seems to abjure the apparently self-evident principle of non-contradiction. Indeed, this was the assessment of Aristotle. However, as Miller explains, Heraclitus does not reject the principle of non-contradiction as such, but only as the ultimate norm of correct thinking. Instead, he replaces it with his own ultimate norm, his understanding of the *logos*, which allows one to recognize the paradoxical truth of the coincidence of unity and opposition, which is none other than the fundamental cosmic structure of all reality.[156] Heraclitus' principle of *noûs*, or combined thinking, does not entail the denial or exclusion of the principle of non-contradiction (in particular because this principle is the basis of analysis, as opposed to synthesis). In virtue of the essential place of analysis in proper combined thought, the principle of non-contradiction is thereby embraced, not rejected.[157] Thus, Heraclitus reveals analysis as only one part of the whole of thought, namely as the contrary of synthesis, both of which are united in understanding.[158] As we shall see, self-knowledge requires a grasp of this paradoxical yet essential concept.

Miller cites two examples which illustrate the syllaptic reality of the world as well as the method appropriate to understanding it, namely the duck-rabbit image and Bach's fugues.[159] Concerning the former, as one looks at it, one may see at one time the duck, whereas at other times one's gaze may shift such that one sees the rabbit. However, both images are intrinsic characteristics of one and the same thing.[160] By considering the image itself and both of its aspects together, one rises to a higher level of insight, thereby recognizing the image as duck-rabbit, a unity constituted by opposition.[161] Furthermore, in Bach's fugues, one can also perceive how unity itself results from opposing parts. In this musical genre, one first identifies a theme, then its counter-point and finally both of them together.[162]

From the consideration of B10, I note two particular insights. First, Heraclitus' unique understanding of opposition applies to all of cosmic reality, including and especially human life. Secondly, the careful study of this text reveals that opposition for Heraclitus is not a mere binary contrast, but rather a dynamic combination in which the opposites are implicated in one another and are constitutive elements of a particular entity. Heraclitus is gesturing towards the challenging observation that unity is part and parcel of opposition, and vice versa.

B12: Rivers

Heraclitus' treatment of rivers provides a final and paradigmatic illustration of his idea of how unity is mysteriously forged from opposition. This section also establishes a connection between Heraclitus' cosmology and his anthropology/psychology, as well as a potential basis for addressing Grand's paradox about personal identity referenced *supra*. In what follows I shall focus on B12: 'On those stepping into rivers staying the same other and other waters flow.'[163] Not only is this text deemed authentic,[164] but commentators have also read this passage as a description of Heraclitus' psychology (even if the term *psyche* itself does not appear in it).[165]

This text – both in its composition and its message – indicates that something possesses stable existence in virtue of flux.[166] Heraclitus employs multiple dative forms, thereby mimicking the sound of running water.[167] Once again, he also exploits the grammatical flexibility of the Greek to introduce multiple meanings. The phrase 'the same' (*toisin autoisin*) could refer either to those who wade into the rivers or the rivers themselves. The fragment thus admits of two distinct possible interpretations. It could be that the rivers maintain their identity, despite the fact that new and different water is constantly flowing and providing the substance of what they are.[168] Alternatively, this text could be interpreted as focusing on human beings as the same.[169] Furthermore, the syntactical ambiguity of these forms also suggests an essential relationship between rivers themselves and those who wade into them, that is, human beings.[170]

Crucially, Kahn emphasizes that this fragment assumes the *continuity of identity* of the rivers in question.[171] Heraclitus seems to be indicating that a river exists insofar as its underlying material is in constant motion.[172] Given the suggested link between the rivers and the humans who wade into them, one can say the same for humans.[173] Rather than envisioning a conflict between constant change and stability of identity, Heraclitus claims that one possesses the latter in virtue of the former.[174] As suggested above, Heraclitus is not interested in flux for its own sake, but rather the paradoxical part it plays in the identity conditions of various entities.[175] The upshot, as Miller writes, is that B12 'hints at the one stable lesson that stepping selves and the rivers into which they step are what they are – in a word, the same – only by some kind of flowing, some kind of perpetual change or *otherness*'.[176] In other words, to be human is to be dialectically constituted. Once again, Heraclitus draws upon ordinary experience to inform his philosophy and develop an account of the human being.

Conclusion to discussion of the union of opposites

As esoteric as Heraclitus' doctrine of opposites may appear, one must recall that it is based on a careful reflection on ordinary experience.[177] The cosmos is replete with paradoxes lying hidden in plain sight. If one is truly attentive, according to Heraclitus, one will gradually perceive how the mysterious coexistence of opposites is universally present. Miller reminds us that whenever one focuses on the unity of the *logos*, one must not leave behind its inseparable multiplicity: 'If this is one logos, one activity, a perfect unity, we must nevertheless refract this one into many whenever we think or speak it.'[178] Heraclitus challenges his audience to question their unreflective way of viewing the world, to reconsider their perspective, to see and think in a new way beyond mere binary opposition. By doing so, one truly heeds the *logos*.

God and man in Heraclitus

Heraclitus' log-ical anthropology

The development of Heraclitus' psychology represents a major turning point in Western history. One can detect an inchoate conception of the self in Greek lyric poetry of the seventh and sixth centuries.[179] While the conception of the *psyche* is present in Homer, as well as Pythagoras, neither develops this idea further.[180] Kahn cites Ulrich von Wilamowitz-Moellendorf's 1931 *Der Glaube der Hellenen*, according to whom Heraclitus was the first to investigate the soul.[181] Reinhardt agrees, claiming that Heraclitus articulates the first 'psychology' in philosophical history.[182] As McKirahan emphasizes, specifically, Heraclitus differentiates himself from the prior Greek tradition by associating *cognitive* functions with the soul, rather than animal life alone.[183] Although he distinguishes human life from animal life on the basis of reason, one should not mistake Heraclitus for a proto-Cartesian dualist. Like other Presocratics, Heraclitus did not conceive of the material and the intellectual in oppositional terms.[184] Rather, mind and body are considered integrally related, even if distinct.[185] Augustine too understands the human person in similar terms.

The Heraclitean self admits of indeterminate if not infinite depth. Heraclitus presents himself to himself as a problem, one which is never solvable.[186] The investigation of B101 ('I inquired of myself'[187]) reveals the deeply enigmatic nature of the *psyche*. The saying itself is striking, as it suggests that one is somehow detached from oneself.[188] Indeed, Kahn finds in this fragment an intimation of later ideas of alienation, for instance in a religious or theological context.[189] A similar concept is present in another fragment which deals with the soul, B45: 'If you went in search of it, you would not find the limits of the soul, though you travelled every road – so deep is its measure'.[190] This fragment reveals a further novel aspect of Heraclitus' psychology with respect to his culture, namely the integration of his psychology with his cosmology.[191] The fact that the soul cannot reach its limits (*peirata*) indicates that it is *apeiron*, unlimited, which evokes both Anaximander and Anaximenes. This suggests an essential connection between the human mind and the cosmic *logos* itself.[192] The *logos* is in Heraclitus' philosophy the highest cosmic principle, yet also deeply connected to individual humans.[193] Thus human existence is integrally related to the fullness of being, and this also means that introspection will lead one to knowledge of the mysteries of the universe.[194] Because the *logos* is an inherent part of one, and because it is other than one, I believe that one can speak of Heraclitus' understanding of the person as *dialectically constituted*. Specifically, one can speak of a log-ical constitution of the human subject.

Classical sources such as Sextus Empiricus (fl. third century CE) seem to have interpreted Heraclitus in much the same way. As Finkelberg argues, Sextus read Heraclitus as stating that the rational (*lógikon*) encompasses the human being and that one derives 'mind' from 'inhaling' the divine reason around one.[195] Indeed, in B78, Heraclitus avers that only the divine has intelligence, not human nature.[196] This would suggest that in virtue of possessing *psyche* – which as indicated *supra* concerns the rational and cognitive functions of the human being – one participates in the divine life.

One may recall that the main lesson of Heraclitus' doctrine of opposition was to see that the world is a *syllapsis*, a simultaneous combination of many and one. As we have seen, the self is integrally related not just with the cosmos, but with its structuring principle. This implies that true self-understanding requires one to think according to the principle of syllapsis.[197] When one thinks about oneself according to synthesis, one sees only the superficial unity of oneself, a fragile unity easily shattered by life experience or the challenge of philosophical enquiry. One uncritically assumes that one is a (mere) unity.[198] As one can surmise, a purely analytical approach will undermine any hope of finding stability and unity of identity. Heraclitus' solution, I believe, is to embrace and enter ever more deeply into the mysterious syllapsis that one already is, to participate in one's log-ical constitution.[199]

According to Miller, syllaptic self-enquiry occurs in the following manner. First, one subjects oneself to analysis, breaking oneself apart. Then, once divided, one responds by achieving a new form of reconciliation. This new unity becomes the basis for further analysis, thus allowing the process of self-reflection to continue indefinitely.[200] It is not simply that one finds oneself in and through this dialectical form of self-enquiry; one *is* this perpetual activity of introspection.[201] In the second sense of the phrase, therefore, one can say that the Heraclitean self is dialectically constituted.

In addition, in this process of self-discovery, one is connecting as well with the divine principle of reality which provides one with

one's being.[202] The connection of introspection with theology is of
paramount importance for Heraclitus, for it is through participation
in the cosmic *logos* that one attains to immortality.[203] Heraclitus
does not endorse metempsychosis; he believes that one has one and
only one life, and hence there is an urgency to the manner in which
one lives it. It is therefore crucial to focus on self-knowledge.[204]
Once one knows *what* it means to be human, one can think about
how to live one's life.[205] According to Heraclitus, the extent to
which consciousness is preserved after death depends on the quality
of one's soul.[206] Those who do not heed the *logos* will continue
to exist after death, but in the state of something like a dreamless
sleep.[207] In contrast, those who recognize the common *logos* within
themselves will have the opportunity for eternal life.[208] Once again,
Heraclitus is interested in a practical and ethical programme.[209]
In a theological idiom, introspection is in the final analysis a
soteriological and eschatological question. As we shall see with
Augustine, his various forms of spiritual exercise serve the purpose
of continuous purification so that he can share in God's life, and not
become detached from it and ensnared in his own existence apart
from God.

Heraclitus' theo-logy

If the human person is essentially connected with – indeed, constituted
by – the divine *logos*, and if introspection leads simultaneously to
knowledge of god, it would be useful to know something about this
mysterious divinity Heraclitus claims to serve. Before concluding, I
shall note two key aspects of Heraclitus' conception of god, both of
which resonate with Augustine's theology. These are that this god
includes opposites in itself and lies beyond human comprehension
and expression.

As already suggested, in Heraclitus, one can associate the
concepts of harmony and *logos*.[210] The foregoing cosmological
insights extend to Heraclitus' theology: *logos* is the principle of
order which god knows, and god *is* this *logos*.[211] Recalling that the
world order is syllaptic, this must be true of god as well. One can
see this understanding present in the first part of B67, which reads,
'God is day night, winter summer, war peace, satiety hunger ....'[212]
Heraclitus, against Hesiod and Greek religion, held that there

are not separate gods of, for example, war and peace, but that both opposing realities are united in the one god, incorporating opposition into unity while remaining beyond opposition.[213]

Furthermore, if, as discussed *supra*, the world itself is ambiguous, and this is reflected in the utterances one uses to describe it, then this will likewise apply to the divine. Heraclitus addresses the difficulty of speaking about god in B32: 'One being, the only wise one, would and would not be called by the name of Zeus [life].'[214] Once again, syntactical ambiguity yields multiple meanings. The word *mounon* (only, alone) can modify either 'the wise one' or 'be called'.[215] Hence Heraclitus is saying that (1) the wise one is one and *only* one, (2) this wise one is only willing to be called Zeus and (3) this wise one is not willing to be called Zeus *only*, but demands other names.[216] All of these names, both individually and collectively, capture something true about god, yet also fail to do so, for Heraclitus' god is ultimately ineffable.[217]

2

Building a Bridge:
Heraclitus to Augustine

The Heraclitean tradition
of subjectivity

Historical and theoretical continuity

Despite their manifest differences and temporal distance, I believe that Heraclitus and Augustine can be read broadly within the same theoretical and historical context. This is due to the fact that Heraclitus' philosophy exerted a profound influence on subsequent reflection on the human person. Porter traces a line of enquiry concerning the self, which begins with Heraclitus and carries through to Augustine.[1] Heraclitus' understanding of the self became paradigmatic for classical philosophy, especially Stoicism.[2] Miller seems to concur with Porter's assessment, stating that subsequent generations of philosophers inherited and investigated the Heraclitean understanding of personality.[3] This makes sense in light of the fact that, as discussed *supra*, Heraclitus' work was well known and annotated throughout antiquity.[4]

According to this view which finds its foundations in Heraclitus, the subject admits of certain essential characteristics, namely (1) vulnerability, (2) imperfect agency, (3) indeterminate character, (4) contingency and (5) opacity.[5] A key facet of this conception is that, in virtue of its profound connection to the cosmos,[6] the self is an insoluble if ineluctable conundrum.[7] Indeed, the works of classical authors bespeak no predilection for certitude or self-mastery, but instead an interest in the harrowing if indefinite search for one's very essence and identity.[8] As we have seen, according to Heraclitus, the self admits of infinite depth and represents a problem which has no clear resolution.[9] Similarly, Porter considers an appreciation of the fleeting character of human life as a unifying feature of Roman accounts of the self.[10] On this view the self is understood as inherently unstable and struggling to remain integrated.[11] As will become clear, all of this is essential to Augustine's own understanding of the human person.

Porter argues, against Foucault and Gill, that this conception of subjectivity as deeply enigmatic is essential to classical philosophy.[12] The views of Foucault and Gill represent reactions to the modern view, which adopted a post-Cartesian and post-Kantian account of the self and saw the classical Greek conception of self as unworthy of the status of 'subject'.[13] Foucault's picture of the antique self is that of an 'elaborately fashioned object'[14] that performs certain acts on itself; it has no need to engage in introspection.[15] Thus subjectivity does not rise to the level of an 'existential' challenge.[16] Whereas for the Heraclitean tradition, the self remains ever removed, mysterious and beyond itself, the model of the self that Foucault locates in antiquity conceives of one as a generic object awaiting formation.[17] Porter particularly misses in Foucault an appreciation of the various threats to identity and the coherence of the self.[18] The respective works of Seneca, Marcus Aurelius and Augustine all testify to this theme.

Seneca

Seneca anticipates several key themes of Augustinian anthropology, such as the attempt to chart the human soul and the discovery of its integral connection with the divine.[19] Both J. Lagouanère and J. Rist claim that Seneca directly influenced Augustine,[20] while A. Michel stresses the mediation of the former through authors such as Plutarch, Lucian and Tertullian.[21] Seneca and Augustine share an interest in the magnitude of the human soul[22] and an interest in ascending to the divine.[23] Seneca urges one to place oneself before the gods.[24] Seneca's dialogues concern an encounter with the absolute within one.[25] In his *Ep.* 41, he describes the beauty of natural and solitary locations, as well as that of a soul in which a god is present.[26] These three elements – self, world and the divine – are all interlocking and inseparable features of one and the same reality. (As we shall see, Augustine shares the same understanding of the structure of reality.) Knowledge of one of these implies knowledge of the others. As Michel writes, Seneca 'découvre l'intériorité dans la nature et dans l'intériorité le sacré'.[27]

Seneca also testifies to the inherent instability of the human person, a key facet of Heraclitean and Augustinian anthropology. In locations such as *Dialogues* 6.11.3 and *Quaestiones Naturales* 6.2.3, Seneca gestures towards the utter nothingness of the self lying hidden in plain sight.[28] He does so through his analysis of an 'abyssal object', that is, a negation of something, and indeed, one that pushes one to the limits of reason and experience and confronts one with one's nothingness[29]. For example, Seneca's account of the fluid nature of time – which reflects Augustine's thoughts on the same theme in *Conf.* 11 – pushes him into the abyss.[30] Of course, one might say that death is the abyssal object *par excellence*. Seneca too acknowledges the overwhelming question of death in his *Ep.* 57, noting how one is forced to address something which exceeds the bounds of reason, indeed, that which is conditioned. One is forced to reckon with the fact that human life appears to hover between being and nothingness[31]. The very essence of the self according to Seneca consists in this precarious state, yet one forms oneself precisely in virtue of being attentive to this sense of destitution.[32]

Elsewhere, Seneca continues his discussion of the impermanence of human life. In doing so, he also suggests a therapeutic programme whereby one can come to terms with and address the insecurity of life. In addition to time and death, Seneca's observation of the natural world bespeaks the unstable and precarious nature of human existence. In light of the sheer force of nature, humans are reduced from subjects to objects, losing the capacity for self-determination.[33] Seneca expounds upon this topic at the beginning of the sixth book of his *Quaestiones Naturales*, which deals with earthquakes. He begins by referring to an actual earthquake that had recently struck the region of Campania.[34] In this respect, Seneca notes how an earthquake is an apparently distinct form of disaster. Other catastrophes, such as fires, plagues or wars, are escapable and have a defined scope. Yet the destructive force of an earthquake seems far more fundamental and comprehensive than anything else humans may experience.[35]

Seneca uses this event to reflect on the contingent nature not merely of human existence, but of the natural world as well. In the wake of such destruction in Campania, many people fled to live elsewhere. Yet what makes them think, Seneca wonders, that any other place will not meet the same fate?[36] In addition to the sheer destructive force of this event, the time of year it occurred was also significant, as it happened during winter, a season traditionally considered safe from such natural disasters.[37] One deludes oneself into believing that one can permanently secure happiness.[38] Seneca sees in one's flight a vain search for certainty and stability in a world that ultimately lacks such.[39] 'Everywhere shares the same condition, and, if not yet shaken by an earthquake, still it can be shaken. Perhaps this spot on which you are standing too confidently will be torn apart tonight, or today before nightfall.'[40] Moreover, and crucially, the extreme case of the earthquake allows one to perceive the utter contingency and finitude at the root of being. Such an observation also allows one to perceive the full force of Porter's critique of Foucault. A proper understanding of authors such as Seneca requires an appreciation of the inherently tenuous nature of human identity. Thus Porter:

> Abstract theoretical problems [in Foucault] are replaced by attention to down-to-earth practices. More precisely, speculations about the self are treated as the secondary by-product of these primary formative practices, if at all. The sheer functionalism of Foucault's procedural analysis of the self falls short of the Senecan reality. How do you *schedule* meditation on the self when the very medium in which that self-reflection is to obtain is itself being shown to be a problem, and an abyssal one at that?[41]

Moreover, one must note that for Seneca, the earthquake, while in some sense an exceptional occurrence, is simply a less common instance of an abiding truth. One's life exists in a constant state of uncertainty, though one often does not recognize it. Thus, the very nature of reality at its foundation is like that of the ground during an earthquake.[42]

This insight, rather than cause despair, can become a source of hope, according to Seneca.[43] We are very frail and susceptible to harm from many sources, including familiar ones.[44] Why be terrified of earthquakes or other disasters when familiar things can cause death as well?[45] 'How foolish', Seneca thinks, 'to tremble at the sea when you know you could be killed by a drop of water!'[46] We fear large-scale events of nature when the same result can come from something close to us.[47] 'What is more foolish than being afraid of [the earth's] swaying or of the sudden collapse of mountainsides and invasions of the sea as it races beyond the shoreline, when death is present everywhere and can attack from anywhere, and nothing is too tiny to be able to bring destruction to humankind?'[48] Regardless of how it happens, death is inevitable for all, and death by one cause is no better or worse than by another.[49] One eradicates fear by realizing that one should be wary of all things.[50] When one acquires appropriate knowledge about the nature of things, one is able to mollify one's fear and live free of such troubles.[51] Through his critical investigation of the natural world and one's experience of it, one can apply a therapeutic balm to the apprehensive heart.

In *Ep.* 104, Seneca addresses the reality of loss in ways which, in my estimation, are congenial to Augustine's thought, as will become clear *infra*. In his missives to Lucilius, Seneca is teaching his friend how to manage the vicissitudes of life, and indeed, how to die.[52] Seneca writes that one erroneously considers the loss of a loved one a terrible tragedy, when in fact it is like mourning a leaf that inevitably falls from a tree.[53] In this respect, Seneca anticipates an objection from Lucilius, namely that those who are lost are permanently changed. This insight, while true, provides an opportunity to bring to light a more fundamental if less obvious truth, namely the fact that one is constantly in flux oneself. The failure to acknowledge this fact will cause one only greater suffering: 'You will not be conscious of these changes, nor will you be able to remedy the afflictions, but you will nonetheless make trouble for yourself by hoping for some things and despairing of others.'[54] The self is slipping away and changing at every moment, though this is easy to overlook, in contrast to the loss of a loved one, which occurs outside of oneself. Thus, as in the example of an earthquake, the loss of another person represents a more conspicuous instance of a constant reality.[55] Ultimately Seneca does not wish for one to avoid pain but to embrace it so as to overcome it.[56] His message is that all things come and go in their due season. One must learn to enjoy things as they are but not cling to them as if they are or could be permanent.[57] As we shall see, it was Augustine's failure to understand this truth that led him to tremendous existential pain, recounted in the fourth book of the *Confessiones*.

Marcus Aurelius

The thought of Marcus Aurelius provides a synopsis of the anthropological tradition in question and reveals significant continuity with Augustine. Marcus Aurelius places a great emphasis on introspection.[58] On his view, when one turns inwards, one can discover, *inter alia*, the incomprehensible mystery of being and one's connection with all things.[59] In *Med.* 4.40, Aurelius notes how all things are woven together.[60] As Porter explains, Marcus' universe is one of a basic porosity or extimity between self and world,[61] a variation on the Stoic concept of *sympatheia*.[62] Moreover, both elements are always beyond or in excess of themselves.[63] Thus the self is inseparable from other selves and the universe as a whole.[64] The world of self and nature are essentially linked, such that introspection yields results for knowledge of the world, and vice versa.[65]

Furthermore, as with Seneca, Aurelian introspection reveals one's inherent finitude and contingency.[66] Ultimately, the self is just as much a non-self as it is utterly transient.[67] This also means that there is no such thing as 'pure' autonomy.[68] 'To speak of selves,' writes Porter, 'is to speak of momentarily circumscribed entities that have a tenuous grasp on identity.'[69] Selves possess only the illusion of continuous, stable existence; they are not individual units, separable from others.[70] Aurelius – like Augustine[71] – situates the consideration of his own self within a network of relations which contribute to the formation of the self.[72] In other words, the self is dialectically constituted, insofar as otherness is an essential and constitutive feature of one's identity. One cares for oneself by conforming to the one true being of the universe, a task which requires the recognition of oneself as paradoxically constituted by flux.[73]

Self-knowledge in the Heraclitean tradition

According to Porter, Augustine inherits and intensifies the notions of self in the respective works of Seneca and Marcus Aurelius.[74] Like Seneca and Aurelius, Augustine's self-formation reveals the self's nihility and turns it outwards and upwards.[75] However, in contrast to Seneca, the Augustinian formation of self, rather than assuaging anxiety, exacerbates it, only finding resolution in eternity.[76] For example, Augustine's initial euphoric encounter with *memoria* quickly changes as he is revealed to himself as a mysterious abyss.[77] His programme of forming the self is ultimately oriented to revealing the self as a conundrum which must be left behind for the sake of a higher truth in which it already finds itself contained.[78] These and other aspects of Augustinian subjectivity will be unfolded in the coming chapters.

In my estimation, the most obvious similarity between Heraclitus and Augustine is in the impetus to self-knowledge and the importance of this pursuit for one's relationship with the divine. Both figures – in their own distinctive ways and unique contexts – obeyed the order attributed to Apollo's oracle at Delphi. One of the commands inscribed on the temple there was the famous *gnôthi seauton*, often translated as 'Know thyself.'[79] Indeed, Augustine construes human life itself as a response to the Delphic imperative.[80] According to R. Shusterman, Heraclitus was the first to consider this imperative in a philosophical context.[81] Through Plato's Socrates, the Delphic oracle became the centre and foundation of all subsequent philosophy.[82] This is especially noteworthy given Augustine's direct reliance on Neoplatonic sources for his understanding of human subjectivity.[83] Furthermore, for the philosophical tradition under consideration, self-knowledge and knowledge of the world and God were not separable from each other, as seen in Marcus Aurelius. For Augustine – as we shall see in sources such as the *Soliloquia* – knowledge of God and self are two sides of the same coin.[84]

Interrogation and introspection

According to Johnstone, the specific sense of *logos* for Heraclitus is the universe's self-communication. In Heraclitus, *logos* designates the 'world's constant, common presentation of itself to us as an ordered and intelligible whole'.[85] This cosmic *logos* becomes available to human beings in experience.[86] The novelty in Heraclitus' use of the term consists in claiming that the universe can present a *logos*, an activity generally reserved for humans.[87] He establishes an analogy between the *logos* of the universe on the one hand and the various communications (*logoi*) of human beings on the other.[88] One can comprehend (or fail to comprehend) the world's *logos* in a manner comparable to a written or spoken text.[89] In B107, Heraclitus compares those who do not speak Greek ('barbarians') to those who cannot understand the *logos*, drawing upon the analogy between human *logos* and universal *logos*.[90] One fails to understand the reports of the senses and their deeper meaning if one's soul is not in the correct state.[91] Furthermore, Heraclitus stresses the importance of differentiating between human *logoi*, which are many and varied, and the one universal *logos*, which is presented in the same way and openly to all, and is thus 'common' (*xunos*).[92] Because the presentation of *logos* is universal, true understanding must be *xunos*.[93] Despite the fact that it is openly presented to all, many people will fail to understand the universal *logos*.[94]

In *Conf.* 10, Augustine presents an understanding of the interpretation of creation in ways which are congenial to Heraclitus' comparison between human *logos* and cosmic *logos*. Augustine begins his search for God by interrogating the world around him. He 'listens' to the various parts of creation state that they are not God, but that God made them.[95] Once he hears this, he turns within himself to continue his search;[96] his *interrogation* has led him to *introspection*.[97] Augustine reports that he made this turn because he was able to understand the world's speaking within himself through a careful consideration of his sense experience.[98] One arrives at understanding by comparing the reports of one's senses with the truth dwelling within.[99] As we shall see, in other locations Augustine makes it explicit that sense experience is private to individuals, while truth is common to all, even if they do not perceive it clearly. Those who are bound by the love of temporal things are incapable of understanding the speech of creation.[100] God speaks to all, but not all understand.[101]

3

Augustine and the Theo-log-ical Constitution of the Human Person

Forms of otherness in the Augustinian self

According to G. Stroumsa, Christianity's novel disposition towards the human person arose from two key beliefs, *imago* and *peccatum* (*originale*).[1] Concerning the former, the new anthropology derived from the biblical understanding of the person as created in God's image (Gen 1:26) had implications which marked a significant departure from Graeco-Roman conceptions of the human person.[2] One key difference was that a new dignity was given to the human being.[3] Furthermore, the body was now included as an essential and even positive element of the person. In contrast to Platonism, one was no longer identified simply with one's mind or soul.[4] The theological understanding of *imago* entailed an emphasis on the unity of the person, resulting from the integration of body and soul.[5]

Augustine's anthropology proceeds from the initial acknowledgement that the human being is essentially a complex creature, that is, differentiated, consisting of parts.[6] According to J. Rist, Augustine's mature position is that to be a person is to be in *relation*, first and foremost in virtue of the relation between body and soul.[7] This suggests that one is originally associated with otherness, indeed, constituted by or in virtue of it. Augustine's understanding of the person includes attention to a variety of aspects of difference included in a single individual. I would like to focus on three kinds of 'otherness' of the Augustinian person, namely (1) the integration of body and soul, (2) the individual's unique history along with the shared history of humanity and, crucially, (3) the fact that to be human means essentially to be in relation, and ultimately related to and determined by something beyond and infinitely greater.[8]

As I see it, this sequence progresses from the 'bottom up' in the sense that one's initial confrontation with internal difference is the awareness that one can distinguish one's 'self' from one's body. Further consideration reveals additional elements of relationality fundamental to human existence, until finally one arrives at the 'higher' form of otherness within one, namely the divine Other. However, this realization allows one to view the question from the 'top down', and indeed, in its original order. God gives one to be, and this creation determines all further and derivative elements of the otherness of the self.

Mind and body

The initial challenge one confronts is the question of the relationship between the human being's physical and the spiritual aspects. Augustine's eventual insistence on the unity of soul and body provokes, as with countless other philosophers, a series of conundrums about the relationship between these two realities and whether they can be understood as constituting a single entity.[9] Although in his early works Augustine appears to identify himself with his soul or mind, his mature view resolutely maintains the inherently integrated, *incarnational* nature of the human being. Thus Rist: 'Augustine's final position is that we are a single thinking and loving person, compounded in some strange and (to him) inexplicable way, of soul and body.'[10] One is never identified merely with the soul or the body; rather, their very union constitutes the human being.[11] (That being said, one should also note that, according to A. Nordlander, Augustine never provides a final resolution to the relationship between body and soul in the human person.[12])

The 19th *tractatus* on the Gospel of John reveals Augustine's commitment to the unity of body and soul in one human being. Discussing the Resurrection of Christ, he states that this is not the end of resurrection in general, for it will extend to human beings as well (*audiant adhuc aliud, ne hic finitam esse resurrectionem putent*). Moreover, the resurrection of the dead will include both soul and body (*ibi erit resurrectio mortuorum, sed corporum*). Thanks to the power God the Father has granted to Christ his Son, humans will be raised in their whole nature, body and soul, the former through Christ as the Son of Man, and the latter in virtue of Christ's power as the Son of God (*animas ergo suscitat Deus, per Christum Filium Dei: corpora suscitat Deus, per eumdem Christum filium hominis*).[13] Furthermore, in the same location Augustine appeals to the unity of two natures in Christ as an analogy for the unity of body and soul in humans (*Filius Dei, quod est Verbum Dei, habet hominem, tamquam anima corpus*). Assuming the classical definition of the human beings as rational souls with bodies (*Quid est homo? Anima rationalis habens corpus*), he states that just as Christ is the Son of God who 'has' a man (*Quid est Christus? Verbum Dei habens hominem*), which is constituted of body and soul, yet remains one, so too does a human being remain one although consisting of both body and soul.[14]

The term that Augustine eventually uses to denote this incarnate being is *persona*.[15] His first use of this word appears in his *Ep.* 137 (Volusiano) of 411. This marks the departure from his earlier endorsement of the (Plotinian) identification of self and soul. The same view expressed in *Ep.* 137 occurs elsewhere in Augustine's corpus, notably *Ep.* 169.2.8 (415); *Trin.* 13.5.22; and *Ciu.* 19.3.4.[16] According to Rist, 'the word *persona* indicates both a relational "mixture" of soul and body *and* that this relationship results in "something single and individual" (*De Trinitate* 7.3.11)'.[17] Though a composite, the person is a discrete reality distinct from its constitutive parts.[18]

Subjective and objective elements of the human person

Rist's treatment of Augustine's conception of *persona* brings to light a crucial feature of Augustinian anthropology, and one which, according to my understanding, has direct implications for the enquiry into the self. Not only does Augustine emphasize the exterior and physical aspects of the human being,[19] but his work is novel in treating this as a distinct matter of enquiry.[20] In virtue of possessing the body as an essential feature of one's identity, one is in some respects an *artefact*, objectively observable and affected by external occurrences in the world. As Rist explains,

> A fundamental derivative from the body's being an ineradicable part of the person is that we are subject to the vicissitudes of history. It is one of Augustine's chief claims to philosophical fame in his mature account of persons that he is aware not only that they must be understood (metaphysically and theologically) as a mixture of soul and body, but also in terms of their history precisely as individuals.[21]

The shared history of humanity contributes to one's individual biography, and in turn one's own story becomes a part of the overall human story.[22] (In due course we shall see a contemporary philosophical approach to how one's deep shared history with humanity plays a part in self-knowledge.[23]) The human person is radically both a subject and an object,[24] which implies that one can be studied both 'objectively' and 'subjectively'.[25] That is, one's individual history can be analysed under various aspects, such as biography and anthropology.[26] Such commitments inform Augustine's introspective methodology.[27] It is not surprising therefore to find that Augustine places such an emphasis on an introspective and narrative methodology.

The human being as essentially relational

A further implication of Augustine's prioritizing of the relationality and historicity of the person is the importance of human relationships as constitutive of and essential to one's identity.[28] In this respect, Augustine's position is consistent with classical Latin reflections on the self.[29] According to Mathewes,

> Against modern temptations toward Cartesian solipsism and alienated autonomy, Augustine offers a picture of selfhood inextricably intertwined with otherness and community. Augustine's anthropology affirms that we are most ourselves when we are most fully related to others, indeed, that *otherness and selfhood intermingle* at every level of the self's reality.[30]

One's very identity is generated by one's relationships, especially with the triune God.[31] The interior presence of God serves as the basis for the inherently relational and other-oriented aspect of human identity.[32] In addition, the importance of interpersonal relationships extends to Augustinian introspection.[33] According to Conybeare, Monnica's death is the central theme of the entire *Conf.*[34] She proceeds to suggest that one could view Augustine's discussion of God and his mother as an extension of his discussion of the self.[35] Augustine finds himself in a set of relationships, not least of all with his mother, whose death provides the occasion for him to re-evaluate the meaning of this 'web of relationships' (Conybeare's term).[36] (We shall return to this question of the interpretation of the events of one's life *infra*.)

The foregoing aspects of otherness are crucial for understanding Augustine's conception of the self, yet all of them are secondary in comparison with the root of human identity, that is, God. It is well known that Augustine follows Genesis 1 in holding that the human being is created in God's own image and likeness. However, I believe that the full importance of this position is seldom acknowledged. Therefore, I shall consider certain locations in Augustine's corpus in which he addresses the manner in which God is essential to the identity of the human person. Thus this research will reveal how Augustine understands the self as *dialectically constituted*. This means that to be human is in some paradoxical yet very real sense not to be entirely identical with oneself. Furthermore, because this otherness is the absolute divine Other, self-understanding requires investigating that which in principle lies beyond human comprehension. One arrives at the question of whether it is meaningful or possible to speak of knowledge and understanding of oneself, a problem which Augustine himself investigates, and in which we shall eventually join him. I also contend that these insights will reveal the way in which Cilleruelo can rightly describe Augustine as a 'Christian Heraclitus' and how the Ephesian's cryptic utterances can inform introspection grounded in Augustinian anthropology. The journey to self-knowledge requires maintaining the constitutive poles of one's intrinsically dialectical nature.

According to Mathewes, Augustine grounds his account of relation – whether of people to God, each other or themselves – in his Trinitarian theology, thereby presenting an essentially *theological* understanding of otherness.[37] One finds an instance of this position

in the third book of *De Genesi ad litteram*, which also establishes
a connection between the understanding of the inherent otherness
included in human identity and its creation according to God's own
image. As Augustine specifies, for the human being to be created in
the *imago Dei* is to say that he is made in the *imago Trinitatis*.

In his treatment of Genesis 1:26, the starting point of his
anthropology,[38] Augustine stresses that when God creates
entities other than humans, the text reads, 'God said: Let it be',
or as Augustine has it, *Dixit Deus: Fiat*. However, in the case of
the creation of human beings, the verb, number and person are
different. As Augustine's text reads, 'Let us make the human being
in our own image and likeness' (*faciamus hominem ad imaginem
et similitudinem nostram*).[39] It seems to me that the change in
verb implies a more direct relationship between Creator and this
particular creature. Moreover, Augustine derives a key implication
from the plural form of *facio*, which will provide a key insight for
this research. The use of the plural indicates that man is created
in the image of God the Holy Trinity; otherwise, the text could
not reasonably have 'our image' (*ad imaginem nostram*).[40] I argue
that Augustine's biblical understanding of the creation of the
human being in God's own image suggests the inherently dialectical
constitution of the human being, specifically because God's own
essence is triunity. In my estimation, it follows that human beings,
made in God's image and likeness, must be understood in reference
to God, specifically God as Trinity. Thus knowledge of self and
knowledge of God will be inseparable, and such knowledge will
require a sustained investigation of otherness and dynamic relation.

The interior presence of the divine

De Magistro

De Magistro 11.38 contains the famous 'inner teacher' doctrine.
Although Augustine never directly applies the adjective *interior*
to the noun *magister*, he does use the adverb *intus* to qualify the
manner of teaching.[41] In any case, I would like to note three points
about this passage. First, Augustine states that learning occurs
not through what one hears but through consulting an inner

truth present to the mind.[42] Clearly my presentation of the claim is simplistic, and it implicates a long tradition of epistemological and semiotic argument. Instead of pursuing this question further, I would simply like to note that the process of acquiring knowledge according to Augustine involves an interior conversation (more on which *infra*),[43] and indeed presupposes an intimate 'otherness' which is necessary for one to arrive at truth. One's rationality, considered essential to one's very being, is inseparable from something which is distinct from yet deeply intimate to oneself.

Secondly, Augustine immediately proceeds to identify Christ with this interior truth (*ille autem qui consulitur, docet, qui in interiore homine habitare dictus est Christus*). Thirdly, by reference to Ephesians 3:16–17 and 1 Corinthians 1:24, Augustine emphasizes the divine and immutable nature of this indwelling pedagogical truth (id est incommutabilis Dei Virtus atque sempiterna Sapientia: *quam quidem omnis rationalis anima consulit*). Thus it becomes clear that Augustine resolutely maintains that the eternal God is an essential aspect of the human person and is operative in one's cognitive functioning.[44]

Certainly, such formulations raise concerns about whether a space remains for human autonomy. On Augustine's view, the activity of learning is a not a zero-sum game between the inner teacher and his pupil.[45] In fact, instead of conceiving of these as mutually exclusive, Augustine would see them as complementary and collaborative. The presence of the inner teacher enables one to locate and develop one's autonomy.[46] Such a position does not seem plausible in a contemporary setting. Part of the reason for this, as already described, is that it is very difficult for humans to heed the *logos*, especially when it summons one to truths which seem not to make sense in binary terms. Furthermore, as heirs to the concept of Enlightenment rationality, one struggles to conceive of the self as anything other than a discrete, autonomous unit. The result is that what seems like a self-evident truth is not identified as a deeply ingrained prejudice resulting from one's intellectual context. In line with both Heraclitus and Augustine, I have argued that one must ever recall the necessity of maintaining an openness to truths transcending apparently intuitive categories. Thus Augustine can hold that being and having oneself is not separate from one's cooperation with God but presupposes it. As Bianco explains, one (re)discovers the divine other present to one, yet through this encounter with the other, one is also (re)introduced to oneself.[47] Paradoxically, one becomes most oneself by giving oneself to what is completely and absolutely Other.

De Libero Arbitrio

The second book of *De Libero Arbitrio* – a dialogue which Augustine began at Rome in 388, but completed *c.* 395, after his ordination (which took place in 391)[48] – contains similar ideas present in the portion of *Mag.* treated *supra*. In Book II, Augustine engages in an extended, introspective dialogue with Evodius, the ultimate goal of which is to establish a rational basis for belief in God.[49] According to Kenyon, the methodology which governs this part of Augustine's corpus 'involves connecting ideas, refining distinctions, spelling out implications, all of which is done through a familiar combination of dialectic and self-reflection'.[50] (Kenyon's observation indicates the essential correlation between dialogue and introspection.) Due in part to the considerable length and intricacy of this argument, I shall not explain it in detail, but rather reference it to the extent that it is necessary to understand the major results of Augustine's joint investigation with Evodius. Along the way to the conclusion that God exists, Augustine discloses significant insights into human psychology and experience. As Kenyon writes, 'Each section [of *Lib. Arb.*] builds on the last, not by providing new premises for a single deduction, but by integrating ever more nuanced considerations within a single explanatory scheme.'[51] In this work, Augustine discusses the facets of the soul, its operations and its capacity for self-reflection, and in so doing attempts to chart the *psychê*.

Augustine begins from the observation that the senses and their respective objects are completely private.[52] What may seem like a trivial and self-evident claim becomes crucial in connection with other aspects of Augustine's tortuous argument. Although one's senses are private, the things that one perceives by means of these senses are external and common, even if in a limited manner.[53] Some objects are only sensed individually, as part of it is transformed and assimilated into one's body, as in the case of oxygen or food.[54] For smell and taste, two perceivers can at best sense only different parts of a general object.[55] For the sense of touch, one may sense the same object, but not the exact same part at the exact same time.[56] Moreover, it is possible that one's touch may have irrevocably changed the object, as in the case of touching a piece of ice. In the case of other objects, one does not damage or destroy them. These are able to be sensed with greater commonality among perceivers, who can sense something together without changing the object.[57] However, considering the fact that sense objects are material, there are inherent limitations to the shared aspect of perception.[58] In contrast to physical objects, Augustine believes there are immaterial realities that all minds perceive together in a way that escapes the limitations of sense experience. As evidence for his position, Augustine discusses some examples of ideas that he considers common to all. He also suggests certain implications for his arguments.

Augustine appeals to cognition as a basis for his claim that number does not come through sense experience, which partially explains his extended discussion of the senses. According to Augustine, sense experience presupposes and is enabled by the *a priori*, eternal concept of *one* or *unity*.[59] All objects given in sense experience are never simple units, but present themselves in terms of diversity and multiplicity. No matter how small something is, it admits of – at least in principle[60] – distinguishable parts, such as a right side and a left side.[61] (Furthermore, there is also the question of a thing's temporal parts or duration throughout time.) Augustine contends that *one* is not a physical object. A perceiver only senses physical objects through the bodily senses, and these are never *one*.[62] Indeed, the concept of *part* presupposes the concept *one*. Otherwise, it would be impossible to speak of parts.[63] The rational agent searches for *one* in an object, with a presentiment of what *one* is, even if *one* as such is undiscoverable in an object.[64] Without *one*, it would be impossible to speak about *many*.[65] Rational agents identify other numbers by how many times they include the number *one*. Thus the agent does not perceive numbers by the senses but thinks about them through reason.[66] Augustine claims that *number* is present to all rational beings and that it remains intact even though people look at it together.[67]

Besides mathematical rules, Augustine identifies other principles which he believes are immaterial ideas perceived by all minds.[68] One of these is that all people desire to be happy.[69] Although the desire is hidden in each human heart, Augustine believes that he can know this truth with certainty.[70] Despite the fact that people disagree about that in which happiness consists, they nevertheless share this common pursuit.[71] Augustine makes similar claims about other principles, for example that lesser things should be subordinated to the better and that one should prefer what is incorruptible.[72] Indeed, various truths seem self-evident and are shared by all, suggesting that all gaze upon a common truth.[73]

Augustine's argument extends a step further as he elaborates on his positions, claiming that the fundamental shared principles of thought that he has enumerated are eternal. For example, he states that mathematical truths hold eternally, in contrast to sensory data, which is always ephemeral.[74] In addition to individual numbers such as 1, Augustine also refers to how eternal law governs the relations of numbers. For example, for a number n, the nth number in a series is $2n$.[75] Furthermore, one knows that one should prefer the incorruptible, which suggests that one knows the 'immutable'. Thus a concept of 'eternity' is seen by all minds.[76] The upshot is that one sees certain immutably true normative principles in common with others.[77]

After reaching this conclusion, Augustine proceeds to argue that the truth present to the human mind is superior to it. He reasons that if this truth were *inferior* to the mind, we would judge it, not according to it. One recognizes in light of this truth that, for example, $3 + 7 = 10$. One does not declare that it 'ought' to be so.[78] If this truth were *equal* to the mind, truth itself would be mutable. However, truth remains whether one acknowledges it or not. In fact, one judges one's mind according to it.[79] By process of elimination, Augustine concludes that this eternal truth is *superior* to the mind.[80] (As he states in *Conf.* 10, Augustine consults with God in himself on every matter.[81])

Augustine concludes that he has established the existence of God through introspective and dialogical research, but I would like to note other implications of his argument. Kenyon indicates that the results of Augustine's investigation with Evodius extend to insights of further interest. As he explains, 'the self-reflective discovery that we have access to norms that are certain, incorruptible and common is instrumental to a larger project of working out the implications of our rational activity as a means to understanding our place in the world'.[82] Indeed, I believe that *Mag.* and *Lib. Arb.* advance the theological-anthropological reflections of Augustine in the following way. Not only does one find otherness within oneself, but the more profound question concerns the nature of this otherness, which seems qualitatively different from, indeed superior to, the human. The condition of the possibility of knowledge includes something qualitatively superior to the human mind. This observation brings one into a more challenging enquiry. How can one maintain a sense of intrinsic identity when one is not only constituted by otherness, but an otherness which exceeds the merely human plain of existence? In the following section, we turn to how Augustine explores this question in his discussion of the creation of the human person in the image of God (*imago Dei*).

Imago

The foregoing section has resulted in several insights into Augustine's anthropology, which can without hesitation be described as inherently 'theological'. For one, sources such as *Mag.* and *Lib. Arb.* reveal that the 'conditions of the possibility' of human cognition require a divine source. Likewise, the opportunity for maintaining and attaining integrity of personal identity across time and space is in the final analysis a theological question. Augustine's understanding of the person as *imago Dei* lies at the basis of these positions. However, I believe that one can go a step further in the investigation of this doctrine, and thus arrive at an even more radical understanding of the human person which, though paradoxical, also discloses further opportunities for introspective exploration.

   In what follows, I would like to explore more fully the implications of Augustine's understanding of the image of God, in particular in terms of its negativity or nothingness with respect to the human person. This part of the investigation is motivated by an observation made by J.-L. Marion on Augustine's exegesis of Genesis. Whereas the rest of creation has a particular form or type of its own, the human person has none whatsoever, save the very image of God. This insight radicalizes Augustine's epistemic reflections in light of *imago*. The human person has nothing of its own, and it is modelled on *no-thing* in the universe, for God is incorporeal, neither temporal nor spatial. I contend that this situation of the human person as grounded yet groundless frames the subsequent drama of the interior move in search of oneself and the divine.

In *Gn. litt.*, Augustine speaks of creation according to two aspects, to begin to be or exist (*creari*) and to be formed and brought to fruition (*formari*).[83] God calls creation into being from 'absolutely nothing'.[84] Once it begins to be, it is gradually completed in time with God's assistance; without this continuous conversion, creation would recede towards non-being.[85] God's creatures are 'formed and perfected' by converting to him, but become formless by turning away.[86] Augustine's understanding of two aspects to creation informs but also complicates his anthropology.[87]

Furthermore, I contend that the general dynamic of *creari-formari* is relevant to the enquiry into the self, and it can be articulated in Heraclitean categories. As we have seen, for Heraclitus, true progress in self-knowledge occurs by 'heeding the *logos*' and continuously responding to this principle which structures the entire universe. One already participates in the *logos*, but this can be appreciated and realized to varying degrees. Similarly, according to Augustine, the human soul is impressed with the image of God, yet this image stands in need of being brought to completion.[88] For the human soul, this turning involves a response to divine grace, by means of which one is able to acquire truth.[89] The soul only progresses insofar as it is oriented towards God from whom it receives its (particular mode of) being.[90] The drama of creation is constitutive of life, especially human life: One is continuously created as one turns towards God, and this is only completed in eternity.[91] In turning away from God, that is, in placing one's trust in one's own ability and one's own knowledge, one deforms the image within one.[92]

Though I do believe that there are significant continuities between Heraclitus and Augustine in this matter, one must stress among other things the *theological difference* of Augustine's account of the continuous creation of the human being. Ultimately, stability is found only in God, and is only attainable by turning to Christ. This suggests, according to M. Drever, that the completion of one's being is an eschatological endeavour, although one may be granted a brief intimation of it on earth.[93] As he writes, the soul moves 'through Christ into the *unity* of God'.[94]

Imago and *memoria*

The notion of *imago Dei* is often linked with considerations of human rationality. In *Trin.*, for example, Augustine writes that one can contemplate eternal ideas because one is made in the image of God.[95] This concept allows Augustine to adapt Platonism to his Christian commitments: Augustine can reject Platonic anamnesis but retain the overall framework for explaining *a priori* knowledge.[96] Similarly, Augustine develops his own account of memory in order to address this philosophical issue, though as we shall see, his interests lie ultimately in distinctly Christian questions.

The soul bears within itself a certain reflection of God, the *memoria Dei*, which is neither *a priori* in a strictly Platonic sense, nor is it purely empirical.[97] According to Cilleruelo, 'God records, imprints, stamps in the human soul the memory "sapientia" […]'.[98] G. Jeanmart notes Augustine's distinction between the *memoria sui* and the *memoria Dei*. The former pertains to memory in the more conventional sense of the term, a catalogue of past experiences. The latter is more fundamental to the human person; it consists of a trace of the divine origin left on every human soul. This trace suggests both a presence and a lack, and thus calls one to the origin whence it has absconded. Thus one might say that one does not so much turn to God as return to God.[99] Faith directs us towards God, even before we know him.[100] In imprinting the soul with the divine image, God leaves there a trace whereby the soul has some inclination and sense of direction to seek God.[101]

Both aspects of memory play a role in the soul's search for knowledge. The soul is able to engage in rational, reflective thought in virtue of a prior internal sense of itself, a habitual awareness of the soul to itself.[102] As Cilleruelo writes, 'The soul has from itself a knowledge which is ontological or pre-ontological, pre-reflective, pre-logical, … which is simply called "the presence of the soul before itself"'.[103] The *memoria sui* mediates the person's experience of the mundane with the eternal.[104]

The *memoria Dei* provides the basis for thinking about how the human person can relate to the infinite God.[105] The good itself is located within one, one is interpellated by it, even if it alludes one's conceptual grasp.[106] The soul has a certain impression of happiness as a memory, a presentiment of the goal towards which it strives.[107]

In *Trin.* 8 Augustine raises the example of justice or righteousness: It seems that we are not righteous, yet we want to be. It seems that we have some knowledge of it, because we recognize it in others and love them for it. This would be impossible if we did not already possess some notion of justice, what Augustine calls a certain acquaintance with this concept.[108] Faith prepares the way for both the love and the knowledge of God. Augustine suggests a hermeneutical dimension to one's relationship with God; although God is not completely unknown or unloved, one's faith enables that love and knowledge to develop further.[109]

In virtue of one's rational nature, one has a certain implicit awareness of God, indeed, not just an awareness, but a basic responsiveness to the divine initiative through which one was created and is sustained in being.[110] Discussing the *imago Dei*, Drever writes that 'The divine image structures the soul's primordial recognition of God and so conditions its basic identity.'[111] This understanding of the soul's relationship to itself and to God casts the very concept of subjectivity in a new light. As C. Mathewes explains,

> (Epistemic) justification, according to Augustine, does take place within the autonomous space of subjectivity, but such justification proceeds only by affirming that an irreducible otherness stands at the heart of subjectivity – the otherness of God. Augustine anchors his realism in the inwardness of our minds discerning God. Objectivity, that is, is realized through subjectivity, only because subjectivity holds, at its heart, an objective reality.[112]

Knowledge is grounded in self-knowledge, which in turn is grounded in something even more fundamental, knowledge of God: Hence the inward turn, not for its own sake, but rather because of a higher, enabling presence which draws one beyond oneself.[113]

It would be a misreading of Augustine to couch his theory of the person as 'subjectivist', at least in a post-Cartesian sense. The return into one's self is not primarily or ultimately a return to *one's* self, but rather to oneself as a locus for an encounter with God; indeed, the very existence of the human person is constituted by its encounter with and response to God's calling one into being by love.[114] This also means that God is implicated in all human reasoning. As Mathewes writes, 'human agency is always already related to both God and the world; thus, it chastens modern predilections for absolute autonomy while still affirming the subject's importance'.[115] For Augustine, turning inwards is not an exercise in self-indulgence, but the very path towards finding God. The conception of the subject in the present is of a far different character than that of Augustine's time.[116] As Ong-Van-Cung makes clear, Augustine understands the human person as that which cannot think itself apart from God.[117] From the other side of things, one cannot access God without also examining oneself; in a sense, one comes to God in virtue of coming home to oneself.[118]

The foregoing insights establish the integral connection between God and the human being, glimpsed through the concept of *imago*. However, I believe that these positions are pushed to a new level in light of J.-L. Marion's treatment of Augustine's exegesis of Genesis.

Nihility, or the 'no-thinglyness' of the human person

In his treatment of *Gn. litt.*, Marion notes the distinction which Augustine introduces between the creation of all other worldly things on the one hand and man on the other. The former are created according to their own distinct form or type. Augustine writes that God declares that things should be made according to their own image. Thus these things have their own proper image and resemble themselves (*secundum suam similitudinem*, Gen 1:11–12).[119] In contrast, God makes man according to *God's own* image, not any other image. Hence human identity is fundamentally premised not on anything that it possesses intrinsically, but rather on God. Marion cites Augustine's exegesis of Genesis in the thirteenth book of the *Conf*:[120] 'After all, you [=God] did not say, "let there be human beings according to their kind", but "let us make a human being after *our* image and likeness"'.[121] God's unique blessing to the human person is creating him without a particular definition; the fact that man is always referred to God means that, among other things, man can increase indefinitely in happiness.[122] I would add that this suggests a continuous, even eschatological dimension to one's self-enquiry.

Augustine's understanding of divine incorporeality introduces a further challenge to human identity. The human being is grounded, in a sense, in *nothing*, for no particular thing is God.[123] Elsewhere

I have written about the importance of divine incorporeality for Augustine. However, here I shall illustrate this idea from a different perspective. According to Beattie, the character Tom in A. C. Grayling's theatre play *On Religion* illustrates the view that God cannot be confined to human categories. This is what Tom calls the 'no-thinglyness' of God.[124] Tom draws upon the story of Moses ascending Mount Sinai. He notes that the closer Moses draws to God, the thicker the clouds become, obscuring Moses' sight.[125] In contrast, the people below forge an image of a calf from gold and worship it.[126] Their idolatry demonstrates the human tendency to place constraints on God. One reduces God to human terms, and loses him in doing so.[127] Rather than opening oneself in vulnerability to the ineffable God, one clings to something as a source of comfort, even if false.[128] It is an error to think of God as a thing or object; one must open oneself to the possibility of conceiving of God in terms which lie beyond human comprehension and expression.[129]

The human person is simultaneously itself and not itself.[130] Likewise, situated within time and space, the soul is ultimately oriented towards that which transcends and conditions it.[131] As Marion writes, the lack of definition of the human person is simultaneously the question and the answer.[132] One becomes most oneself by ceasing to cling to what is one's own and revealing oneself as created by God, or in Marion's words, bearing the style of God, as a painting reflects the style of an artist.[133] Human identity is paradoxical; one can only find oneself by forsaking oneself.[134] The ground is also the goal; God draws the soul by attracting it, pulling it beyond itself.[135]

A further element follows: grounded in the unconditioned God, the human person admits of inexhaustible depth.[136] Augustine strikes at the heart of the human drama, the challenge of life itself. Oriented towards the infinite, and increasingly aware of one's limitations, one can find true happiness and fulfilment of desire in acknowledging one's own inadequacy and placing one's hope in God.[137] This apparently devastating realization, W. Desmond writes, can orient one in a positive direction.[138] The realization of one's nihility should lead, according to Augustine, to *confessio*, which, as Marion notes, admits of two parts.[139] One is the negative *confessio*, the acknowledgement of one's lack of understanding, but this coincides with the acknowledgement that one is in fact known by God.[140] With the *confessio*, a certain communication takes place between

God and the soul in the silence of one's heart.[141] (Cf. *infra* for more on the importance of the heart in Augustinian introspection.)

Implications for introspection

As already suggested, one can derive certain epistemic implications from Augustine's theological anthropology. If God is essential to human identity, and God lies beyond human comprehension, then there will always be something to the human person that escapes one's knowledge. In the *Conf.*, Augustine's conversion is a lifelong process; yes, one has located God and re-oriented one's focus. However, one continuously explores the divine *mysterium*.[142] According to Desmond, this experience of mystery becomes for Augustine the occasion for the pursuit of further investigation, not an excuse to withdraw from it.[143]

Furthermore, as a result of the soul's conversion, it can see its experiences in a new way. In due course we shall return to the consideration of how the retrospective analysis of previous life experiences is a fundamental feature of Augustine's introspective method. For the moment, one can note that in the *Conf.*, Augustine indicates that experiences which were once obscure or unintelligible have become clear and meaningful.[144] For example, Augustine notices how he failed to place his trust in the One who alone is trustworthy; rather, he looked to human beings and their inventions, but found these inadequate.[145] In looking to these as sources of support, Augustine simultaneously wandered from God and himself.[146]

Augustine's understanding of the creation of the human being discloses the dramatically precarious state of human existence. One's very being is not a given, but rather an objective towards which one must unceasingly strive, as suggested by the twofold aspect of creation as *creari-formari*. The image of God within the soul is *dynamic*; it constitutes the very (possibility of) *relation* between the person and God.[147] As it pertains to the human being as the image of God, this exists in a *tensile* form, that is, is constituted by the spiritual resonance generated between God and the soul.[148]

Human nature admits of a fundamental ambivalence in virtue of its creation simultaneously *ex nihilo* and *ad imaginem*. Because of one's finitude, one has the propensity to recede towards the non-being whence one was called.[149] In *Trin.* 8, Augustine distinguishes between the mind (*animus*) as an entity possessed of value and as that which can deliberately turn towards God and be fulfilled. The same idea can be expressed in negative terms, meaning that when one turns from the good, one does not thereby cease to *be*, although one does in fact lose contact with the highest good.[150] Despite the *a priori* presence of God to the human soul, this presence is not thereby self-evident to the mind. As Ong-Van-Cung explains, the realization of the presence of God's light to the mind is a result of one's *exercitatio animae*, by means of which one can *see* how God is present to one.[151] The imprint of God within the soul is not clearly perceived; therefore, it must be recovered through a process of introspection.[152]

The doctrine of *imago Dei* has a variety of implications, but ultimately it is soteriological.[153] Among other things, this means that drawing closer to God is not accomplished through rational or ethical judgement but by *loving* God.[154] This is why Augustine believes that love is essential for growth in knowledge.[155] In this respect one can see the theological difference in Augustine brought to the fore, as love alone is capable of bridging the gap between the finite and the infinite.[156] Moreover, I believe that the current discussion of Augustine's anthropology can be related to his understanding of pride – a false trust in oneself – and the way in which it is mutually exclusive with love.[157] To reiterate, alone the human being tends towards nothingness, a movement which is accelerated by pride. In contrast, one is only oneself to the extent that one places oneself in the source of one's being.

We have arrived at the paradoxical concept of the creation of man in the image of God, an image which is not any particular 'thing' or model but relies upon one's self-exploration in search of one's divine ground. It requires that one truly love and seek God, place one's entire being in him. In the *Sol.*, for example, Augustine's inner dialogue moves from a trust in his own rational capacities to the recognition that he requires God's help to advance in knowledge. Moreover, it is Augustine's unique approach to the dialogical method which leads him to this position. For the moment, however, let us dwell further on the way in which the human being derives its identity from God. For this purpose, I turn to two of his *Sermones ad populum* (75 and 76), in which he portrays Peter as an archetype of the constant human struggle for personal stability.

I argue that Peter symbolizes the fluidity of the human person, vacillating between trusting completely in God and losing oneself in the sundry tempests of the *saeculum*.

Peter as model of the drama of human life

Augustine views the biblical Peter as a symbol of the overall human condition and the condition of the Church in the midst of the world. Although the focus has been and will continue to be the constitution of the individual self, the ecclesiological aspect of Augustine's treatment here is not altogether out of place. In addition to the aforementioned importance of interpersonal relationships in the self's identity, Augustine would eventually come to see the Church as the ideal community in which one can attain full self-realization. One might even say therefore that the respective analyses of Peter and the Church are inseparable if distinct themes. Augustine states that Peter is the foundation of the Church which is in turn founded on Christ. This suggests that, just as the identity of Peter as a symbol of the Church refers its identity and sustenance to Christ, so too should the human person be grounded in God.[158]

Let us first consider the passage in which Christ asks his followers about his identity. They report the various answers they have heard, but directly addressing them, Jesus asks what *they* think. Peter responds on behalf of the others. In confessing that Christ is the Son of the living God, Peter represents the *firmi* of the Church. Shortly thereafter, Peter is horrified about Christ's plan to proceed to his death; in attempting to prevent this, he represents the *infirmi*[159] and elicits the infamous rebuke, 'Get behind me, Satan.' The apparent rapidity with which Peter could change from blessed to banished is due to his understanding, more specifically the *way* in which he interpreted his experiences. When Peter confesses that Jesus is in fact the Son of the living God, he relies upon revelation not from human ability but from God alone. However, when Peter attempts to prevent Jesus from proceeding with his plan, which would involve suffering and death, he begins to think and understand in human terms, that is, not orienting his reasoning to God but rather fixating on himself and his own humanity,[160] which detached from God is sheer nothingness. He ceases to consider the things of God but those of human beings.

In virtue of this twofold sense to Peter, a symbol of the Church, Augustine suggests that the Church consists *essentially* of both the *firmi* and the *infirmi*.[161] The *firmi* are those who are strong in faith and morals and have a clear sense of their goal; rather than exclude the weak and the struggling, they are called to assist them.[162] However, Augustine also challenges the very categories of *firmi* and *infirmi*, suggesting that they can switch very quickly or appear misleading. The greatest obstacle to becoming strong is the idea that one is strong in oneself, in virtue of one's own powers (*Multos autem impedit a firmitate praesumptio firmitatis*).[163] Rather, one must be weak (in oneself) and acknowledge this weakness, so that one can become strong in God (*Non firmaretur, si non infirmaretur, ut abs [Deo] in [Deo] perficeretur*).[164] The apparent paradox disappears when one recalls that the human person is created and always referred to God's own image. In the soul's turning to its author, it is completed, fulfilled and indeed, made firm and secure.[165]

One can relate Augustine's theological anthropology and epistemology to his exegesis of the gospel passage in which Jesus walks on water. From their boat, Peter and the other disciples see a man (Jesus) walking on the water in the midst of the storm. Peter asks this man to order him to walk on the water, too, if it is truly Christ. Augustine identifies in Peter's request an implicit confession of faith in God and in one's dependence on him.[166] When Peter steps out of the boat and walks on the water, he becomes a symbol for the *firmi* of the Church.[167] Because of his faith, Peter is able to walk to meet Jesus. Though Peter is the agent, his ability to complete the action comes from his recognition of his own powerlessness and nothingness and his dependence on the divine.[168] He only begins to sink when he is distracted from the Lord and begins to trust in his own powers.[169] Despite this momentary lapse, Peter is rescued after calling upon the Lord. In addition to Peter, the other disciples also illustrate the importance of total reliance on God. (This dynamic seems to reflect that of *auersio* and *conuersio*, more on which *infra*.) In the midst of the storm, had the disciples raised the sails, it would have done more harm than good. This symbolizes the ultimate futility of all (merely) human efforts and the need to place one's trust in the divine.[170]

The resolution of the scene of walking on water witnesses the winds subsiding and the comforted disciples with the Lord in the boat. According to Augustine, this situation prefigures eternal life, a peaceful dwelling with the source of all creation, where God will be both known and loved (*et cognoscitur et amatur*).[171] All people are pilgrims in this world, yet not all desire to return to their origin.[172] In this life, one suffers the storms of the world, yet the ship, a symbol of the Church, can carry one safely to one's destination.[173] Augustine closes *S. 76* by complementing theological speculation with pastoral realism. Just as Peter called upon the Lord for help once he began to sink, so too should one do so when one begins to sink in the maelstrom of worldly desire.[174] Even by acknowledging that one is perishing, one opens oneself to Christ's saving hand (*Dic*: pereo; *ne pereas*).[175]

The 'constantly inconstant' Peter represents the tenuousness of the human condition: Given to be towards God's image, the soul only maintains its identity to the extent that it refuses to cling to it. Indeed, the *imago* is not a distinct thing or model itself, but rather consists of the dynamism generated between God and the soul which has turned to it. This paradox informs Augustine's account of rationality and interiority. Whilst all of these arise within and respond to certain philosophical questions, they have both their origin and goal in the Christian economy of salvation. One's love of God ultimately bridges the insurmountable gulf between the human and the divine. We see that love is the way that leads to the goal and origin, for all things proceed from God's being, which is love itself.

Enarrationes in Psalmos[176]

Augustine's *Enarrationes in Psalmos* is a work of particular interest for the study of Augustine's narrative and dialogical methodology as well as interiority. These extended reflections reveal not only the profound and essential interiority of God but, in working through the implications of this theological principle, anticipate ideas which will be discussed at greater length in the following chapters.

The form of *enarratio* accommodates both a simple recounting as well as a retrospective interpretation of one's experiences.[177] As J. Bouman notes, the genre of *enarratio*, used since the time of Varro (116 BCE to 27 BCE), combines exegetical commentary with attention to both grammatical and literary components of the text.[178] According to Stock, Augustine's *Enarrationes* 'constitute a metanarrative, or internal conversation, within himself, that is carried on during his entire lifetime'.[179] Indeed, this series of commentaries deals especially with the coincidence of knowledge of God and of the soul.[180] The treatment of this source is crucial because, according to Hankey, 'the essential connection between self-knowledge and the knowledge of God is most thoroughly worked through *practically* in the *Enarrationes in Psalmos* and *theoretically* in the *De Trinitate*'.[181] Furthermore, the *En. Ps.* contain extensive introspective commentaries, for instance on the theme of the *cubiculum cordis*.[182] In what follows, I consider Augustine's understanding of the reciprocal interaction of head and heart as one interrogates oneself and the nature of created reality.

The presence of God in the heart

In Matthew 6:6, Jesus enjoins one to enter into one's room, shut the door and pray to God ('But when you pray, go into your room, close the door and pray to your Father, who is unseen.'). In *En. Ps.* 4, Augustine links Psalm 4:4 ('search your *hearts* and be silent') with Mt 6:6. Augustine identifies the 'chamber' of Mt 6:6 with the inner sanctum of the heart, the *cubiculum cordis*.[183] According to Ong-Van-Cung, Augustine understands the heart as 'the place in us where God speaks and where it is necessary to return to find truth'.[184] However, one must also note that the heart is a place of restlessness and dynamic activity.[185] Augustine states in *Conf.* 10 that the heart is the centre of his identity.[186] It is a locus of contact with God: God sees one's heart, the seat of one's desires and thoughts.[187] In *En. Ps.* 35.5, Augustine describes the heart (*cubiculum cordis*) as a locus of intimate encounter with God.[188] In this respect, Augustine is in continuity with Ambrose, who invites one to enter into one's into one's private inner chamber, a location of 'profound intimacy' (*alta praecordia*), and then to shut the door.[189] Moreover, as Huian suggests, not only does the language of an inner chamber indicate a sense of closeness, it also surpasses categories of 'possession' in favour of 'mutual indwelling',[190] such that one can describe 'the human as a home for the divine and the divine as a home for the human'.[191]

One finds in the *En. Ps.* evidence for Augustine's understanding of the human person as 'dialectically constituted'.[192] In *En. Ps.*

17.7, Augustine states that God always already dwells within and enlivens the soul.[193] Hence the retreat into oneself for Augustine is never a solipsistic movement. When one enters within one's heart and shuts the door behind, one allows oneself to be regarded by God, to bask in light of the divine countenance.[194] One's inner space is supported by prayer to that which is other than one and is always already a response to God's initiative.[195] Furthermore, Huian argues that this divine inner presence also has methodological consequences. In virtue of the human person's relation to the infinite God, the soul can rightly be called unknowable.[196] Just as the incomprehensible God challenges conventional language and categories and demands an apophatic method, the same can therefore be said for the investigation of the self. 'If the hidden face of God', she writes, 'requires an apophatic approach, so does the hidden heart of man'.[197]

The door to one's heart

We have considered what it means to enter into one's heart; what is the significance of leaving the door opened or closed? To explore this, let us consider the distinction Augustine draws between two intentions of prayer. He distinguishes between praying to God for certain things and seeking God alone (*Aliud est aliquid inquirere a Domino, aliud ipsum Dominum inquirere, En Ps.* 33.2.9, PL 36). Those interested in the former leave the door to their hearts wide open, allowing fear of loss and desire for gain to become established. These unwelcome guests cause turmoil within the soul, urging it constantly to flee from itself. One must cleanse one's soul, which is only possible through prayer, confession and divine help. God is always present, but from one's purification, God can dwell within one more profoundly. Moreover, when one's *cubiculum* is in order, one is able to perceive spiritual goods and to seek them above all other things.[198]

Augustine presents a similar vision in *En. Ps.* 35, wherein he distinguishes between those who find joy in present things on the one hand and those who place their hope in the 'shadow of God's wings' (*En. Ps.* 35.12), a future[199] or perhaps an eschatological good. Augustine draws on the same text to differentiate between Adam and Christ. Those who prefer earthly goods belong to the former.[200] To enjoy full humanity, however, requires clinging to God ('*Tamdiu est aliquid homo, quamdiu illi haeret a quo factus est homo. Nam recedens ab illo, nihil est homo, et cum haeret illis [hominibus]*'[201]). Anything that God could give one is less than God himself (*Quidquid tibi dedero, uilius est quam ego*), and God wishes to give the soul only the greatest of all gifts (*meipsum habe, me fruere, me amplectere*).[202]

One must ask God for goods of the internal order, God himself, and not external goods.[203] In *En. Ps.* 12, Augustine states that God's gifts are spiritual and do not pertain to the *saeculum* (*bona spiritalia, non ad humanum diem pertinentia*).[204] Closing the door means asking God for what only he can give. While knowledge of God lies beyond human power, one can raise oneself to some knowledge of the divine when one frees oneself from mundane concerns.[205] When we ask for this, writes Favry, we ask for more than we can possibly imagine: 'une prière dans la nuit ne peut demander que la vraie lumière'.[206] Although one should seek God and God alone, this capacity lies beyond human capacity on this side of the veil (*nondum potes totus*). One's hope lies in reaching out to God in faith (*ex fide continge me*), from which one will be able to attach oneself to him (*inhaerebis mihi*).[207]

Those who are interested in particular things of the world leave the doors of their hearts wide open, allowing the fear of loss and desire for gain to become established within them.[208] Ps 18:7 states that the foundations of mountains shook, for God was angry. This symbolizes the divine attempt to eradicate the love of temporal things from human hearts, especially of the proud.[209] God never hides his face from one, though scripture employs this term to describe a lack of knowledge of God for a soul which is not yet sufficiently purified.[210] The unwelcome guests of false desire and sin distress the soul and urge it to flee from itself. If returning to a troubled home causes disturbance, how much more so to a troubled conscience.[211] Indeed, as Augustine suggests in the fourth book of the *Conf.*, if one's soul is in torment, where can one go to flee from oneself?[212] One remains in spiritual adversity until one returns to one's soul, at which point God can direct the soul to knowledge of himself.[213] Purification is only possible through prayer, confession and divine help.[214] One may find encouragement in Ps 4:3: 'The Lord will hear me when I cry unto him.' Augustine interprets this passage as an exhortation to the soul to beseech God for help in a spiritual manner: 'I believe that we are here warned, that with great earnestness of heart, that is, with an inward and incorporeal cry, we should implore help of God.'[215]

In addition to the interior dwelling of God, Augustine's treatment of the Psalms provides insight into the pursuit of integration. Efficacious prayer includes the recitation of the Psalms themselves, through which one can redirect one's heart to God (*En. Ps.* 32.2.1–2).[216] Augustine understands the chanting of the Psalms as a means to recover a prelapsarian state of psycho-physical integrity,[217] which means that 'the body and the passions are always subject to reason'.[218] A lack of personal harmony implies that one cannot be in harmony with others – especially the Church – and God.[219] As the opening lines of the *Conf.* indicate, the praise of God is necessary for full human flourishing.[220] One flees from God to God (anger to grace) by a non-spatial, inner movement or transformation.[221] When one's *cubiculum* is in order, one is able to perceive spiritual goods and to seek them above all other things.[222]

In tribulatione dilatasti mihi

To shut the door of one's inner chamber is to seek God alone.[223] However, progress in one's relationship with God results in knowledge which causes one pain. Augustine distinguishes between two types of tribulation. One pertains to the ineluctable misfortunes of human life. In *En. Ps.* 49, however, he describes a second sense of tribulation as that which reveals one's finite condition. One experiences pain as a result of recognizing that in this world one is not yet with God, one must continue to suffer and no temporal consolation will ever make one happy. Though difficult, this kind of tribulation must be actively sought, for its discovery is essential to one's progress in wisdom.[224]

The Psalms provide Augustine with, in Favry's felicitous phrase, 'une riche théologie des larmes'.[225] Augustine develops such a theology in dialogue with the Psalms and with reference to the consolation promised in Mt 5:4 ('Blessed are those who mourn, for they will be comforted.').[226] The sadness of human life is poignantly symbolized through birth: a child enters the world crying, not laughing,[227] and that is the good scenario. Throughout the *En. Ps.*, Augustine envisions from one perspective both the severity of death and the hope of deliverance[228] (cf. e.g. *En. Ps.* 38.18). A consistent refrain of Augustine's preaching on the Psalms is the necessity of Christ's saving activity, freeing one from the consequences of sin, which one is powerless to accomplish on one's own.[229]

Fallen human nature is characterized by an enslavement to *imagines falsae*.[230] A key lesson that post-lapsarian humanity must learn is that there is no rest from trouble in this world.[231] One must suffer and be tested, yet eventually God will free one from all troubles.[232] As long as one is in this life, that is, situated within time (signified by 'day' in the Psalm text), one will endure sadness. This also suggests a prayer for things eternal and freedom from the world.[233] In *En. Ps.* 37.11, Augustine states that the human condition remains in sadness until it is healed in soul and body (hereby he also confirms the *incarnational* nature of the person). This twofold healing consists in removing the soul from illusions and granting the body true health, that is, immortality.[234] Sin empties human nature, makes it like a puff of wind (*homo uanitati similis factus est*).[235] As a result of sin, human life itself becomes temptation (*Versuchung*).[236] One prospers in this world only through a vain and illusory felicity; human hearts are hardened against God so that no spiritual fruit can prosper[237] (*En. Ps.* 124.1).

In *Doctr. Chr.* (2.7.9–11), Augustine develops a seven-part spiritual itinerary, the third stage of which consists in *scientia*. However, this particular kind of knowledge is troubling and results in tears.[238] In *En. Ps.* 83.5, Augustine notes that the one who ascends the stages of spiritual ascent and arrives at 'knowledge' understands from Scripture that there is a 'secret' or 'hidden' kind of tribulation. This is unknown especially to those who think that they are happy, living in blissful ignorance and unaware of the trouble surrounding them at every moment.[239] The 'vale of tears' is the start of the ascent to God, an itinerary which proceeds by degrees (cf. *Conf.* 9.2). One begins in this vale, yet ultimately escapes from it (*in conualle plorationis* vs. *a conualle plorationis*).[240] The vale of tears refers to humility: seized by holy fear, one renounces one's pride[241] (*S.* 347.2; Ps 83:6). Hence one can say that the acquisition of this troubling knowledge is ultimately therapeutic, as it disabuses one of false hope, thus providing consolation.[242] 'Le progressant,' writes Favry, 'échappe donc à l'illusion des consolations d'ordre temporel.'[243] The third stage brings one to knowledge, which leads to tears, not pride.

By these tears, one is led to prayer, which in turn obtains for the soul divine help to prevent it from hopelessness.[244]

The tears of true piety must be distinguished from the tears of carnal desire, for the latter do not lead to true consolation, as Augustine states in *S. 53*.[245] Augustine provides the example of a father who loses one son and mourns this dead child. However, he subsequently receives another son and rejoices. It is possible that this father is still bound by the logic of the world, the fear of loss and desire for gain. In wiping away tears, one still harbours the fear that something will happen to occasion them yet again.[246] The son who is lost is a subject of sorrow, the other is a cause for fear.[247] Thus in neither case does this person find true consolation.[248]

In *En. Ps.* 136.5, Augustine distinguishes between finding tribulation and being found by it. The latter case involves the common experiences of human life.[249] However, the other kind of tribulation involves discovering the truth that as long as we are in this vale of tears, we must continue to suffer, and that this condition will only be lifted after death. In several locations, Augustine specifies a tribulation that must be sought, even and especially in the joys of the world (Ps 114:3–4).[250] Without searching for tribulation, one risks living in illusion and self-deception.[251] *En. Ps.* 122.6 states that those not knowing about the other kind of tribulation have more to fear than those who know it. A key passage in this respect is Ecclesiastes 1:18, according to which those who add to their knowledge add to their sorrow.[252] Searching for this kind of tribulation shows one's love for Christ and true desire for the eschatological homeland.[253] To be sure, the life of faith is inherently demanding: 'Augustin évoque fréquemment l'affliction des fidèles au cours de leur montée vers Dieu.'[254] He suggests that the true love of God results in the rending of one's heart (*Quis est autem humilis, nisi timens Deum, et eo timore conterens cor in lacrimis confessionis et paenitentiae?*).[255] Nevertheless, Augustine maintains that in spite of difficulties, these need not cause harm to the hearts of one who hopes in God.[256]

4

The Methods of 'Augustinian Self-constitution'

Dialogue in (late) antiquity

Recent scholarship has recognized the complexity of the dialogue genre within early Christian literature and the pressing need for a multifaceted contextualization and analysis of this form of discourse. Academics have questioned the adequacy of speaking in general terms about 'dialogue' as a literary genre in antiquity, even and especially within Christian literature. Hirzel (1895) provides a starting point for talking about dialogue in more precise terms. R. Thiel paraphrases his definition of dialogue (*Erörterung in Gesprächsform*) as 'rational-diskursive Argumentation' among two or more interlocutors.[1] One can speak of a spectrum (*Skala*) of dialogue forms, although this spectrum does not exhaust the full extent of dialogical literature.[2] Thiel sets a broad definition so as not to preclude certain works from consideration in this genre.[3] However, he also distinguishes between pedagogical dialogues and more speculative ones.[4] Thiel claims that rational argumentation is the distinguishing feature of authentic dialogue which separates it from works which are merely 'didactic' or even 'catechetical' in nature.[5]

The phrase 'Augustinian self-constitution' is Remes's formulation. Remes, 'Inwardness and infinity of selfhood', 174.

Indeed, a major intuition concerning the authentic expression of the dialogue genre is that the conclusion should not be predetermined, leaving room for the discussants openly to pursue truth.[6] According to A. Cameron, S. Goldhill's 2009 volume on dialogue in antiquity articulated and elaborated on this idea. Christianity, in search of certainty and binding orthodoxy, could not brook 'genuine' dialogue in the Socratic sense of the term, that is, as open-ended, since the answer was already settled. Rather, Christian 'dialogue' could only mimic authentic dialogue for the sake of convincing one of a particular position rather than ingenuously seeking truth. Thus one could claim that classical dialogue ended with the rise of social and political Christianity.[7]

In her 2014 monograph *Dialoguing in Late Antiquity*, A. Cameron presents a view which strongly contrasts with those expressed in the Goldhill volume. Similar to Thiel, Cameron argues that it is difficult to define 'dialogue' in the first place, and any *a priori* definition runs the risk of begging many questions.[8] She writes that no one composed a treatise on the dialogue genre itself, and as such it contrasts with rhetoric, for which many formal rules existed.[9] In fact, rhetoric and dialectic were viewed in opposition to one another,[10] the former orderly and the latter more spontaneous and informal.[11] The inherent malleability of the dialogue genre could accommodate a number of tasks, such as introspection, meditation (on solitude), consolation and prayer.[12] Furthermore, Cameron concurs with Van Hoof (2010), stating that a desideratum of the scholarship is attention to the complexity of early Christian literature, and in particular the place of dialogue in this broader framework.[13]

It is also noteworthy that earlier, non-Christian sources displayed a tendency towards a more predetermined form of dialogue. One witnesses in Seneca's oeuvre in particular – in contrast to the tentative methodology of Cicero, for example – a shift from an open dialogue to a didactic monologue, wherein a teacher directs a neophyte. The philosophical basis of this methodology, according to A. Michel, is Seneca's 'dogmatic' epistemology. Though he does demonstrate a certain tolerance in his work, Seneca sees it as his duty to instruct and disabuse others of their false beliefs.[14]

Although her stated focus lies with the literary elements of the early Christian dialogue, Cameron also stresses the importance of the dialogue's place within the socio-political setting of late antiquity. In this respect, she challenges the claim that dialogue died with the rise of Constantinian Christianity. Dialogue remained a significant genre throughout antiquity; it continued long after and in various ways.[15] Moreover, although Byzantine emperors, inspired by Constantine's example, did attempt to suppress questioning and discussion, official doctrines were often openly challenged.[16] 'The reality', Cameron writes, 'was continual struggle, reinvention and resistance, above all, continual talk and continual arguing'.[17] In fact, dialogue served the purpose of Christianization and the striving for unity and orthodoxy.[18] According to R. Miles, Augustine himself expressed this opinion, although he specified that theological debate was the prerogative of the bishops.[19] (However, Miles also notes that Augustine's practises in composing and circulating his missives belie his bold pronouncement.[20]) In any case, the attempt to stifle open discourse on doctrine in the hope of establishing certainty and thereby stability often had the opposite effect.[21] Doctrinal uniformity remained an ideal, never actually achieved in the sixth century. The attempt to secure it came through the use of coercion and political power.[22] Cameron urges scholars to take official doctrinal declarations with a pinch of salt, following the method established in other areas of late antique historiography.[23]

Augustine in the context of classical dialogue

In light of the foregoing observations, I believe it is reasonable to situate Augustine's more didactic and monological dialogues (e.g. *De Musica*) within the broader scope of the dialogue genre; they need not be omitted *a priori*.[24] Similarly, the spectrum of the genre seems to be sufficiently flexible as to accommodate Augustine's less conventional dialogues, in particular the *Soliloquia* and the *Confessiones* (more on this topic *infra*).

These general considerations inevitably raise the question of dialogue in Augustine's own intellectual biography. The fact of the matter is that as a bishop, Augustine did not write any dialogues. One interpretation of this change in Augustine's methodology is that he underwent a radical intellectual shift, such that the dialogue genre became not only obsolete but even scandalous. Brown and O'Donnell would see this as a result of Augustine's increasingly dogmatic attitude,[25] while those sympathetic to Goldhill may see this as a part of a larger trend in late antiquity among Christian authors.[26] Indeed, scholars such as Baumgartner, Catapano, Ritter and Silva Santos distinguish between a 'first' Augustine and a 'second Augustine'.[27] Similarly, Mohrmann draws a sharp distinction between the Cassiciacum dialogues and the rest of Augustine's oeuvre.[28] The early dialogues, which are more open-ended, reflect what Conybeare calls the 'liminal, enquiring state' of Augustine's intellectual development.[29] Mathewes suggests that the early Augustine, as opposed to the 'apologetic Augustine' of *Ciu.*, engages in a more open and less dogmatic form of dialogue.

However, even though some scholars maintain a strict separation between the earlier and the later Augustine, certain observations can nuance the claim that Augustine simply abandoned the dialogue genre altogether.[30] For one, Clark suggests that Augustine's move away from dialogue was primarily pragmatic rather than intellectual, motivated by the crucial difference between the activity of a philosopher and of a bishop, respectively.[31] In his capacity as the latter, Augustine had to be particularly sensitive to his public persona.[32] The main reason that he no longer composed any dialogues, in Clark's words, is 'not that he is a Christian, but that he is a Christian bishop'.[33]

Furthermore, although Augustine composed no dialogues after the 390s, that does not mean that he abandoned the writing technique of dialectic itself. Rather, he incorporated the dialogical form into other works, such as exegetical commentaries.[34] In addition, these dialogical elements consisted at least in part of edited records of actual conversations in which Augustine himself had participated.[35] Indeed, other genres such as *sermones*,[36] *epistolae*[37] and *enarrationes*[38] admit of dialogical elements.[39]

Certain scholars hold that the letter was a form or extension of the dialogue genre.[40] For example, Lim (2008) argues that epistles served as a 'surrogate dialogue form' within the context of late antique Christianity.[41] This understanding of letters extends to figures such as Cicero, according to whom they were part of a larger conversation.[42] These texts were widely circulated by the sender, somewhat like a social media post.[43] The *audience* of the letters was wider than that of the individual recipient. 'These letters were no more private documents,' writes Miles, 'than dialogues were private discussions'.[44]

Some of Augustine's epistles reflect this overlap with dialogue. For instance, through their correspondence (*Epp.* 158–64, 169), Augustine and Evodius continued the dialogue they had begun in *Quant. An.*[45] Although it found no permanent foundation in Milan, Augustine's model of a dialogical community did meet with modest success across the Mediterranean in North Africa.[46] Augustine addressed twelve of his earliest letters, *Epp.* 3–14, to Nebridius beginning in the winter of 386–7.[47] According to Köckert, Augustine composed *Ep.* 3 in Italy and *Epp.* 4–14 in Africa; in particular, *Epp.* 4 and 13 originated at Thagaste.[48] She writes that Augustine and Nebridius seem to have understood their correspondence – redolent of Neoplatonism – as an extension of the Cassiciacum project and its search for happiness.[49] In their letters, Augustine and Nebridius provided a sketch of a philosophical life, even though it eluded their grasp. The missives themselves became a substitute for this unattainable philosophical ideal.[50]

Scepticism

Since the nineteenth century, scholars have extensively discussed the works of the early Augustine, especially the Cassiciacum dialogues.[51] The interest in these and related questions persists.[52] While twentieth-century scholarship largely focused on questions of historicity or doctrinal development, E. Kenyon has pioneered a new method in recent years. Instead of looking at the dialogues in light of Augustine's intellectual biography, this new approach treats the dialogues on their own terms, investigating each of them as accomplishing a particular philosophical goal. Furthermore, previous treatments of these texts have been only partial, divided along methodological lines, meaning that Augustine's early dialogues do not find an obvious location in contemporary scholarship. Philosophers and historians, Kenyon writes, are not sufficiently attentive to the texts' structures, whereas literary scholars focus on formal and stylistic qualities while ignoring their content. Kenyon seeks to merge both approaches and thereby to illuminate Augustine's larger project in the dialogues.[53] His work has advanced two major claims, namely (1) the identification of the method underlying all of Augustine's dialogues and (2) a recognition of the positive role of scepticism in his thought.

Concerning the first, Kenyon[54] argues that Augustine's dialogues are structured according to a tripartite pedagogical-philosophical method (ARP). First, through aporetic debate, one becomes aware of one's contradictory beliefs. Secondly, one reflects on the operation of reason, thereby generating novel insights and enabling a new perspective. Finally, one proposes a *probabile* conclusion about a particular topic. As for the second, Kenyon has argued that Augustine recuperates scepticism in his early *dialogi*.[55] He argues that, in contrast to Descartes, who seeks utterly to undermine the sceptical position, Augustine retains some aspects of scepticism to advance his arguments.[56] In a 2014 article, Kenyon reads *Acad.* as a paradigmatic example of Augustine's scepticism in action. He claims that this dialogue is not intended to refute scepticism but rather to appropriate it in service of a Platonic objective.[57] According to A. Nordlander, openness to and acceptance of aporia is a fundamental part of Augustine's methodology.[58] In his investigation of Augustine's approach to *interrogatio*, Mathewes elaborates upon this insight.

Charles T. Mathewes on dialogical methodology in Augustine

Charles T. Mathewes argues for the legitimacy of dialogue within the Christian tradition and responds to the foregoing controversy about different forms of dialogue.[59] He indicates a way that the tensions in the dialogue genre can be reframed, such that the motivation for dialogue itself arises *in virtue of*, as opposed to in opposition to, the firm commitment of faith.[60] Though he is addressing contemporary theological interests, Mathewes nevertheless looks to Augustine and the Christian tradition for inspiration.[61] As we have seen in the previous chapter, the human person is 'dialectically constituted', which means, among other things, that difference is paradoxically an essential part of who one is. Clearly, the place of God in one's being is paramount. Thus the first motivation for dialogue emerges from the theological-anthropological fact of one's identity as a human being.[62] Indeed, rather than deliberately engaging in dialogue in one's rational or social activity, Mathewes stresses that one is always already in dialogue as a simple fact of dialectical human being.[63]

Continuing the reflection on theological anthropology, one could also say that in virtue of one's finite and limited condition, truths about the incomprehensible God will lie beyond complete comprehension by the human mind. Augustine himself suggests this, and we have seen the importance of this idea in his theological anthropology. Mathewes too indicates that one's faith is never static, but always a summons to a deeper commitment to and exploration of one's beliefs, truly a *fides quaerens intellectum*.[64] In light of this observation, one can reasonably balance both the centrality of confession with the tentative searching for truth in collaboration with others.[65] To be sure, this position envisages an ideal, hardly a lived reality. But the importance of this reconsideration I believe is to say that the ostensible tensions between faith and dialogue are a result of human limitations rather than fundamentally opposed ways of thinking about the Christian life.

In addition to considering dialogue *ad extra*, Mathewes also stresses the importance of interior dialogue (more on which anon). The dialectic here again develops from the recognition of one's divided self, that every believer is imperfect and in search of complete belief: *I believe, Lord; help thou my unbelief*.[66] Dialogue therefore serves the Christian life by enabling and promoting conversion in the individual believer. Thus one can say, as Mathewes puts it, that dialogue is a 'theological imperative'[67] demanded by Augustine's overarching view of the human person and one's enquiry into the incomprehensible God.[68] Remarkably, it is *in virtue of*, not in spite of, his Christian beliefs – especially those about the nature of God – that Augustine embraces a position which avoids complete dogmatism.[69] As Michel writes, Augustine looks to dialogue as a way of striking a balance between making claims to truth while respecting one's own limitations: 'le dialogue apparaît donc comme le double refus du doute et de la suffisance: l'homme ne trouve pas en soi la certitude mais il la trouve en Dieu'.[70] One's knowledge and very identity must ever remain grounded in God.[71] This Augustinian vision is a fundamental lens through which I interpret Augustine's approach to dialogue and enquiry.

Interrogation in Augustine's *Confessiones*

In a 2002 article, Mathewes proposes a novel interpretation of Augustine's thought, arguing that Augustine is 'more centrally dialogical than metaphysically dogmatic'.[72] The conventional reading of Augustine as the dogmatist *par excellence* misses the true nature and importance of questioning in his oeuvre in general and the *Conf.* in particular.[73] Mathewes notes that in his 1992 commentary on the *Conf.*, O'Donnell contends that the original text of the thirteenth and final book ends not with 'Amen' as some editions have it, but rather 'aperietur'.[74] The former was likely a later scribal addition, perhaps seen as implicit in the text, or as the result of a deeply felt need to provide some sort of closure for the work.[75] In any case, Mathewes argues that this later interpolation completely changes the interpretation of the *Conf.*, in particular the work's understanding of faith and the philosophical life.[76] The original manuscript suggests that the *Conf.* is not intended to provide clear resolution or conclusion.[77] Rather than reading the end of the *Conf.* as a terminus, one should read it as a beginning, an opening to ever further questioning.[78] This suggests I believe a dialectical nature to the work and the methodology underlying it.

A further implication of Mathewes's study is to reconsider the nature of faith itself. Instead of thinking of faith as a final destination and a *regio certitudinis*, one can conceive of faith as a point of departure and as a continuous search for understanding through interrogation.[79] Indeed, Mathewes claims that the 'dogmatic' (my gloss) understanding of faith and belief is 'fundamentally flawed'.[80] This claim makes more sense if one considers that as inexhaustible depth and mystery, God will always exceed human comprehension.[81] If faith cannot be construed in intellectual terms, perhaps it is better conceived as an ongoing relationship. As Mathewes puts it, for Augustine, 'faithful life is a project of resisting our always premature attempts at conclusion, in order better to see the project of "inquiry into God" as an infinite undertaking'.[82] Augustine presents an understanding of faith very far from a simple assent to a series of propositions. Rather, it is a dynamic, ongoing encounter. According to Mathewes, 'questioning, and "seeking" more generally, is not simply a prolegomenon to faith or praise but, in fact, a vital expression of it'.[83] For Augustine, life itself is the continual process of entering ever more deeply into one's enquiry.[84] Life as questioning means occupying a tensile position.

Life as questioning is the fulness of life. One must – in a Heraclitean manner – cast oneself into this process, rather than resist it.[85]

The foregoing 'interrogative' configuration of faith requires a further discussion of the precise nature of questioning at work. Questioning is not first and foremost about a lack of merely intellectual understanding. Rather, it implies a deeper sense of uncertainty. Mathewes likens this unto ice skating, when one begins to move freely on the ice. In interrogation, this feeling of instability results from a sense of being grasped, compelled, called by something beyond oneself. Thus the need to pursue it arises more from an existential need, indeed, a sense of one's nothingness, rather than from there mere interest in filling a lacuna.[86] Questioning discloses one's inexhaustible depths to oneself, but also makes one aware of one's ultimate potential. In this, however, it also reveals one's own inadequacy in pursuing ultimate truth.[87] As we shall see, I believe that Augustine presents this insight in the *Sol.*, among other locations.

Augustine ultimately arrived at a disposition of 'eschatological patience' towards questions of profound significance, rather than officiously demanding an immanent resolution.[88] He shifted from expecting immediate and unequivocal answers to gradually understanding his experiences over the course of time.[89] This disposition, I contend, is a further indication of the way in which personal self-understanding is dialectical in relation to the divine. In other words, if as a human being one is essentially constituted by the divine, and the divine is incomprehensible, then there is something about each person that lies beyond complete understanding. However, rather than viewing this as a discouragement or an excuse to avoid searching, one is encouraged to enter into an inexhaustibly deepening search for truth, which always involves both God and the soul. Thus one could say, to borrow Mathewes's aforementioned fortunate phrase, 'eschatological patience' is the attitude proper to introspection (and in this respect, I believe Augustine is in continuity with Heraclitus).

The *Soliloquia*[90]

Augustine consciously follows the venerable tradition of classical dialogue initially established by Plato and mediated to the Latin world through Cicero, according to which the optimal method for pursuing philosophical investigation was the dialogue.[91] As Augustine himself avers, the term 'soliloquy' itself is both a neologism of his own invention and a novel form of the classical dialogue genre. B. Stock defines the soliloquy as a dialogue taking place within a single individual which combines elements of literature and philosophy.[92] J. Lagouanère offers a similar definition, describing the soliloquy as 'l'interrogation intérieure de soi face à sa Raison'.[93] Thus the form of the *Sol.* simultaneously imitates and challenges the conventional genre category of dialogue, as on the one hand, two characters are speaking, yet on the other, they are both – so it seems[94] – part of the same individual.[95] The *Sol.* therefore resists precise categorization, occupying a liminal space between monologue and dialogue.[96] On a similar note, W. Otten stresses that in addition to, or even in connection with, the dialogical style of the *Sol.*, the unique *intimacy* of the work demands careful attention.[97]

In contrast to *De ordine*, *De beata uita*, and *De Academicis/ Contra Academicos*, the *Sol.* does not include any of the other members of the Cassiciacum cohort. This observation, coupled with the enigmatic nature of the origins of Augustine's interlocutor Ratio, has led scholars such as B. Voss and I. Milusheva to characterize the *Sol.* as 'non-scenic'.[98] T. Uhle refers to the 1920 *Handbuch der Altertumswissenschaft*, in which the *Sol.* is identified as an 'inner dialogue'.[99] This unique term captures the aspects of both monologue and dialogue contained in the *Sol.*[100] Stock too seems to accept this assessment,[101] as reflected in the title of his 2010 monograph, *Augustine's Inner Dialogue: The Philosophical Soliloquy in Late Antiquity*. Fuhrer too appears to subscribe to this position, stating that the neologism *soliloquium* conveys Augustine's novel concept of a discussion with(in) oneself, as well as an innovation on the traditional genre of the dialogue.[102]

In recent years a new development has occurred for understanding the method of the soliloquy as of crucial significance for the interpretation of Augustine's oeuvre. Stock argues that the early Augustine's discourse on the self – which he understands as the works composed between *c.* 386 and 401 CE – happens in and through the soliloquy. According to Stock, 'when we analyze the topic of the self in works written before 400 … we are almost always talking about what he says in soliloquies …'.[103] Moreover, Catapano and Lagouanère have suggested that the soliloquy is in fact the *normative* form of dialogue in Augustine. As Lagouanère writes of Catapano's position, 'il est possible de considérer que le soliloque ... constitue le paradigme même du dialogue authentique pour Augustin'.[104] From these insights I draw a further conclusion which is of special importance for this research, namely that for Augustine, an *essential connection* obtains between *introspection* and *dialogue*.

In recent years a further insight has been added to the *status quaestionis* of the *Sol.* M. Foley has brought to light the significance of its inherently *dramatic* character, thus revealing a further important fusion of content and methodology. Foley identifies and endeavours to address two lacunae in the scholarship on the *Sol.* First, one has tended to neglect the text in terms of Augustine's overall approach to theatre and drama. Secondly, critical treatments of the *Sol.* are usually confined to the philosophical content of the work and do not address its dramatic and dialogical method.[105] My work applies some of his findings – especially concerning the latter topic – to the analysis of the introspective project of the *Sol.*

The dialectical self in the *Soliloquia*

A key motivation for considering the soliloquy is that it integrates both style and substance. As Stock notes, 'Augustine maintains this link between content and form throughout his early writings, where some of his most interesting discussions of the self are found.'[106] In my estimation, this union reflects the challenge of certain topics of enquiry, namely that their very nature circumscribes the manner in which one approaches them. I believe that introspection is this kind of activity. Just as for Heraclitus, in the search for oneself, one must enter into one's syllaptic constitution, so too for Augustine, the inner dialogue provides the way by which to realize integration. In other words, the method proper to self-enquiry is dialectical. This form or modality of enquiry is especially suited to the nature of its intended object. The method of the soliloquy allows one to regard oneself, albeit obliquely, thus enabling one to unravel the layers of the self.

In Augustine's use of the inner dialogue, there is an essential link between the form and method of the dialogue on the one hand and the conception of the self on the other.[107] The text also calls attention to the mode and methodology that Augustine demonstrates, and indeed invents.[108] The *Sol.* appears to be a dialogue representing division or inner conflict or otherness.[109] Foley cites Barish, who sees an intrinsic connection between one's understanding of theatre and anthropology. Investigating the former gives one insight into the latter.[110] Augustine explores the dramatic nature of being human through the use of drama itself, and also reveals humanity's theatrical nature.[111] Augustine uses two characters or plays two roles in the *Sol.*, suggesting an internal differentiation which, when appreciated, can be enriching and move one beyond the difference itself.[112] Because of the use of the present tense in the text, *Sol.* also bespeaks a performative character, rather than something Augustine is simply recounting.[113] In other words, I believe one can say that through his soliloquizing he is both dramatizing his inner division and otherness yet also forming and speaking himself towards an integrated unity.

Moreover, for both Heraclitus and Augustine, the inner movement is always integrally connected with the ultimate ground of one's existence, which *de iure* lies beyond human comprehension. Early in the *Sol.*, Augustine states his twofold intention for the work, namely knowledge of God and the soul (*Sol.* 1.2.7), the latter of which, according to Fischer, is understood as the finite subject (*die Wirklichkeit des endlichen Ich*).[114] Thus from the outset of Augustine's enquiry, the search for God and the search for the self are inseparable.[115] Interestingly, according to Michel, this twofold search for God and the soul encapsulates the entire history of the dialogue genre in antiquity.[116] He indicates that classical philosophers opted for dialogue because every dialogue involves God. One sees this especially in Augustine's *Sol.*, in which both Ciceronian (dialogical) and Senecan (monological) elements are present, as Augustine speaks with(in) himself/his reason, which connects him with God.[117] Furthermore, in linking the question of the transcendent God with that of the finite self, Augustine raises a revolutionary question which has remained fundamental for philosophical posterity (e.g. Kant and Heidegger).[118] Indeed – in Heraclitean fashion – Augustine's *Sol.* suggests an integral link between God, self and world.[119] According to Otten, one should interpret 'the *Soliloquies* not just as a work about the self, or about the self and God, but also about the cosmos, as a kind of natural extension of self from which it cannot be distinguished by hard and fast boundaries'.[120] These three realities (as also in Heraclitus) are integrally related, thus suggesting a dialectical constitution of the self.[121] The self – intrinsically determined by and related to the infinite God as a source of its identity – is likewise ultimately unknowable. (Recall Heraclitus' pronouncement that one will never find the limits of the soul.) Therefore, one must be in dialogue with this divine Other for the sake of progress in self-knowledge. One sees the essential link between content and method: A dialectical method is appropriate to a dialectical subject (and 'subject' both in the general sense of a matter of enquiry as well as the 'subject' as a synonym for the self).

In addition to the internal differentiation of the self, the form of the *Sol.* reflects the philosophical challenge of the mediation between unity and plurality in the knowledge of God.[122] According to Uhle, the central focus of the *Sol.* is the attempt to resolve the conundrum of unity and difference in a specifically *theological* manner. Augustine desires to know God and the soul. However, God is the perfect unity, indeed, unity itself, while human knowledge is always conditioned by the ineluctable polarity of subject and object, knower and known.[123] The speakers in the dialogue – Ratio and the character Augustine – reflect the problem of unity and multiplicity.[124] Uhle looks to the introductory prayer of the *Sol.* (1.2.1–1.6.3) to substantiate his position. This prayer evokes each member of the Trinity independently in succession – Father (1.2), Son (1.3.1–3) and Holy Spirit (1.3.4–6) – and finally the entire Trinity (1.4.1–8). This passage especially demonstrates a strong link between form and content.[125] Augustine's prayer suggests the Christian response to the challenge of reconciling the unity of God with the inherent plurality of the world. Succinctly put, it is found in the Incarnation.[126] As Uhle writes, 'der dreieine Gott selbst – durch die Inkarnation Christi – in die Welt eingetreten sei und dadurch die Trennung zwischen Einheit und Vielheit überwunden habe'.[127]

Trial and error in the *Soliloquia*

As noted *supra*, Augustine believed that the optimal way to seek truth was through dialogue.[128] However, this method is effective in virtue of revealing one's errors and failures, hardly an inviting proposition. Thus the challenge of philosophical enquiry is a kind of 'Catch-22', in that the pursuit of the highest truths requires vulnerability, yet due to the potential for embarrassment, one may avoid taking the necessary step of engaging in dialogue.[129] The

Sol. offers a means of avoiding this problem by providing a way to reproduce the dialogical method within oneself, shielded from the critical eyes of others.[130] Indeed, Augustine avers through the character Ratio that the motivation for this novel genre was to enable one to pursue truth without feeling self-conscious. When one discovers one's errors, for example, one need not feel ashamed, but simply address the problem and continue (*Sol.* 2.7.14) The important thing is to acknowledge errors and learn from them,[131] which is precisely what Augustine does as the *Sol.* proceeds.

The early stages of the *Sol.* set Augustine on a collision course with disappointment and failure. At 1.2.7, Augustine boldly states that he wishes to know God and the soul. In stating his truest desires, Augustine places himself at risk, rendering himself vulnerable to criticism. He must subject not only his ideas and arguments to critical scrutiny, but also his entire inner life, revealing his self-deception and risking embarrassment (*Sol.* 2.17.31). The cost of wisdom is the opening of oneself to interrogation, not simply from within but also from without. In a way that only it can – for it is internal to Augustine[132] – Ratio probes Augustine's deepest and most inscrutable thoughts, revealing the woeful inadequacy of Augustine's soul for seeking wisdom. Throughout the *Sol.*, Augustine continues to break himself down in ways that would be counterproductive if applied to others (*Sol.* 2.5.8). Ratio demonstrates this in two major ways, namely through revealing Augustine's contradictory beliefs and his numerous instances of self-deception.

At various points in the *Sol.* (1.2.7–4.10; 2.4.5–5.8; 2.6.10–7.14), Ratio's interrogations lead Augustine to discover his incoherent beliefs and poor arguments. This is not incompetence on Augustine's part, but rather a deliberate choice in service of his literary strategy. Augustine intentionally includes flawed arguments to reveal what presuppositions need to be repudiated.[133] One sees here, I believe, the formative element of Augustine's writing. As Foley notes, Ratio plays an ambivalent, almost mischievous role in the text, in particular by deliberately leading Augustine to dead ends.[134] One example arises from Augustine's efforts to define truth and falsity (2.6.10–7.14). At 2.6.10, Augustine defines the false as that which is other than it appears. Ratio proceeds to take Augustine through a number of examples which seem to confirm this hypothesis, leading Augustine to agree with Ratio that 'the likeness of things, which pertains to the eyes, is the mother of falsity' (*Sol.*

2.6.10). Ratio continues to lead Augustine through an elaboration of the argument and a distinction between two different forms of likenesses. Augustine readily agrees with the ostensible conclusions reached by Ratio (2.6.12). As Ratio reiterates, and as Augustine agrees, 'we still name the things false that we observe to be similar to the true' (2.6.12). In the next paragraph, Ratio summarizes its previous arguments, noting Augustine's impatience to continue (2.7.13). Soon thereafter, Ratio leads Augustine to contradict his prior position: Whereas Augustine had endorsed the claim that the false is that which appears to be like the true (2.6.10), Ratio has now gradually brought him to the conclusion that in fact 'likeness is the mother of truth and *unlikeness* the mother of falsity' (2.7.13). Augustine realizes his error and regrets how his haste has revealed his lack of careful reasoning (2.7.13). The following paragraph (2.7.14) contains the aforementioned statement about how the soliloquy provides one a safe haven or 'low stakes' environment in which to try and fail at various arguments. Despite the frustration Augustine experiences, he demonstrates how the soliloquy can in fact accomplish its intended purpose. At 2.8.15, after Ratio's assurance and encouragement, Augustine proceeds to disclose (confess?) his thought process and how it only leads him into confusion and contradiction. If the original motivation for the soliloquy is to provide the student with the necessary encouragement to pursue truth, then it seems like Augustine's text has suggested a path for effectively achieving this goal.

Ratio also focuses on exposing Augustine's self-deception, especially as it pertains to his true desires and motivations (e.g. *Sol.* 1.9.16–11.19). Augustine attempts to hide his sinfulness from Ratio,[135] though Ratio ultimately brings this duplicity to light. For example, while Augustine initially maintains that he desires goods such as wealth not for their own sake but for the sake of wisdom (*Sol.* 1.11.19), Ratio later compels Augustine to acknowledge that this is false (*Sol.* 1.14.25). Ratio foregrounds the imperfections and self-deceptions latent in Augustine's mind, such as the presence of fear, which suggests that he loves goods other than wisdom. This fear detracts from love, thus jeopardizing his ability to discover truth (*Sol.* 1.9.16). Ratio suggests that because certain worldly goods are still appealing to Augustine, his previous desires are dormant rather than dead (*Sol.* 1.11.19), contrary to what Augustine had previously claimed.

According to Foley, through the *Sol.* Augustine attempts to formulate a new form of theatre that simultaneously reflects the dramatic character of one's life and assists one in philosophical enquiry. As already noted, one of the tendencies of philosophical debate was to lose focus on the true goal and lapse into sophistry (cf. Michalewski 2014). Augustine condemns this desire for the appearance of victory in debate over discovering truth.[136] The term that Plato uses for the desire to conceal one's faults is *thumos*.[137] The result of *thumos* is to shift one's focus from truth to one's appearance, which leads one to the very opposite of wisdom.[138] Augustine borrows a term taken from drama to describe how one's ego affects philosophical enquiry – it ruins the discussion of a reasonable topic by expelling it.[139] In the *Sol.*, Augustine construes human life – specifically the search for wisdom and self-knowledge – in dramatic terms, as a conflict between genuine enquiry and *thumos*.[140] Human life for Augustine is a series of performances for various audiences, for which one wears different masks to conceal one's true self.[141] As a result, one can become firmly attached to one's own beliefs and feel defensive when one is challenged or refuted. Instead of being led to question one's beliefs, one 'doubles down' and holds ever more firmly to one's opinions, or one even seeks to exact revenge on one's opponents.[142] The result of one's dismay at being refuted is the weakening of one's desire for finding truth.[143]

In the *Sol.*, both dialogue partners are engaged in duplicity, but for different ends. Ratio engages in obfuscation for the sake of truth, whereas Augustine tries to hide himself for appearance's sake.[144] Both characters of the drama are aspects of the 'real' Augustine, suggesting that Augustine himself is *bifrons*.[145] The term *bifrons* refers to having two faces or foreheads, and is an epithet for Janus.[146] As Foley writes, 'the *Soliloquies* is a play wherein Reason and the character Augustine are two different projections or masks of the same individual, namely, Augustine the author'.[147] Through the *Sol.*, Aug is attempting to reconfigure drama, envisioning a new kind of theatre taking place on the inside to counteract the negative aspects of the classical tradition of theatre, especially as it is enacted in human life. Nonetheless, the risks of theatre still remain, even if they are somewhat counteracted. Even inside of himself, Augustine reveals his tendency towards (self-)deception and projection. The goal is to provide a new way of conceiving of one's acting, in particular treating God as the audience, not oneself or others.[148] The first step for this is to make sure that one is good inside and that this is realized in the public world, rather than doing good deeds which are meant to present a spectacle for others.[149] A way to accomplish this is through the 'therapy' of soliloquy.[150] The reader can see in Augustine a model for a soliloquy, but perhaps more importantly can be reassured at the affective level that one is not alone in one's imperfection.[151] As Foley states, the *Sol.* offers an opportunity for learning how to dialogue with oneself and to replicate this wholesome kind of drama in one's life.[152]

The aporetic terminus of the *Soliloquia*

The problem of course is that Augustine is still subject to self-deception and lacks the inner goodness necessary even to begin to ascend to knowledge of the divine. Ratio chastises Augustine for his presumptuous desire to know God when so many faults remain in him (*Sol.* 1.9.16). Indeed, this reiterates and intensifies Ratio's earlier rebuke of Augustine for his desire to attain the knowledge of God to the point that he could know 'enough' about God and thus view his search as complete (*Sol.* 1.3.8). God as infinite and inexhaustible depth can never be comprehended by the human mind, let alone by unaided human effort.[153] Indeed, as Ratio reminds Augustine, he even lacks sufficient knowledge of himself (*Sol.* 1.3.8). How then, forsooth, can he expect ever to have adequate knowledge of God? Ratio stresses the importance of patience in Augustine's enquiry; one must respect the eminence and depth of the objects of one's search. Knowledge of these requires time, effort, sacrifice and above all, purification (*Sol.* 1.4.9), which, as Augustine learns, he desperately needs (*Sol.* 1.9.16). Augustine's inner dialogue has disclosed to him his true state and enabled the first step to purification, namely the acknowledgement that he stands in desperate need of it. He has realized just how far he is from God. Furthermore, it has also revealed some knowledge of God, namely that God must be sought with a pure heart, and that the kind of effort that is required to seek him effectively.

After the revelation of Augustine's self-deception, his need for purification, and his many contradictory positions, Augustine crucially shifts from reliance on his own efforts to dependence on

God alone (*Sol.* 1.14.26).[154] The soul is powerless to re-orient and re-integrate itself, to convert or revert to its divine source, through which one becomes oneself.[155] Augustine is pushed to the realization that his own activity is not adequate for attaining to God.[156] Furthermore, as a result of Ratio's discourse, Augustine no longer attempts to assess his own worthiness (*Sol.* 1.14.26). Whilst it is true that no outside observer can know the state of another's soul, one can only understand it for oneself through the internal light of Christ. Indeed, in Book II, Augustine reiterates his desire to know God and the soul, but now he adds his request for God's help in pursuing such knowledge (*Sol.* 2.5.9). The exercise called the soliloquy is intended to prepare Augustine eventually to achieve some knowledge of God and the soul (2.20.34). Although the practise of soliloquizing does not guarantee success, it can nonetheless be effective in disabusing one of the false notions about oneself and setting one on a correct course.[157] The various dead ends and false starts of the *Sol.* could be seen as disappointments as well as encouragements to try again. The frustrations Augustine experiences can in themselves still be a form of intellectual progress.[158] Despite the aporetic nature of this inner dialogue,[159] Augustine has achieved some important self-knowledge, and this provides a basis for advancing and deepening his introspective enquiry.

Conclusion to the *Soliloquia*

Despite the progress Augustine has made, the dialogue clearly ends in *aporia*. I have already stated that this terminus need not imply an absolute failure, but can rather be a form of progress. However, there are two further observations on a larger scale relevant to Augustine's overall search for the self. First, it seems that Augustine had intended to add a third book to the *Sol.* but never did; this text is now known as the *De immortalitate animae*.[160] Secondly, as Otten claims, the performance of the soliloquies reveals the limitations of the method itself. The *Sol.* combines both discursive and contemplative modalities, yet Augustine seems unable to formulate a satisfactory approach that harmonizes these.[161] The *Sol.* ultimately fails due to its inability to open the dialogue to include God, a form, so she claims, he realized in the *Conf.*[162] Michel too suggests a normative trajectory to Augustine's genre of dialogue, namely that it terminates in *confessio*.[163] We now turn to further developments of the dialogue genre in Augustine, *narratio* and *confessio*. I believe that Augustine's use and development of these methods afford him new opportunities for introspection, yet also confronts him with new challenges.

Narratio

My contention is that Augustine employs various dialogical methods to articulate the full implications of one's dialectical constitution. His eclectic introspective method incorporates elements of rhetoric, classical philosophy[164] and other literary sources.[165] In the *Sol.*, Augustine experimented with situating the philosophical dialogue within himself, calling attention to the internal differentiation of the self. In addition to inner dialogue, narrative arose as a key method for introspection.[166] One constitutes one's identity through the things one says.[167] This technique is especially present in Seneca and Plutarch.[168] Indeed, Michel locates in Seneca's *De uita beata* an anticipation of Augustine's genre of *confessio*, in particular in the former's admission that he does not live according to his own standards. (Nonetheless, Seneca maintains that his awareness of his limitations and his faults makes him superior to his critics.)[169]

As indicated *supra*, Rist stresses Augustine's crucial acknowledgement of the essential embodiment and historicity of human life. After Augustine, the temporal nature of the human being becomes an essential feature of identity and thus of introspection.[170] The mutability of the soul entails that there are numerous paths one can take in developing one's self.[171] In my estimation, it follows that the sequential assembly of events and experiences of one's life is integral to the understanding of the person. Due to Augustine's growing appreciation of the essentially historical nature of the person, he opts for narrative as a method for discerning how to live one's life.[172] In multiple works, Augustine seeks to achieve this goal by *narratio* (Herzog's term). I would describe *narratio* as the pursuit of achieving coherence and meaning through putting one's life in the form of a narrative. According to Augustine, reflection on and interpretation of experiences and memories constitute the path to self-understanding and the discovery of hitherto unrecognized meanings.[173] In *Ep.* 80 Augustine remarks that God speaks to one through one's experiences.[174] Written to Paulinus *c.* 404/5, herein Augustine suggests that one discerns God's will precisely in and through the things which are happening to one, and indeed, in relation to a particular set of circumstances, the consideration of which can alter one's decision-making process.[175]

Certainly one finds God's will in the actions of one's life, and indeed, in relation to the particularities of one's own unique situation. However, autobiography becomes for Augustine not simply a recounting of past experiences but an interpretation of those experiences in terms of their potential meanings, including their 'counterfactual' possibilities. There is a meaning latent in the experience which, when recalled, can grant one deeper insight into the activity and call of God operative in one's experiences. Thus autobiography deals with events 'as they might have been experienced'.[176] Stock suggests that Augustine anticipates Freud, insofar as both hold that 'the unraveling of the self's history by means of conversations with oneself is a way of deciphering the self's meaning'.[177] Thus *narratio* is not merely retrospective but also normative and a method for projecting future possibilities. Indeed, Stock claims that this narrative methodology provides the pathway to attaining the goal of the philosophical life: '[Augustine's] rhetorical talents are deployed in persuading the reader that such an exercise, involving *a reinterpretation of one's life*, can provide counsel on how to reach the ancient goals of wisdom and happiness.'[178] Augustine's compositions are not merely descriptive or historical; rather, they skirt the boundaries between fact and fiction, gesturing towards possibilities and ever-expanding meanings to be mined from his life. Thus Parsons:

> Augustine used his own life experiences in conjunction with literary sources to construct an archetypal self that transcends his own biography, speaks to the universal human condition, and functions as an instructive discourse concerning the nature, limits, and possibilities of human transformation. Augustine's teaching—his theology, so to speak—is found transmitted through a rhetorically crafted historical narrative. In rhetorically weaving his narrative, Augustine "makes the truth," and hence sublates the distinctions among autobiography, theology, and history.[179]

Likewise, Stock contends that Augustine's early writings should not be viewed as definitive historical records but as various attempts to understand his own life from different perspectives and under different aspects.[180] One must distinguish therefore between the historical Augustine and the literary character 'Augustine'.[181] As numerous scholars have argued (e.g. Courcelle, Ferrari, Jonte-Pace, McMahon), this is especially true of the *Conf*.[182]

Though Augustine composes and recomposes the narrative of his life, his story is not merely his own invention. Rather, Scripture provides the framework within which to assimilate and render meaningful his experiences. For this reason, Mathewes describes Augustine's understanding of life as 'fundamentally exegetical'.[183] Augustine's biography is the story of his search for God.[184] Without Scripture his life is a sequence of events, viewed as a stream of consciousness.[185] Augustine seizes upon the idea that one gives meaning to one's life by situating its events within a narrative structure and develops it in light of his theological commitments.[186] The Bible – especially the theme of Christ as the new Adam – provided Augustine the framework through which to tell the story of his life.[187] Human identity for Christians was determined in relation to the drama of the paschal mystery. Thus the task of the Christian was to discover oneself through the prayerful and reflective reading of scripture and other sacred literature.[188]

This method reflects the more general religious significance of sacred stories. Through ritual, especially rites of passage, one internalizes the stories of one's tradition and then replicates them in one's own life. One is then able to conceive of oneself as a character in a story which already has a general structure, though one has the freedom to continue the story in new and creative.[189] It appears therefore that this form of *narratio*, like the form and content of some of Augustine's introspective literature suggests, constitutes a kind of prayer. Furthermore, in seeking meaning in one's life, one is simultaneously attentive to how God is acting in and through one's experiences (cf. *Ep*. 80). Stock captures these two points, stating that 'Augustine likewise considers the rehearsing of narrative as a "spiritual exercise", whose purpose lies beyond the streams of memory from the meaning of the text to the eternal message of God.'[190]

Confessio

Augustine and dialogue with God

Following his experimentation with the inner dialogue in the *Sol.*, Augustine introduced further innovations on the classical dialogue genre, in particular by including God in his dialogue. To appreciate the full importance of Augustine's shift, let us briefly consider Mircea Eliade's study of religious experience.

The twentieth-century Romanian scholar Mircea Eliade was renowned for, among other things, his study of the *phenomenology* of religion in general and religious experience in particular. In his research he identified a common pattern or structure of experience across various world religions. In his *Tradition and Incarnation*, W. Portier enumerates five elements of religious experience according to Eliade. First, one begins from the ordinary (mundane or profane) world. Secondly, the sacred irrupts within the world. This is followed by the natural response of worship on the part of the one undergoing this experience. One is compelled by what Rudolf Otto calls the *mysterium tremendum et fascinans* which is the divine; one cannot but fall prostrate in worship, which combines both fear and reverence. Fourth – and this is the crucial step for our consideration – the sacred issues a particular command or calling to the individual. In other words, the apex of the religious experience reveals its essentially *pragmatic* function: The sacred calls upon the human because it wants the human to *do* something. Finally, one returns to the world, although in a new way, not least of all because one is charged with a new mission on God's or the gods' behalf.[191]

What I would like to emphasize is that the foregoing account of religious experience is linear in nature. It has a beginning, a middle and an end, and is formulated as an arc, with a clear purpose and outcome. The sacred, though never truly absent from the profane, manifests itself in a unique and unmistakeable way, and then withdraws from human attention. Portier discusses two examples from sacred literature. One is Arjuna's theophanic experience of Vishnu through his avatar Krishna, and the other is Moses's encounter with the Lord through the burning bush in the desert. In the former, Arjuna receives clarification on a moral dilemma, whereas in the latter, God commissions Moses to liberate his people from Egyptian bondage. In both stories, the divine addresses a specific point of interest that directly leads to human action.[192] Herzog's discussion of the dialogue between God and humans in ancient religious texts is consistent with Eliade's analysis. He writes that, in general, communication between God and man is pragmatic: God calls, and the human being responds. There is no room for exchange, except to the extent that the recipient of a vocation gives one's *fiat* or asks for clarification or further information. Herzog too refers to Moses's encounter with God. He concedes that this episode is somewhat unique, as God speaks to Moses as one person to another. Nevertheless, this is the exception that seems to prove the rule.[193] Augustine's discussions with God are not exclusively or even primarily about discrete actions demanded by God, but rather a continuous and spontaneous exchange between partners. In this sense, Augustine's dialogical method represents not only a departure from the conventions of ancient religious texts but also bespeaks the question of the fundamental purpose of Augustine's formulation of a dialogue with God in general, and especially in his *Conf.*

Herzog notes a further remarkable aspect of Augustine's dialogical method with reference to certain passages of the *Conf.*, namely the *familiarity* with which he addresses God. He enumerates a few examples from the *Conf.* In the opening lines of Book IX, Augustine writes that he 'chatted' with God (*garriebam tibi*). Shortly thereafter (at 9.4.4), Augustine relates how his reading of the Psalms filled him with a passionate love for God. He writes that in his praying of these sacred texts, he considered, in God's presence, his most intimate feelings (*coram te de familiari affectu animi mei*).[194] Finally, in *Conf.* 12.10.10, Augustine says to God, 'Converse with me, commune with me' (*tu me alloquere, tu mihi sermocinare*).[195] Such expressions, Herzog argues, appear odd and even scandalously informal for an address to God. However, the consistent use of such formulations throughout the *Conf.* demonstrates that this form of familiarity in speaking to God is a deliberate choice.[196] Though Herzog notes that part of the difficulty for a contemporary reader can result from a post-Enlightenment understanding of the expectations of religious language, Augustine's own context still would not have supported such intimacy in speaking to God.[197]

On a related note, scholars such as P. Brown, L. Douglass, and A.-I. Bouton-Touboulic have remarked on the surprising candour with which Augustine speaks about himself in the *Conf.*[198] Augustine, so it seems, reveals the innermost depths of his soul, in all of its imperfection.[199] Bouton-Touboulic notes the counterexample of Plotinus, who was reticent to share anything about his family or personal life.[200] 'Augustin brave', writes Bouton-Touboulic, 'l'indécence antique à parler de soi, et qui plus est, en ces termes, car il donne l'impression de *mettre à nu* son intimité'.[201] This complete disclosure of oneself was almost completely unprecedented and would have been scandalous in antiquity.[202]

In the tenth book of the *Conf.*, Augustine also reveals some of the motivations for his performance of confession in general and his remarkable candour in particular. In *Conf.* 10, Augustine presents a 'meta-commentary' on his prospective readers, acknowledging that his confessions recorded in written form will be openly available.[203] He writes that the publication of his innermost thoughts is a form of service to others; indeed, it is his duty as a bishop.[204] Augustine's past misdeeds can provide encouragement and consolation to the weak who are despondent of the ability to improve. His reflections can also be a source of joy to those who live righteously, since the evils recounted no longer exist.[205] Augustine's readers can benefit from his confessions by growing in love and righteousness. Whether they disapprove of his sins or delight in his goodness, they sincerely love him.[206] He does not miss the opportunity to address potential critics, openly wondering why some are so interested in knowing about *him* when they are unwilling or unable to undertake a similar form of introspection.[207] While Augustine recognizes that some will be sceptical about his writings, he states that those motivated by love will accept them as true.[208]

Questioning in the *Confessiones*

True appreciation of the *Conf.* requires viewing *questioning* as central to the work,[209] as it is fundamentally about how Augustine learned to question correctly.[210] Through one's questioning, imperfect though it may be, one begins the process of *conuersio*.[211] 'The *Confessions*', writes Mathewes, 'turns out to be a story of Augustine learning to accept the dynamic of questioning as an energy moving him toward God'.[212] Augustine in turn challenges his audience to embrace questioning as a way of life, with the *Conf.* serving as a guide drawn from his own experience.[213]

Mathewes reads the *Conf.* in the following way. In books 1–9, Augustine recounts how he learned to question. Then in books 10–13, he models how to do so. Book 10 demonstrates the inadequacy of questioning as an individual and interior activity, while the remaining books elaborate enquiry as a form of scriptural interpretation performed in community.[214] Again I quote Mathewes:

> Far from a text seeking "resolution," where that is conceived as an ending, Augustine aims to produce a text showing us what it means to begin: He wants us to picture life as a way of inquiry, conceived not as a narrowly intellectual project but as a whole way of seeking God, exercised not simply in contemplative interiority but in the ecstatic communion with others in the world, framed and formed by the reading of Scripture.[215]

The form of exegesis Augustine propounds in the *Conf.* includes all members of the community. It is essentially communal, for even in reading the *Conf.* one is in conversation with Augustine.[216] The indefinite openness of enquiry, while in some sense horizontal, is also vertical – the scriptures are an expression of the infinite, inexhaustible goodness of God, which means that one's investigation of them is never complete.[217] Even creation itself as given to be by God is continuously unfolding.[218] A form of knowing and questioning in univocal terms is thus an expression of a vicious desire for control.[219]

Confessiones I

The question of otherness provides the point of departure for and continuing basis for the *Conf.* Throughout the work Augustine envisions human life as a response to the divine other[220] which one finds somehow mysteriously present within one, thus escaping simple binary categorization.[221] The basis of Augustine's *confessio* is the insoluble mystery of his being.[222]

Lotz's analysis of otherness in the *Conf.* draws upon Martin Buber's renowned conception of the I–Thou relationship. Beginning from the perspective of merely human interpersonal interaction, one must acknowledge that the other can never be reduced to a mere object. While this may seem self-evident, the real force of this position is that the other as other is not analogous to any particular thing given in experience.[223] 'Being the other', writes Lotz, 'is based on an *absolute* distinction. Otherness must mean an *epistemological* distinction between the subject and what this subject experiences, as well as an *ontological* distinction between the subject and what remains other to the subject.'[224] This implies, *inter alia*, that the mode of one's engagement with the other must adapt accordingly.[225] In my estimation, Lotz's observation is pertinent to the aforementioned 'no-thinglyness' of God, which applies just as much to other humans as it does to oneself. As with Heraclitus' observations, the world given in experience also presents 'stumbling blocks' which reveal the inadequacy of apparently intuitive categories of understanding, thus forcing one to think beyond them. Furthermore, following Derrida, Lotz writes that this irreducible otherness of one's interlocutor entails an ever-deepening dialectic.[226]

If the human other outstrips objectification, then *a fortiori* so too God, and even more so.[227] As Lotz writes, God '*per definitionem* and as Thou – is beyond any intentional content and beyond any possible representation'.[228] As a result of this observation, Augustine opts to shift the mode of his discourse. Instead of talking about God, he talks to God, for only in this way can he – to the extent possible – truly appreciate and do justice to the otherness of God, and indeed, relate to God.[229] Augustine focuses especially on praise, which is intended for the other *as* other.[230] Augustine's address to God as Thou renders possible Augustine's engagement with the otherness of God.[231] In the *Conf.*, Augustine is consistently renouncing himself in front of God.[232]

In his *L'appel et la réponse*, J.-L. Chrétien speaks of any rational activity as always already a response from the human side, in particular to the invitation of being, which is grounded in God. I believe that for Augustine, whom Chrétien discusses in his work, human reason is always already a response to the divine initiative. Even the inward turn, by which one searches for God, results from God's invitation.[233] Moreover, in the *Conf.*, Augustine portrays life itself as a response to God's initial call.[234] True, Augustine calls upon God, but this call is itself a response to God.[235] Indeed, one's very being is already an implicit response to God's creativity, calling one into existence.[236] Boven speaks of Augustine's *Conf.* as a dialogue with God, whose agency is primary in the act of dialogue.[237] God initiates and completes. The soul plays a role to the extent that it renounces itself.[238] Augustine's life is defined by the interruptions originating in the agency of the divine other.[239] However, according to Boven, the divine voice emerges within the activity of Augustine's confessing: 'the two voices emerge within the discourse of a single speaker, incorporating true otherness within the discourse of the self'.[240]

Augustine's invocation of God raises at least two distinct if related problems. First, Augustine wonders whether and to what extent it is possible to call upon God. Does he or does he not know God? God seems to be characterized by a remote presence, a familiar strangeness. Augustine's answer to this problem is that faith, a gift of Christ's humanity, enables Augustine's invocation of the not-yet-present God.[241] Faith therefore underlies all speech and responsiveness from the human side.[242] Secondly, even if Augustine can address God, he does so in expectation of a response, unsure of when, whether and to what extent it will ever come.[243] One thus opens oneself in vulnerability to the unconditioned Thou, which also reflects the general condition of human life.[244] In this respect, some form of faith and hope is always necessary.[245] If one's address to God is always a response, and this response is enabled and sustained by the *theological* virtues, then it suggests that the dialogue with God itself is a gift into which one is invited.

One need only look to the *Confessiones* to discover a wealth of images for the self and its relation to God in Augustine's thought. One particularly famous phrase comes from the third book, in which he describes God as *interior intimo meo, superior summo meo*, which Hammond renders as 'deeper within me than the most secret part of me, and greater than the best of me'.[246] This enigmatic phrase may provoke a series of questions. How can someone or something be more interior to one than oneself, and likewise for being greater? How can one make sense of what seems not to make sense? One response, and a very reasonable one I think, is to content oneself with the observation that Augustine, no stranger to rhetorical flourish, is using such utterances to express his overwhelming love of God and inner experience of him. Certainly something of this is true, not only for Augustine but for Christian sources and myriad forms of religious language. However, I also believe that Augustine would not understand his words as *merely* poetic in nature, or that this sense would be mutually exclusive with the following. An expression such as *interior intimo meo* is not simply a pious and emotional aspiration, but rather the product of profound intellectual enquiry into and reflection both on experience and the given elements of a faith tradition which in turn demands rigorous critical treatment. Viewed in this way, Augustine's paradoxical statements become so many *loci philosophici-theologici* which, when subjected to scholarly attention, promise to demonstrate a plethora of insightful connections to other conversations in philosophy, theology and psychology and yield insights into ongoing research in those fields as well as for perennial questions of the *condition humaine*.[247]

Early in the *Conf.*, Augustine raises a series of difficulties about how to 'locate' God, whether with respect to creation or to the self. Augustine asks how or in what sense God can be present within one or how one can dwell in God.[248] For example, the scripture says: 'I fill heaven and earth' (Jer 23:24). The phrase *caelum et terram* is a comprehensive formula for all of creation, in other words, all reality that is not God.[249] How, then, could God, who fills all things, enter into Augustine?[250] Do I exist, Augustine wonders, because God is in me (*non ergo essem, Deus meus, non omnino essem, nisi esses in me*), or perhaps because I am in God (*an potius non essem nisi essem in te ...*)?[251] If one is already in God, as Romans 11:36 indicates, then is it redundant to invoke him?[252]

Augustine pursues this line of enquiry in the next paragraph (1.3.3), though he does not immediately present any particular resolution. What may seem like a vain diversion or dilatory word play is in fact theologically significant. O'Donnell links this preoccupation with the spatial or local characteristics of the divine with Augustine's Manichaean background.[253] The importance of this topic becomes clear in such parts as Book VII, wherein Augustine stresses the key role that Neoplatonism – in particular its conception of incorporeality – played in his conversion from Manichaeism.[254] Moreover, this intellectual puzzle bears direct implications for this study, insofar as it reveals the paradox at the very heart of the human being.

The problem of the 'location' of the divine raised in Book I resurfaces in Book X, in which Augustine maintains that God is certainly to be found within *memoria*.[255] However, the 'locus' or 'part' of the memory in which God resides is ultimately unattainable.[256] Thus Augustine: 'Even if no human individual knows what is proper to that individual except their spirit (which dwells within them), nevertheless there is a part of each person that not even that person's spirit within them can know.'[257] Certain parts of oneself lie beyond one's grasp and comprehension.[258] Augustine must also acknowledge that whatever he knows about himself he only knows because of God's illumination.[259] In addition, Augustine can even say that he knows more about God than he does about himself.[260] I believe that this statement is momentous and must not be overlooked.

This particular part of Augustine's *Conf.* brings us to a central contention of this research. One of the crucial elements of my argument is that Augustine's theological anthropology is founded on and is developed as a response to the following challenge. The human being is created in God's own image and likeness. This means that God forms an essential part of the human being. One can speak therefore of the self's 'theo-log-ical' constitution. One cannot speak about man without also speaking about God. Furthermore, a given of Christian theology is that God escapes all comprehension and understanding. Therefore, man is also ultimately unknowable to himself. Note that this unknowability is not simply *de facto*, for instance the result of a practical limitation, as in one cannot know oneself because one lacks the time in today's highly charged society. Rather, the incomprehensibility of the human being, like that of God, is *de iure*: 'If you went in search of it, you would not find the limits of the soul, though you travelled every road – so deep is its measure.'[261] Coming to terms with this truth, I believe, is what Augustine is trying to do in a significant portion of his corpus. Thus one cannot avoid speaking of the foregoing mystery with respect to Augustine's thought in general and his theological anthropology in particular.

Augustine's recognition of the challenging insight that one will ever remain incomprehensible to oneself must not be confined to one particular portion of the *Conf.* In fact, O'Donnell provides evidence for thinking that this paradoxical understanding of human identity in connection with divine incomprehensibility permeates the entire work. In this respect, he comments on Augustine's quotation in 10.5.7 of the first half of 1 Cor 2:11,[262] the latter half of which he includes near the end of the *Conf.* itself, at 13.31.46. According to O'Donnell, 'The verse [sc. 1 Cor 2:11] thus brackets the meditative Bks. 10-13 with a scriptural text that declares the unknowability of humanity and divinity.'[263] Augustine's use of these two parts of the same verse underscores his eminent interest in the theme of the incomprehensibility of both God and the self.[264]

Augustine raises several paradoxical claims about God early in *Conf.* 1, all of which stem from the tension between the immutability of God on the one hand and on the other the activity and presence of God in the mundane.[265] Augustine writes that God is immutable yet changes all things; he is never new and never old, is always both active and at rest, and he constantly seeks even when he lacks nothing.[266] This section contains an implicit critique of the Manichees. In this respect, one wonders if Augustine's emphasis on paradox reflects a reaction against his former Manichaean beliefs. Whereas the Manichees took a bifurcated and oppositional approach to, for example, the Old and the New Testaments, respectively, Augustine stresses how apparent contraries harmonize.[267] In addition, I believe that this section of the text provides a further point of contact between Augustine and Heraclitus. Indeed, here Augustine speaks about and to God in paradoxical language that could easily encapsulate Heraclitean ideas.[268] Augustine's understanding of God seems to encapsulate the essence of Heraclitus' *logos*, which unites tensile elements and points to a greater reconciliation beyond apparent opposition.[269]

O'Donnell draws attention to how several formulations in early portions of the *Conf.* indicate Augustine's profound interest in navigating enquiry into the divine through the fallible means of language. One can see how from the very foundation of this work Augustine is preparing himself for engagement with theological paradox. For instance, the early sections of Book I under consideration contain several rhetorical questions, to which Augustine often resorts when he finds himself at the limits of language.[270] According to O'Donnell, 'it is the elusiveness – the incomprehensibility – of God that reduces [Augustine] to the rhetoric of paradox'.[271] At 1.4.4, Augustine addresses God, describing him with a series of superlative adjectives in the vocative. One of these is *omnipotentissime*, which is a 'superlativized' form of the already-superlative adjective *omnipotens* of Augustine's own formulation. The use of such a term suggests how Augustine is grappling with how to express the ineffable.[272] Indeed, I believe we see here on a smaller scale what Mohrmann has described has Augustine's improvisational style. It is obvious that the professor of rhetoric possessed an exceptional and thorough understanding of Latin grammar.[273] Like Braques and Picasso, who knew well the rules of perspective and chose to flaunt them for a particular artistic purpose, Augustine innovates and experiments with language when it reaches its limits.[274]

A further example derives from Augustine's attention to speaking about God and praising God. In the opening lines of the *Conf.*, Augustine twice writes that man wishes to praise God (*laudare te uult homo*; *et tamen laudare te uult homo*). After the former instance, Augustine proceeds to mention the weakness (*homo circumferens mortalitatem suam*) and fallibility (*circumferens testimonium peccati sui*) of human nature.[275] The second instance is preceded by the phrase *et tamen*, which occurs twelve times in Book I and a total of fifty-nine times in the *Conf.* and reflects Augustine's embrace of contradiction and paradox.[276] O'Donnell stresses that in this location Augustine does not use *laudat* but *laudare uult*, since his attempt to praise God remains inadequate.[277] A little while later, Augustine suggests a similar idea with respect to speaking. One *must* speak about God (*uae tacentibus de te*).[278] But as the context makes clear, this seems like an impossible task. Augustine echoes this seemingly intractable dilemma in *En. Ps.* 102: 'therefore, if we cannot speak, and because of our joy it is not permitted for us to remain silent, we may neither speak nor remain silent. What therefore should we do, not speaking and not remaining quiet?'[279] We are permitted neither to speak nor to remain silent. The human being is caught in an intractable situation.

These observations reveal the inherently conflicted nature of being human. As we have seen, man wishes to praise God, not least of all because God has made it so that it is pleasing (*tu excitas ut laudare te delectet*).[280] According to Brown, delight (*delectatio*) is the primary motivation for action according to Augustine.[281] One might even say that man is *commanded* to praise God while he is inherently incapable of doing so. One cannot speak about God, yet one must speak about God. Moreover, Augustine famously holds that the heart is restless until it rests in God.[282] The foregoing insights suggest that human life is descriptively if not also normatively characterized by the continuous and ever-deepening (syllaptic) enquiry into God and the self. The tension Augustine describes here seems remarkably consistent with a contemporary postmodern world.[283] Once again, if speaking of God presents insuperable difficulties for expression and understanding, and it is necessary to connect the enquiry into God with the enquiry into the self, then introspection will remain an ever-present mystery. For Augustine, then, the upshot is that the centre of human identity is paradoxically the haunting question of what one truly is.[284]

Dialectical constitution
in *Confessiones* X

The tenth book of the *Conf.* represents, according to O'Daly, a paradigmatic example of moral introspection.[285] Furthermore, I argue that in this text one locates Augustine discussing both senses of the self's dialectical constitution. Augustine realizes that God is within him, and he turns to God and speaks with him in pursuit of self-knowledge and integration.

Here Augustine repeats certain ideas we have previously noted. He states that introspection and reflection on experience lead to the recognition of the divine presence within himself.[286] Augustine writes to God, 'you are with me even before I am with you'.[287] However, this divine Other cannot be precisely located or conceived in spatial terms; it is neither purely within nor without.[288] This inner divine reality, while present to the mind and intrinsically connected with oneself, is nonetheless transcendent of the self.[289] This is what Hwang terms the 'paradoxical place of the self'.[290]

Furthermore, he recognizes that truth itself has always been present to him and that he has looked to it to evaluate and make sense of his experience.[291] He also depends on divine assistance for the correct understanding of the contents of his memory.[292] God already knows Augustine, who seeks not only to know himself, but to know himself as God does.[293] Augustine realizes that self-knowledge consists in listening to God.[294] If we frame the *Conf.* as a dialogue with God[295] in which the divine voice emerges within Augustine's own speaking,[296] this means in my estimation that one must *confess* to heed God's voice. However, it seems that some form of ethical introspection is a prerequisite for the performance of this act: 'Confession', writes O'Daly, 'is exposure to divine goodness. Self-examination and self-revelation are means to this end'.[297] Augustine states that he writes confessions so as not to hide God from himself.[298] He also suggests a performative aspect to confession, in particular with regard to truth: 'I want to accomplish truth in my heart, in making my confession openly before you.'[299]

One of Augustine's discoveries in the midst of his *confessio* is the enigmatic nature of subjectivity. As he examines the oddity of how one can 'remember' forgetfulness, he steps back and recognizes that he is struggling to understand himself.[300] Again, one is confronted with perplexity: How is it possible that one cannot understand oneself? As Augustine writes, 'So is the mind too restricted to appraise itself, forcing the question: where is that part of itself which it does not understand? Surely it is not outside the self rather than within the self? So how can it not understand?'[301] Interestingly, Augustine seems content with the lack of a clear answer to this conundrum.

Despite the lack of clarity he finds within, Augustine still arrives at certain conclusions about his identity. One of these is his internal differentiation: 'What kind of nature am I? A complex and manifold life and one that is utterly incalculable.'[302] According to Hammond, Augustine generally considers multiplicity to be negative.[303] He also locates division within himself at the ethical level. Augustine describes an inner conflict between his desire for God – Truth itself – and the lies of his current life.[304] He wants to rise to heaven, but lacks the necessary strength.[305] Augustine avers that it is with God's assistance that he can achieve and maintain integration: 'I find there is no safe place for my soul except in you; you bind my shattered self together, and no part of me can fall away from you.'[306] He focuses especially on his relation to God and the precise way in which he seeks truth.[307] The formation of the Augustinian self can only be accomplished by focusing on the transcendent and eternal God. One seeks by God in particular by looking to the image of the Trinity present within oneself. Such a way of situating and orienting oneself enables one to experience the world in the correct manner.[308] The divine presence is realized in the interaction with the soul as it simultaneously seeks God and itself.[309] Through dialogue – specifically dialogue with God – Augustine has hope for securing his identity.[310]

5

The Dialectical Self
and the Abyss

Polarity

Polarity as a primordial theological challenge

We have seen how Mathewes locates otherness at the centre of Christian theology, as well as how Heraclitus understands god in fundamentally dialectical terms. Looking to the long tradition of mystical and apophatic discourse, I believe one can view God in polar terms, which would then ground the twofold aspect of human being and knowing. The incomprehensibility of God suggests a juxtaposition of God and emptiness.[1] To be clear, this would not be a radical dualism, akin to that of the Manichees, which Augustine rejected. Instead, thinking of the divine in this way is motivated by the primordial revelation and experience of God as intimately related to every individual, yet always exceeding human comprehension, an idea to which Augustine eloquently testifies in his *Conf.* For example, in Book VI, he writes, 'you are both transcendent and immanent, entirely unknowable, yet close at hand'.[2] The key I believe is to hold both of these elements together, not in alternation, whereby one would succumb to the tendency to assimilate the divine to the limited perspective of human categories.

Turner echoes a related understanding of theological language in his description of the relationship between cataphatic and apophatic theology. One might think that cataphatic articulates truths about

God to a certain point and, when it reaches its limits, hands the baton to the apophatic and the mystical, as if theology consisted of two separate methodological chambers. Instead, Turner argues that these two ways of speaking about God are present together in every form of theological discourse.[3] Moreover, such a dynamic is a fundamental aspect of theology *qua* theology: 'it is this interplay of negativity and affirmation which structures all theological discourse *precisely as theological*'.[4] The presence of the paradoxical tension in theology is not only essential to it but *always remains*.[5] One might even say that the coincidence of positive and negative elements in theological language is a function of the inherent polarity of the divine nature, an idea articulated by the contemporary theologian Erich Przywara, whose thought took inspiration from Augustine.

Przywara and the *Polaritätslehre*

Przywara's account of polarity should be situated within the context of his overall thought, which addresses the inherently 'dialectical' structure of reality.[6] Przywara analyses polarity with respect to two major types of sources: (1) philosophers who dealt with the theme of polarity and (2) by attending to such structures in other realms of human life.[7] Concerning the former, he located in Augustine a foundational principle for the *Polaritätslehre*, namely the simultaneous immanence and transcendence of God, *interior intimo meo*, yet beyond all conceptualization.[8] In the *Conf.*, for example, Augustine addresses God as 'both transcendent and immanent, entirely unknowable, yet close at hand'.[9] As a result, human experience is always characterized by tension and opposition.[10]

Diversity moulded Przywara from an early age, and this directly influenced the development of his thought.[11] Przywara was raised in a remarkably heterogeneous environment. He was born in 1889 in Kattowitz in Upper Silesia, near the intersection of Austria, Russia and Germany, and raised near both an industrial centre and a pristine forest. His context was also religiously diverse, consisting of Catholics, Protestants and Jews.[12] Additionally, following the Great War, the idea developed that one truly found oneself in orientation to other, and indeed reciprocity (*Austausch*) with that other.[13] This would seem to suggest that for Przywara, one could not speak of the self without speaking of the other, and especially of the ultimate Other.[14]

To illustrate Przywara's understanding of polarity, Schütz references an example drawn from Herman Hesse's *Das Glasperlenspiel*.[15] In this novel, a teacher tells his student that first, one must learn correctly to identify opposites *as* opposites, and subsequently to understand them as two poles of a more basic unity.[16] However, such a notion leads not simply to confusion but frustration: It is difficult to determine whether one can say anything meaningful or true at all, as Hesse's character Josef Knecht suggests in Hesse's roman. One loses any sense of certainty or meaning.[17] Indeed, Schütz describes Knecht's plaintive cry as 'nostalgia' (*Sehnsucht*). One longs for clarity, univocity, precision, beyond all ambiguity.[18] Yet a resolution or final synthesis is not the Przywara's understanding of polarity. Rather, he envisions reality as an internally layered and differentiated whole.[19] This implies, I believe, that one must maintain the tension and the resonance generated by two poles, as a result of which a unity is also possible.

According to Schütz, the logic of polarity and unity in opposition can inform contemporary theological anthropology.[20] In this respect, he presents certain observations which are consistent with a Heraclitean hermeneutic. He notes how Przywara thinks that human life itself must be understood as a tensile, multifaceted polarity.[21] The individual represents a collection of pieces and fragments, lacking coherence. One is never completely present or identical to oneself.[22] A person is simultaneously many and one, yet somehow also one being.[23] The essentially dialectical structure of being is also that of the human being, and this structure encompasses knowledge as well.[24] The dialectical constitution of the universe suggests that true knowledge, including knowledge of oneself, requires openness and attention to the other.[25] From a perspective informed by the *Polaritätslehre*, true insight results from the contemplative and patient looking at being.[26] Indeed, as the nature of being itself suggests, one must always maintain a tensile and dynamic state in one's search for truth.[27] As Schütz writes, 'Diese Polarität zwischen dem Gewonnenen und einer stets wieder zu versuchenden Auskehr ist die echte Herausforderung der Existenz.'[28] This is especially true in the enquiry into the mysterious God who lies beyond human categories, yet is also the path to finding oneself.[29] Ultimately, the search for God is essential because only in divine love can oppositions be reconciled.[30]

The dialectical self

Leib und Körper

The fact of possessing a body is itself a form of otherness which is paradoxically inherent to the self.[31] We have seen how for Heraclitus, one both is and is not oneself. For Augustine, several elements of differentiation are present within the person, such as the distinction between body and soul. Plessner (1970), under the influence of Husserl, looks at human existence as inherently divided, in particular in virtue of one's corporeality.[32] The fact of possessing a body entails that one's identity is always somehow found in relation to or negotiation with otherness. According to Plessner, living beings are not only defined by their relationships with their boundaries (*Grenzen*), but 'the borders of living beings are part of those beings themselves'.[33] One both is and is not oneself, or rather, that which is other than one is a constitutive part of one. Furthermore, as Rist notes, Augustine stresses the importance of the entire history of humanity as a constitutive feature of one's individual history. From a contemporary philosophical perspective, one could hold essentially the same position, arguing that both our individual and collective histories are integrated into the person.[34] Citing Merleau Ponty, Wehrle writes that one is shaped in ways difficult for one to comprehend, in part due to the sheer temporal distance of past events.[35]

The universal experience of growing older represents a paradigmatic example of the intrinsic division within oneself.[36] Whether from one's reflection, looking at photographs of oneself, or thinking about one's past, one develops a general image of oneself. However, at a certain point, one will notice a striking difference with how one once looked.[37] Furthermore, others' perceptions of one will inevitably influence one's own self-perception.[38] In the confrontation with the divergence between one's own image of oneself and others' perceptions, one becomes an 'other' to oneself.[39] Virtually all people experience distress in the face of ageing. According to Wehrle, this disquiet results from one's failure to acknowledge 'the dynamical tension inherent in every human embodiment',[40] in other words, an ignorance of the *logos*. Moreover, I believe that the universal experience of growing older also includes an intimation, however faint, of one's inevitable demise, thus placing one at least implicitly in contact with the abyss.

These observations about the self and otherness indicate that one can conceive of oneself in both subjective and objective terms. In addition to being a self, in virtue of one's body, one is also essentially material, even if not reducible to it.[41] In response to this twofold aspect of lived experience, Husserl developed the distinction between two aspects of corporeality, *Leib* and *Körper*. Simply put, the former refers to the subjective nature of embodiment, that which lives, moves, feels, etc. (being a body), while the latter indicates the objective aspect of possessing a body. Wehrle refers to Al Saij's (2010) example of one hand touching another to illustrate this concept. Both the touching and the sensation of being touched occur simultaneously, yet these can neither be collapsed into each other nor separated.[42] When the left hand touches the right hand, one could attend primarily to two simultaneous and inseparable aspects of this action. One could focus on the right hand as an object, or one could prioritize the left hand and its subjective action of sensing.[43]

Husserl's *Leib* versus *Körper* distinction is intended to show that being a body and having a body are two inseparable 'poles' (Wehrle's term) or aspects of life.[44] Indeed, objectivity is infused with subjectivity: The experiences one feels or realizes in one's body are registered within oneself. One has a certain disposition towards them, one *relates* to them.[45] That being said, the subjective dimension to human existence is primary. The perception of oneself as an object presupposes the sensing subject.[46] Through the experience of oneself as an object, one is able to realize that one was already a subject.[47] In other words, one's own intrinsic otherness enables and enhances subjectivity. Human life consists in a continuing mediation between subject and object with respect to oneself.[48] Wehrle speaks of one as possessing a 'twofold constitution'.[49] Husserl emphasizes that holistic being is essential to being human. He reacts against the Cartesian understanding of the body as a *mere* object. He encapsulates this in the term *Leibkörper*. The body is part and parcel of one's entire life.[50] Human life requires a constant reconciliation of two poles which arise from our ruptured existence,[51] a maintenance of two polarities in harmony.

Personal identity: A psychological perspective

Both common sense and contemporary psychology assume the existence of a stable, internal self which maintains its identity across time. However, K. Komatsu challenges this firmly established and apparently self-evident position.[52] He describes the prevailing psychological view as the representational – as opposed to a presentational – self.[53] According to the representational understanding of the person, the self pre-exists any interaction and can be brought forth more or less on command. One assumes that there is sufficient ability on the part of the subject to produce and articulate this inner reality.[54] Such assumptions manifest themselves in research methodologies, such as questionnaires: One assumes that the self can be brought forth to respond to particular questions when and however they are posed.[55]

Komatsu raises several concerns about the foregoing understanding of the self. One problem concerns the precise source of these presuppositions. Komatsu believes that this idea of the self is assumed on the basis of intuition or convention rather than established by critical research.[56] This challenge is exacerbated by the fact that daily interactions reinforce the preconception of a stable self.[57]

Furthermore, Komatsu believes that there are in fact scholarly reasons to question the idea of the person as a discrete entity. He argues that psychological methodologies generally assume only one version of the self while ignoring plausible alternatives.[58] Attention to these is motivated by the struggles conventional psychological research faces in understanding the dynamism of the self, especially in light of significant changes over the course of one's life.[59] Remarkably, according to some psychologists, the existence of a stable self seems to lack a firm evidential basis.[60] As Komatsu writes, 'Metzinger (2011) insists "there seems to be no empirical evidence and no truly convincing conceptual argument that supports the actual existence of "a" self" (p. 279). From this viewpoint, psychologists' assumptions about the self are based only on intuitive soundness, that is, on common sense.'[61] The opinion Komatsu shares with Metzinger remarkably echoes that of such sources as Cavadini in his discussion of Augustinian subjectivity.[62] Given the pervasive historical influence of Descartes, it is not difficult to see how a particular philosophical position could become so entrenched that it comes to seem like common sense.

Komatsu also critiques the prevailing sense of the self in terms congenial to Heraclitean philosophy. He argues that the fact of constant change presents a significant challenge to the idea of the self as a discrete unit.[63] Because of the nature of time, nothing is ever truly stable or fixed.[64] Rather, it seems that something like the *logos* to which Heraclitus' texts point provides true insight into subjectivity and identity. Furthermore, as we have seen with Augustine's approach to *confessio*, the linear flow of time is fundamental to one's experience and how one develops.[65] As Komatsu writes, 'we are constructing a stable world and stable selves in spite of the fact that almost everything is changing. In other words, our environments have similarity – not the exact sameness, and these fundamental structures lead to our sense of sameness.'[66] Komatsu articulates the conundrum raised by Grand in a psychological context.

Komatsu proceeds to discuss the opposition between sameness and difference and the crucial role this dialectic plays in the formation of personal identity. In agreement with Sovran (1992), Komatsu claims that the opposition of same/not-same is a ubiquitous feature of human life and plays a significant role in human development.[67] One cannot even speak about sameness without invoking its opposite, non-sameness, and vice versa. In the case of Komatsu's study, a child may provide the same answers to certain questions, yet the manner in which she does so may vary. In contrast, if the child gives different responses, it is still the *same* child who does so.[68] The continuing movement from identity to difference is interwoven with one's relationship to others and one's environment.[69]

A significant implication of the foregoing observations is that the self cannot be understood in reified or discrete terms, but rather must be conceptualized as an ongoing *process*.[70] Moreover, if the self is a dynamic reality, then this also means that the conventional language one uses to attempt to quantify or circumscribe it will be inadequate.[71] Once again following Sovran (1992), Komatsu suggests that binary language will not suffice to capture the self which intermingles with yet is not reducible to such categories.[72] However – and again, in agreement with Heraclitus – Komatsu contends that the self is not merely flux; the presentational self is consistent with the idea of continuity, but this continuity is manifested in repeated activity.[73]

The dialectically constituted self in psychology

Besides Heraclitus, the significance of Komatsu's analysis also extends to Augustine, in particular my interpretation of his anthropology as speaking of a 'dialectically constituted' self in two major senses. First, the self is a *combinatio oppositorum*, the paradoxical product of two contrasting elements, which for Komatsu amounts to the 'same' and the 'not-same'.[74] Indeed, these two poles are inseparable.[75] This oppositional relationship is always held in tension and constitutes the crucible, so to speak, in which meaning and identity are forged.[76]

Secondly, Komatsu's research suggests that the relationship to otherness is essential to the formation of the self.[77] Komatsu argues that the results of empirical research demonstrate that identity construction occurs through an ongoing conversational interaction with others.[78] Beginning from the attempt to construct meaning through the use of language and signs, the self results both from the dialogical interaction with the other and with the speaker's configuration of oneself with respect to or in reference to others.[79] This means that one's identity is partially constituted by the other(s) to whom one is speaking.[80] The self is found in the process of those interactions with others.[81] In addition to ordinary interactions throughout one's life, Komatsu also holds that the self emerges in part through the activities of psychological research, whereby the self is 'called forth' by the researchers, who ask questions that would not occur to the individual. The self is drawn forth in continuous conversation.[82] It seems therefore that the subjects of such research whose selves are emerging through the questioning and responding are discovering themselves as they proceed.[83] In fact, this speaking (narrative about oneself/one's experiences) has a 'refractive' effect, in that it reveals many selves within the individual.[84] This insight suggests that identity, in addition to being continually developed, is also inherently multifaceted. From conversation, a conception of the total self emerges which is irreducible to the sum of the individual kinds of interaction with others.[85] As Komatsu writes, 'the self is an abstraction taken out from the constant flow of a person's relationship with the world'.[86] The self is more than the sum of its distinct interactions with various others. All of these must be understood together, and in relation.[87] In my estimation, the foregoing implies that the self cannot be understood apart from its constitutive relationships, a position consistent with that of Augustine.

Otherness and negation

Interaction with others always involves some kind of negation. According to Komatsu, the self is constituted by the attempt to negotiate opposition.[88] Indeed, the process of interaction seems to provoke an encounter with oneself as other. This is because conversation draws one's attention to external elements of one's environment, which in turn leads to a greater awareness of one's previously implicit thinking.[89] One's subjective construction of meaning, according to psychological research, seems to require the negating interaction with others.[90]

Komatsu refers to a study on conversations between a mother and her daughter (a toddler) to illustrate how dialectical exchange includes negation as an essential aspect of forming oneself. Families share the same setting, yet are also unique persons. Conversation is a means to negotiate the otherness of the family members, to reconcile it with the sameness.[91] One sees opposition in identity construction in the daughter's recounting of her own experiences.[92] The conversation differentiates the child from the mother on the basis of unique experiences, thus bringing the child into a greater sense of individual identity.[93] By talking with her daughter, the mother assists her in articulating her own experience and discerning meaning within it. Thus from an early age the child develops the ability to relate to her own experience.[94] Such interactions are structured according to the dialectic of identity and difference, or the same and not-same.[95]

Negation and the abyss

Hegel is the most renowned modern figure to have dealt with the ontological and epistemological question of dialectic. Like Przywara, Hegel argues that one can only find truth and come to oneself with the assistance of the other.[96] As Yountae emphasizes, 'the Hegelian dialectic incorporates exteriority/otherness into the structure of being (and knowing)'.[97] For Hegel the person is constituted by the continuous movement in the midst of polarity and opposition, and this process remains open indefinitely in a continuously unfolding dialectic.[98]

Though the other is an essential part of (the formation of) one's identity, there is a shadow side to dialectical relationships. As indicated by Komatsu's research in a psychological context, the confrontation with otherness initiates a process of differentiation, and indeed, negation. One cannot arrive at self-knowledge without the other, yet, paradoxically, one must relinquish oneself in this encounter with the other.[99] For Hegel, negation structures the entire dialectical process,[100] such that otherness and loss are inseparable.[101] As Yountae writes, 'the Hegelian negative represents the ineluctable and constant failure of subjectivity that is the subject's confrontation with the limits of its own *knowing and being*; it renders finitude a *constitutive* structure of being'.[102] In the encounter with otherness, one's assumed truths are called into question. This experience is more than merely epistemic or intellectual. Rather, one's entire being is made vulnerable in a holistic and existential way. By placing oneself at stake, one begins to feel a sense of groundlessness.[103] The experience of otherness and negation provides an entry point into the simultaneously de- and re-constructive abyss.[104]

Prior to Hegel, the 'abyss' was a philosophical-theological concept pertaining to the self and God, in particular the insuperable gulf between them within the context of Neoplatonism.[105] In the work of Jakob Boehme, a major influence on Hegel as well as Schelling,[106] the abyss comes to refer to the division and opposition within both God and the human soul.[107] Interestingly, Augustine anticipated Boehme's understanding of the radical groundlessness of both the divine and the human.[108] For Boehme, God's nature consists of opposition, both the fulness of being and utter nothingness.[109]

In Hegel's hands, the concept of the abyss is applied exclusively to the self, understood in principle as a constant work in progress.[110] The Hegelian abyss is a non-place of utter groundlessness, 'the limit of being in which all stability and sense of substance dissipate'.[111] One realizes that the self always stands at the precipice of this groundlessness.[112] One's sense of being and identity is radically undermined.[113] However, one should not identify the abyss with the negative.[114] As Yountae explains, the abyss 'is inseparably characterized by the movement of crossing, or "passage", from determinacy to indeterminacy and then to a renewed form of determinacy again: a dialectical journey that entails both *de*-construction and *re*-construction'.[115] The abyss as negation is simultaneously the locus of new possibilities.[116] Within a theological context, one can say that both elements, one of destruction and the other of unification, belong to Przywara's *Gegensatzlehre*.[117]

Therapeia

Augustine's non-self

Although Augustine extensively explores his inner world, he also likens this interiority unto an abyss.[118] Cavadini's account of Augustinian interiority takes as its central principle the fact that one cannot truly speak of 'the self' in Augustine. He disputes scholarship over the last few decades which purports to have established the antecedents of the modern conception of selfhood in Augustine,[119] stating that such observations are really the result of anachronistic eisegesis.[120] One has such a strong expectation of locating a clear discussion of 'the self' in Augustine that one easily projects this onto the sources.[121] Cavadini also points to linguistic challenges and problematic translations as reasons for the erroneous attribution to Augustine of an understanding of the self as a discrete reality. Part of the difficulty stems from the fact that in Latin, there is no particular term for the self.[122] This subtle if crucial difference is then easily lost in translation.[123] As Cavadini explains, certain translations 'can sound like there is a thing called "self", which is "mine", and towards which I am turning, when in Latin all we have are forms of the first person reflexive pronoun'.[124] He cites the example of Boulding's (1997) translation of *Conf.* 10.6.8, wherein 'interioris hominis mei' is rendered 'inmost self'. Cavadini argues that this translation overlooks the analogy of the body, thus presenting interiority in terms more suited to the conceptuality of space or place, although this is not consistent with the context of the passage.[125]

Instead of the self as a determinate thing, Augustine actually envisions the reverse, namely the self as a 'non-self', lacking stability, integration and clarity.[126] According to Cavadini, 'the closer one examines the imagery which Augustine uses to express the content of self-awareness, the more one becomes convinced that he does not use it to describe a stable reality called "the self" that becomes more and more clearly visible as one's interior vision becomes purer, but rather something that *defies reification*'.[127] Even with terms such as *interior homo* – a metaphor for the mind (*animus*) employed in the *Conf.* – the emphasis falls on obscurity and complexity.[128] As in the aforementioned examples of Seneca and Marcus Aurelius, introspection yields a surprising and disturbing realization of the confusion and contingency of oneself.[129] The Augustinian self is given to be by God, but is also a constant work in progress, never fully completed in this life.[130]

This depiction of the self as more a 'non-self' admits of certain implications. If one finds a lack of stability and clarity within oneself, one is compelled to employ a vocabulary capable of expressing one's experience, which may require one to adopt the language of paradox.[131] Furthermore, as we have already seen, in one's endeavour to mitigate the troubling effects of the realization of one's groundlessness, one may turn to an introspective method capable of overcoming the self's disintegration. In this respect, Heraclitean syllapsis offers a promising opportunity. Augustine relates introspection to the interpretation of a complex text, as in exegesis.[132] Such a model entails a continuous and ever-deepening interrogation of one's interiority, for which, once again, Heraclitus offers helpful resources.

Classical philosophy as therapy

Before considering Augustine's own therapeutic narrative, I shall situate him within the context of classical philosophy as therapy which influenced him. On this basis, I shall argue that the relevant portion of *Conf.* 4 should be read as an instance of such introspective *therapeia*.

P. Hadot has demonstrated how classical philosophy, at least as early as Socrates (469 BCE to 399 BCE), was construed primarily as a way of life.[133] R. Cushman confirms this interpretation of early philosophy, in particular in Plato's corpus.[134] Indeed, as the title of his monograph suggests, Cushman describes Plato's philosophy as a form of *therapeia*. He explains how Plato understood the human soul as trapped in a disordered state, with the desire for inferior, material reality dominating. Plato realized that to convince others of their error, he needed more than mere intellectual argument.[135] According to Cushman, Plato articulates his philosophical-therapeutic model to address the challenge presented by the disordered state of human nature.[136] In other words, Plato called for a renovation, indeed, a *conversion* (*metastrophe*) of the self, which involved ethical and affective transformation.

As Cushman explains, Platonic philosophy – in particular dialectic – is *therapeutic* to the extent that it disabuses one of false beliefs and leads one to truth.[137] For Plato, philosophy is the therapy necessary to correct one's incorrect perception of reality. This comprehensive therapeutic process can be described as conversion.[138] Plato recognizes that proper knowledge requires a full renovation and reorientation of the mind. Hence philosophical education is without exaggeration a form of *therapeia*.[139]

According to Plato, one grows in knowledge, and indeed, knowledge of self, by engaging in a full reflection on one's experience and its implications.[140] Ultimately, introspective philosophical investigation leads one to realize one's errors and brings one to a crossroads: either one will remain in intolerable contradiction with oneself, or one will renounce one's quondam false beliefs and open oneself to growth. This latter step, continues Cushman, involves an *ethical* choice and requires humility.[141] I contend that in locations such as *Conf.* 4, Augustine is doing precisely this, namely drawing out the implications of his experience through a reflective narration.

Before continuing, I would like to note two further links between Cushman's discussion of Plato and Augustine. According to Plato, knowledge depends upon the mind's correct disposition towards reality.[142] As Augustine relates concerning his mental state *c.* 375/6 CE, he held a flawed understanding of the world, which was only corrected through a confrontation with the phenomenon of loss and grief. In addition, Plato himself acknowledges the limitations of his own philosophical pedagogy. This focus on philosophy as therapy involving conversion, as well as the apparent necessity of extrinsic assistance, further motivates a consideration of Augustine. In due course I shall consider Augustine's understanding of the process of *conuersio*, in particular in the *Conf.* I hold that the 'theological difference' of Augustine is a necessary complement to Platonic pedagogy.

As D. Praet states, through a programme of ethical and intellectual praxis, philosophers of antiquity addressed not only life's various challenges, but also the challenge constituted by life itself.[143] According to Cicero – who was a key figure in mediating Greek philosophy to the Latin world in general and Augustine in particular[144] – the soul may experience great suffering in this life. Unlike physical ailments, the causes of and solutions to which originate outside of the body, the soul is the source of its own suffering. However, as J. Brachtendorf writes, the capacity to counteract such pain also lies within its power, namely the *therapy of philosophy*.[145]

Other philosophers in the Latin tradition engaged in introspection and dialogue to deal with the challenges posed by the fleeting and unstable nature of human existence[146]. One of these was Seneca, who, according to C. Star, devoted significant attention to the problem of the self and even developed a unique vocabulary to discuss it.[147] (Notably, Rist claims that Seneca was a source for Augustine's conception of self-care,[148] although the connection of these two thinkers remains relatively unexplored.[149]) Seneca's philosophy focused extensively on the self. He advocated a life of contemplation and introspection.[150] Furthermore, Seneca was active during a period in which the lived experience of philosophy was paramount.[151] As Star writes, 'The practice of philosophy itself came to be not only a process of self-discovery, but also a continual process of *therapy* and self-creation. For the Stoics, philosophy was not simply confined to the lecture halls, but a lived experience.'[152]

This survey of classical philosophy is relevant to the present task because it illustrates the understanding of philosophy that Augustine inherited and, in some ways, transformed. What I want to suggest is that insofar as one is talking about the *Conf.*, one is speaking of Augustine's own attempts at philosophical therapy. Indeed, according to Köckert, in his early career, Augustine deliberately operated within the classical philosophical tradition of seeking happiness through various practises, a tradition which even in his time was truly ancient.[153] According to Cushman, Augustine inherits the Platonic tradition of philosophy, in particular in virtue of his emphasis on the necessity of moral transformation for the attainment of knowledge.[154] The psychologist P. Woollcott interprets the *Conf.* as a form of therapy,[155] describing Augustine's work as a 'great therapeutic effort'.[156] Furthermore, he identifies therein a certain playful spontaneity which seems to be consistent with contemporary therapeutic methods.[157] In his comparative study of Augustine and Freud, W. Parsons also characterizes Augustine's *Conf.* as a form of therapy.[158] These insights indicate, I argue, that the (or at least a) proper hermeneutical framework for the interpretation of *Conf.* 4 is that of philosophy as *therapeia*.

Classical philosophy was a holistic form of therapy that one could apply to oneself. It served not only to address *ad hoc* concerns arising throughout one's life, but more fundamentally to help one to deal with life itself. One should note that within the context of classical philosophy, therapy was arduous work, not primarily a means of self-assurance. The encounter with oneself, writes Porter, 'is like facing an abyss. All the techniques of the self, of self-introspection and of self-recollection, do nothing to assuage the pain of this kind of confrontation, which is both existentially and spiritually threatening and anything but an assuring index of self-discovery'.[159] These insights will provide a framework for my reading and interpretation of *Conf.* 4 as a paradigmatic instance of Augustine performing philosophical therapy.

Confessiones IV

Augustine is able to identify in retrospect the subjective features of his experience that caused him such suffering, in particular the improper love of worldly things. In ontological terms, Augustine failed to understand the finite and contingent nature of mundane reality; he did not heed the Heraclitean *logos*. After considering the psychological effects of this position on Augustine's own state, I turn to a distinctively Christian theme, namely the interplay of divine presence and absence. The events of Augustine's life bespeak God's activity and presence therein.

The account of the death of Augustine's close friend, which occurred *c.* 375/6 CE, and thus at least two decades prior to the composition of the *Conf.*, appears in the fourth book. This book, writes J. O'Donnell, is the one most concerned with death.[160] When his friend – whom Augustine leaves anonymous – fell severely ill, Augustine hastened to see him. Initially he lay unconscious, during which time he was baptized. Afterwards, his friend briefly recovered, during which time Augustine mocked his baptism. However, Augustine's friend rebuked him severely, leaving Augustine utterly astonished. In his retrospective account, Augustine believes that his friend ultimately died so that he could be safe from the 'heretical' Augustine.[161]

Shortly thereafter, the friend's condition deteriorated, and he soon expired.[162] As a result, Augustine describes his heart as being 'completely darkened' (*contenebratum*) with grief (*dolore*).[163] He provides a haunting account of how his entire lived experience was transfigured, resulting in tremendous pain (*cruciatum immanem*).[164] Augustine's familiar haunts became unbearable after his friend's death.[165] Even his home no longer provided any comfort.[166] I shall return to this point about God's absence *infra*, for I believe it provides an insight into the deeper theological stakes of this particular passage of the *Conf.*

Continuing with the narrative of Book IV, Augustine recounts how at that time he believed in a false God (*phantasma*), and thus his soul would not obey the psalmist's command to hope in God.[167] At this location one observes a deeply traumatic experience of grief which begins to disabuse Augustine of certain false notions he had, for instance about the impermanence of human life and his understanding of God. Furthermore, in combination with his narrative reflection in the *Conf.*, Augustine came to realize the truth of the immediacy of self-presence. In performing this reflection on his experience, it seems that Augustine is engaging in a form of philosophical therapy. Indeed, Augustine's own observations support this claim, in particular how his grief and its aftermath led him to become a question to himself.[168]

As Augustine's narrative reflection continues, it discloses further psychological insights, which, when properly interpreted and applied, can have a therapeutic effect. At 4.5.10, Augustine considers his own (apparently natural) response to his friend's death, namely weeping. Among other things, he notices that weeping replaced the friend in bringing him any kind of delight. Although Augustine's grief gave him some relief, this was a false peace.[169] Why, Augustine wonders, did he cry so much? And why did he cry out to God in particular? According to O'Donnell, Augustine raises several possibilities for why his tears may have been pleasant, but the conclusion appears to be that although they are sweet in relation to the pain one is experiencing, tears are actually bitter.[170] That is, his tears were comforting only to the extent that he was otherwise miserable. Perhaps weeping, Augustine suggests, is bittersweet.[171] Augustine ultimately concludes that he resorted to tears because he had not yet learned the appropriate way of loving his friend.[172] When Augustine loved his friend as if the latter would never die, he emptied himself entirely; he lacked one of the marks of true Ciceronian friendship, namely *stabilitas/constantia*.[173]

In the wake of his loss, Augustine realized other notable aspects of his psychological state. He felt that his deceased friend was his counterpart. O'Donnell notes that the Augustine of 375/376 would have looked at his grief in terms of classical myth.[174] In other words, Augustine was afraid to live (as half a person) and afraid to die (lest his friend too be utterly destroyed). Thus he reached an impasse: he was afraid to die, yet hated living.[175] In my estimation, this passage shows that Augustine's false beliefs about the nature of created being, combined with the death of his friend, led him to an unbearable inner state. Because of this incoherence, Augustine tries to escape from himself, rather than confront his inner turmoil. Notably, this reflects the critical point to which Platonic *therapeia* is designed to lead the soul. When one reaches this fork in the road, one has the opportunity to renounce one's false opinions and grow in truth.[176] In Augustine's case, however, he had to await comprehensive moral transformation.

Despite his various attempts to flee from himself, Augustine was unsuccessful. It remained that he was constantly reminded of his loss by the absence of his friend, and only groaning and tears could provide any relief, however partial. Ultimately, Augustine changed his surroundings and moved to Carthage, for at least in this new place his eyes were not accustomed to seeking his friend.[177] In fleeing to Carthage, Augustine was still engaged in the misguided and ultimately unattainable desire to escape himself.

The sudden and irrevocable rupture in Augustine's relationship with his friend reveals to him what was always already the case, namely that he is ineluctably with and present to himself. In *Conf.* 4, Augustine recounts how he carried his wounded soul like a burden (*portabam enim concisam et cruentem animam meam impatientem portari a me, et ubi eam ponerem non inueniebam*).[178] He tried to place his soul somewhere where it could find rest, but it only fell down upon him again.[179] He could neither stand to be with himself, nor could he escape from himself.[180] Augustine relates his

unsuccessful attempts to find refuge in sense pleasures, with which
he was already familiar.[181] As O'Donnell states in his commentary
on *Conf.* 4.7.12, Augustine had rested in the *concupiscentia carnis*
and subsequently the *concupiscentia oculorum*.[182] However, when
confronted with the death of his friend, these distractions no longer
sufficed as an escape from life's challenges.[183] Thus Augustine
becomes for himself an *infelix locus*. Indeed, where could one go,
Augustine wonders, to escape from oneself?[184]

In the aftermath of his friend's death, Augustine suffered acutely
from the bitterness of God's absence.[185] Augustine's soul should
have been healed by God, but he lacked both the desire and the
strength.[186] Indeed, in describing the darkening effects of grief,
Augustine suggests the opposite of God's inner presence in the form
of divine illumination (*quo dolore* contenebratum *est cor meum*).[187]
According to O'Donnell, grief has an inherently restless character
throughout the *Conf.*, which stands in opposition to the *requies* of,
for example, *Conf.* 1.1.1.[188] We have seen how after the death of
his friend, everything is transfigured in Augustine's sight, becoming
a constant torment.[189] As M.-A. Vannier notes, in *Conf.* 4.10.15,
Augustine writes that one feels pain in all things that are not God,
even in good things when they are not enjoyed in relation to God.[190]
O'Donnell characterizes Augustine's description of his grief at 4.4.9
as 'almost literally God-less'.[191] He still believed in a pseudo-god,
a *phantasma*.[192] Thus not even prayer could provide any relief for
Augustine; a false god was no source of consolation in the face of
a true loss.[193]

As O'Donnell suggests, the Augustine of this location in *Conf.*
4 – that is, 375/376 – remained in a state of restless wandering
from God.[194] In addition, he had not yet encountered the *libri
platonicorum*, which taught him of God's incorporeality, a truth
crucial to his conversion.[195] Augustine's bitterness, coupled with
his inability to find any relief from God, invites one to consider
a theme of fundamental significance not only for the *Conf.* but
for Augustine's entire life and thought, namely the dialectic of
auersio a Deo and *conuersio ad Deum*.[196] According to Vannier,
this original theme appears first in *De Genesi contra Manichaeos*
(388/389), is developed in the final three books of the *Conf.* and is
also present in *De Genesi ad litteram*.[197] In the earlier *Sol.*, *auersio
a Deo* results in foolishness and misery.[198] As Vannier writes, in
Conf. 4, *auersio* is 'synonymous with dispersion, suffering and

precariousness'.[199] Later in the *Conf.*, *auersio* is interpreted in terms of *distentio*, a kind of disintegration and distance from God.[200] The thematic interplay of aversion and conversion represents 'the result of [Augustine's] personal experience of first painfully facing his separation from God and, after that, finding in his conversion'.[201]

This consideration of conversion is relevant to classical philosophy, which was often conceived in terms of *therapeia*, not least of all by Plato. However, as Cushman argues, Plato himself recognized the inherent limitations of his therapeutic approach to philosophy: Philosophy endeavours to make people good, but only people who are already morally good will be open to doing philosophy.[202] In light of this observation, Cushman suggests that the Platonic theory of philosophy as therapy eventuates in the need for some sort of divine help or grace. Indeed, Augustine himself appropriates Platonic elements and incorporates them into his theological conception of one's personal interaction with the divine. God supplies the necessary aid to complete Plato's philosophical-therapeutic programme; God draws the soul in a way that dialectic cannot.[203] This idea – namely that God is the *sine qua non* of successful philosophical therapy – was, as Cushman writes, 'the impulse and the ground for [Augustine's] own *Confessions*'.[204] Following Cushman, I would like to suggest that the portion of the *Conf.* under consideration constitutes just such an example of early Christianity's distinctive addition to classical philosophy, namely that God is always implicated in one's pursuit of philosophical therapy, completing the conversion process.

The (re)turn to God, the essential activity of human life, combines ethical, intellectual and ontological aspects.[205] In Augustine's case, conversion 'required his intellectual and volitional transformation and his acceptance of God's plan for his life – a "full" renovation, which was both *epistrophe* [intellectual conversion] and *metanoia* [moral conversion]'.[206] Indeed, Plato too understood his *therapeia* as involving a *metastrophe*, or conversion.[207] As Vannier continues, the activity of conversion is essentially a cooperative activity between the soul and God, or more specifically, the free human response to the initiative of divine grace.[208] The importance of *gratia* is present even in the early works of Augustine, including the Cassiciacum dialogues. It also recurs throughout the *Conf.*, for example, 8.12.30.[209] Essential to Augustine's conversion was the encounter with Christ, which cleansed him of his pride, leading him to humility.[210]

Furthermore, I argue that if *auersio* and *conuersio* obtain in a dialectical relationship, then present within the text of *Conf.* 4 lies an indication of divine presence, even in Augustine's *auersio a Deo*. One finds some warrant for my claim in the previously quoted passage from O'Donnell, in which he continues to suggest that God is still present in some sense in this experience: 'The depiction of grief [at 4.4.9] is almost literally God-less: only in a vain attempt to enjoin hope does God appear'.[211] N. Fischer presents a similar observation, stating that this painful event, to the extent that it moves Augustine to look for God, becomes a kind of contact with God, albeit oblique: 'Die schmerzhafte Erfahrung des Todes eines Freundes wird ihm zur Berührung Gottes, zur Anregung ("excitatio"), auf Gott hinzudenken.'[212] My claim is that through such experiences recounted in the *Conf.*, Augustine experiences a faint and fleeting contact with the divine, which invites him to continue to search for it ever more vigorously.[213] Paradoxically, one can experience God intensely in his very distance.

Recent scholarship has acknowledged a similar dynamic at work in another part of the *Conf.* In the Ostia vision, Augustine attains a fleeting glimpse of God, but he cannot sustain this due to his carnal habit.[214] According to Parsons, 'we can detect a distinct *therapeutic* effect of the visionary experience on Augustine's life, understood as an ancient form of *therapeia*. This effect, mediated through and shaped by the language of Neoplatonism and Christianity, instilled discernible shifts in Augustine's character and helped cultivate specific dispositions, virtues and capacities, as well as occasional insights into the nature of the soul that anticipated psychoanalytic theory'.[215] As Parsons argues, Augustine had glimpsed the divine, yet he needed to train himself to return to and maintain such a vision, something like psychology or therapy over the course of his life.[216] It is precisely this form of therapy, I contend, that Augustine is practising throughout the *Conf.*, not least of all in Book IV.

I further argue that the foregoing analysis reveals that Augustine's thought suggests a nuanced approach to divine presence and absence, which can be discussed in at least two distinct senses. First, as Vannier observes, one's flight from or return to God in this life is always provisional. In the *Conf.*, *auersio* and *conuersio* enjoy a dialectical relationship, in that one cannot be discussed without the other.[217] Thus the interplay of these two moments is a constant process throughout one's entire life.[218] Secondly, as scholars such as Huian note, apart from the consideration of sin, evil and one's (potentially) voluntary separation from God, the divine nature itself challenges human conventions and demands an apophatic theological method.[219] Indeed, Huian characterizes Augustine's theological anthropology as essentially 'apophatic'.[220] Apophaticism is not a matter of negating cataphatic pronouncements. Rather, it is a comprehensive way of thinking which attunes one to one's *own* unknowability.[221] While Augustine does not have a systematic negative anthropology, certain fundamental commitments nevertheless imbue his entire thought.[222] As Huian argues, Augustine suggests a view according to which 'binary patterns [...] have little to no relevance at all'.[223] The ultimate mystery lying within and beyond being challenges one to reconsider one's conventional categories. Thus one can say, in Huian's words, 'The superlative of hiddenness is the mode of manifestation of God, even in his most intense presence.'[224]

The foregoing observations suggest that the question is not so much *God's* presence or absence, but rather the human perspective or disposition with respect to the divine summons. In this case, God simply *is*, but due to the finite and fallible nature of humanity, one projects an inner dynamic experience onto the divine. My 'transcendental' gloss on an Augustinian theme can also be expressed in eschatological terms. As Vannier writes, one's conversion to God is always a continuous process and is only completed in the afterlife.[225] As Heraclitus would say, the task is to locate the coincidence of opposites, situating them within a more fundamental unity.

Confronting the abyss

Nietzsche's appropriation of Heraclitus

Although Heraclitus rebuked his contemporaries for their failure to heed the *logos*, such an oversight cannot be confined to his time alone. This suggests for Miller that there is a more fundamental human attitude at work which is resistant to the inherent dynamism of the cosmos.[226] The relentless, destructive force of time disturbs one at an existential level.[227] One's utter powerlessness provokes one to reclaim some semblance of control.[228] Furthermore, people resist the *logos* because it forces them to confront the abyss underlying all being.[229] Miller 'diagnoses' this condition as 'nostalgia'.[230] In the effort to prevent the flow of time and solidify things as they flow into and out of being, one betrays one's deafness to the *logos*.[231]

Nietzsche, a faithful disciple and interpreter of Heraclitus, articulated the ethical application of this doctrine.[232] Instead of striving in vain to counteract the movement of time, Nietzsche's Zarathustra advocates acquiescence to it.[233] The proper attunement to the *logos* reveals the mysterious truth of the twofold oppositional structure of reality.[234] One will recall that Heraclitus does not understand opposites as related sequentially or alternately, but rather as present together simultaneously.[235] Therefore, insofar as anything is existing or living, it is also dying.[236] According to Nietzsche, human life itself is already an implicit acceptance of the log-ical cosmic order. Because all things are constituted by their opposites, whenever one affirms life, one is also accepting of death.[237] This entails that the realities which one fears have really been with one all along.[238] The abyss is always within one, indeed, is even a constitutive element of one.[239] One cannot truly understand the unity-in-opposition of life and death until one has conceded to it.[240] Only then can one learn to live at peace with the abyss within one.[241] In a spirit of cosmic humility, one must accept this ineluctable duality as the divinely ordained constitution of the universe.[242]

The impermanence of human life in Heidegger

According to R. Coyne, Heidegger revisited the question of the ontological identity of the self for the first time in modern philosophy.[243] The starting point for Heidegger's critique was his claim that since Aristotle, philosophy had been concerned with 'thinghood', thus overlooking a separate category of being, 'existence'.[244] The two main targets of Heidegger's polemic consist of Aristotle and René Descartes. However, in proposing an alternative, Heidegger was influenced by early Christian sources, in particular Paul and Augustine.[245] Whereas the former pair had, so to speak, failed to heed the *logos*, and hence reified the self, the latter two were attentive to the inherent dynamism of the human person, as well as how this form of existence is structured according to one's relationship with God.

The *Natorp Report* (1922) contains Heidegger's main critique of Aristotle.[246] He observes that Aristotle's ontology was grounded in the study of motion. For Aristotle, being in a normative sense became associated with discrete objects and completed products.[247] In contrast to the apparent stability of things and artefacts, human be-ing was construed as somehow inadequate or lacking, and unfavourably compared with pure intellection.[248] Instead of noting and respecting the uniqueness of human life, Aristotle applied to it the same concepts as he did in other aspects of his physics and ontology.[249]

According to Heidegger, Descartes committed a similar error in failing to distinguish between two fundamentally different kinds of being. Heidegger argues that Descartes equated the existence proper to human beings (*Dasein*) with 'thinghood', or the state of being an 'object at hand'.[250] Hence even the Cartesian self is understood in objective terms, as a thing which is open to inspection on request.[251] After Descartes, philosophy focused solely on the mode of being of *Vorhandensein* and conflated this particular mode of being with being itself.[252]

Though critical of Descartes, Heidegger wished to recuperate his insights and incorporate them into a new philosophical worldview.[253] In *Sein und Zeit* (1927), he takes the Cartesian *cogito* as the point of departure, but wishes to interpret it differently, mainly by questioning Descartes' understanding of himself as a *res cogitans/existens*.[254] Heidegger proposes to interpret human existence as a distinct and irreducible mode of being. Specifically, this would mean not to reify the human subject and to develop a set of categories which could adequately describe human life as a unique way of being in the world.[255]

Heidegger's critical-constructive treatment of Descartes led him to Augustine in 1921,[256] in whom Heidegger located a radically different conception of human being. He was especially interested in the *Conf.* which, according to his argument, provided resources for clarifying the ontological status of the self which had been left unresolved since Descartes.[257] Informed by Augustine, Heidegger interprets human life in 'Heraclitean' terms (my gloss). That is, he refuses to apply formal and reified categories to the essentially dynamic form of being enjoyed by human existence.[258] Whereas

Descartes' philosophical anthropology rested on the bedrock of the certitude of 'Je pense, donc je suis', Augustine's departs from the groundlessness of the self.[259] According to S.-J. Arrien, the 'dogmatism' of Cartesian certainty is undermined by Augustine's probing account of his own psyche.[260] Indeed, the Augustinian subject is deeply enigmatic and opaque.[261] Furthermore, as already seen with such scholars as Cavadini, Augustine does not understand the self as a stable, given reality.[262] On Heidegger's reading of Augustine, the human being is in fact a 'non-being'[263] whose existence is called into question and challenged through one's experiences.[264] Human life is therefore characterized by a constant restlessness and instability.[265] Thus Heidegger, in continuity with Heraclitus, admonishes one against falsely conceiving of the self as a product rather than a continuous process.[266]

In a manner consistent with Heraclitus' methodology, Heidegger too seeks to discern possibilities for understanding oneself through a careful investigation of experience.[267] Heidegger sees the Christian experience as paradigmatic for lived experience in general, which is called the hermeneutical phenomenology of factical life or the hermeneutics of facticity.[268] He focuses in particular on Augustinian questioning as a means for arriving at knowledge of oneself.[269] Heidegger notes how in *Conf.* 10, Augustine places himself in God's presence by construing himself *as* a question.[270] Interestingly, Heidegger defines human being (*Dasein*) as *Fraglichsein*, 'being-questionable'.[271] One experiences oneself as a question, to which there is no final answer.[272] According to Heidegger, one possesses oneself to the extent that one interrogates oneself.[273] The subject is not simply the one from whom the search begins or within whom the search is executed; rather, the act of searching, as Heidegger states, is *constitutive* of the self.[274] In other words, Augustine does not merely interrogate himself; he becomes a process of interrogation, by which he enters into the essence of his being, which for Heidegger is *Fraglichsein*. This view coheres with that of Heraclitus, for whom the subject must enter more deeply into its syllaptic constitution, whereby it discovers itself as the simultaneous subject and object of its search.

In contrast to Descartes, who not only located certainty and stability within himself but even established this as the foundation for subsequent philosophy, the self-interrogation which Heidegger locates in Augustine and which has been shown in Heraclitus is anything but comforting or reassuring. Rather, self-interrogation undermines certainty and opens one to the possibility of uncovering the ever-present abyss lurking within one's being.[275] The correct response is to face this nothingness as an ineluctable fact of one's existence. One must acknowledge that life is paradoxically had in the privation of itself.[276] This privation however is inherently linked with the fullness of God's being. Introspection is inherently connected to the search for God, insofar as the path to (or away from) God lies within.[277] However, as indicated in the foregoing treatment of Augustine, the search for God is an ongoing process. In the act of searching, one both finds and fails to find God.[278] Augustine describes how the more one approaches God, one also realizes one's distance from him. It is impossible to overcome this challenge without divine intervention. Such an observation bespeaks, according to Heidegger, an acknowledgement of finitude.[279]

The inadequacies and conundrums raised by one's seeking God reveal one's radical dependence on the divine. As with Peter walking on water to meet Christ, the human being becomes most itself in relationship with the divine Other. According to Heidegger, Augustine attains to self-possession when he truly cares for himself in renunciation before God.[280] The soul must hold to its nothingness before God to avoid the risk of returning to or collapsing on oneself. The soul possesses itself to the extent that it relinquishes itself.[281] This suggests that for Augustine, as with Heraclitus, the search for the self is an activity in which one must be constantly vigilant lest one reify or isolate oneself from the ground of one's being.[282]

As with Heraclitus' early successors and with Augustine, Heidegger identifies ethical implications to this ontological reimagining of selfhood. When the human being erroneously considers itself a product, it lapses into delusion and ignorance of reality; in another idiom, it fails to heed the *logos*.[283] That is, one resists acknowledging the ephemeral nature of being and one's inordinate attachment to it. In response to the threat of annihilation, *Dasein* clings to things as if they could be permanent, only generating greater difficulty in the long term.

Heidegger is critical of the human tendency to be deluded by the apparent stability of the world and its constituents.[284] However, certain experiences, such as anxiety, reveal the true abyssal quality of one's existence.[285] One acutely experiences one's powerlessness and finitude, for instance in not being able to do something one wants, or being obliged to do what one does not want to do.[286] According to Augustine, the true characteristics of human being are *priuatio* and *carentia*.[287] In response to this troubling realization, one often attempts to avoid this truth – and indeed, escape from oneself – by clinging to things in the world.[288] The human person, constantly assailed by the threat of nothingness and the temptation to hide from itself, experiences life as a burden.[289] Nonetheless, according to Heidegger, one can never fully escape from oneself, and indeed, one still encounters oneself in one's attempts to hide from oneself.[290]

Heidegger articulates this dynamic in §30 of *Sein und Zeit*, in which he treat of the fear-structure of *Dasein*. In this passage, Heidegger discusses how the complex experience of fear bespeaks the precarious nature of human life. He distinguishes three aspects of the phenomenon of fear: (1) the fearsome, or the thing in the world that causes fear, (2) the act/experience of fearing and (3) that about which or on behalf of which we fear. In virtue of being-in-the-world, fearing is always a possible state-of-mind for oneself.[291] Indeed, Heidegger even describes the state of one's existence as 'fearful' (*furchtsam*).[292] This fearfulness can be understood as a result of the self's suffering of *molestia*, which is realized both in fear of loss and desire for gain. Such an analysis reveals the temporal and ephemeral element of each moment of life, revealing the self's mode as one of waiting or expectation with respect to the future, *die Zu-kunft*.[293]

Through fear, one experiences oneself as lacking and needy[294]. By its very nature, *Dasein* is bound to things and expresses its being in the form of concern. When a thing is placed in jeopardy, one's own being is affected.[295] When one fears about another, one is ultimately afraid about oneself, more specifically the loss of one's opportunity for Being-with another.[296] As Heidegger explains, one identifies the fearsome even before it draws close.[297] The matter which one finds threatening is not yet in one's immediate vicinity. However, it draws nearer, and in so doing acquires a threatening character.[298] As Heidegger writes, 'it can reach us, but it may not. As it draws close, this "it can, and yet in the end it may not" becomes aggravated'.[299] In other words, that which is feared may continue to approach, yet it may just as well recede and cause no harm. Nonetheless, this constant uncertainty exacerbates one's anxiety: 'This implies that what is detrimental as coming-close close by carries with it the patent possibility that it may stay away and pass us by; but instead of lessening or extinguishing our fearing, this enhances it.'[300] The desire to secure oneself against the nothingness one finds in being and in oneself leads to a constant state of anxiety for those who fail to heed the *logos*.

Those who continue to hold to the objective world in the futile attempt to escape the abyssal challenge of one's being run the risk of utter collapse and dispersion, which Heidegger calls *Ruinanz*.[301] The correct form of living according to Augustine is marked by *continentia*, which Heidegger describes as a counter-movement, which counteracts dispersion.[302] When one ceases to seek refuge in the familiar, one is opened to the experience of *Unheimlichkeit*, of not being completely at home in the world.[303] Though this revelation is by no means comforting, philosophical insight and praxis can enable one to address the true nature of one's existence.[304] Heidegger advocates not holding fast to temporal things but allowing them to come and cease to be according to the world's ontological ebb and flow. In this way, one can preserve oneself from unnecessary suffering. In the words of S. Hannan, 'As shepherds of Being, not of beings, it is not our role to preserve beings in their particularity (thus risking adikia), but to instead remember the rhythm in which they arise and pass away.'[305] With Heidegger I believe we see a more recent instance of the ethics of 'active concession' advocated by Seneca and Marcus Aurelius.[306]

Concluding Thoughts

The abyss is a constant feature of human life of which one is at least implicitly aware at every moment. The dialectical structure of being, whereby opposites exist together, means that loss, negation and death are an ever-present part of life. As we have seen previously, sources such as Seneca and Marcus Aurelius embraced this difficult reality and addressed it through a philosophical programme one could describe as therapeutic. Indeed, according to Cushman, one could interpret Platonic philosophy as a form of therapy. One should add to this the observation that Socrates famously defined philosophy as preparation for death.

Augustine too engaged in a form of philosophical therapy which anticipated contemporary therapeutic techniques. While Augustine was informed by the classical tradition of dialogue, he also innovated, under the inspiration of his Christian beliefs. In his works, one sees a movement from external to internal dialogue (*soliloquium*), and then a reopening of that dialogue to include God, the ultimate Other, as a consistent interlocutor. In this way, Augustine's dialogical method takes the form of *narratio* and *confessio*.

The therapeutic and psychological aspects of philosophy and theology which have been considered in the foregoing pages provide an organic point of intersection with contemporary psychology. However, from a theological perspective, one may critique psychology's apparent theoretical and methodological limitations, which have a real effect on patients. Aside from the many serious and non-trivial problems one faces in life, all of these are situated within the more basic setting of the abyssal confrontation with one's inescapable mortality. As Porter suggests in his critique of Foucault, specific practises intended for the care for oneself are moot if the self is a process in constant flux. The pre-reflective awareness of the abyss causes deep distress, and this distress extends beyond that which is immanent and conditioned.

I argue therefore that, without conflating theology and psychology, the latter must not ignore the former. Rather, one must respect the inherently dialectical constitution of the human person, which includes an orientation to transcendence and ultimate questions as an essential feature. Contemporary psychology has acknowledged the importance of the religious and spiritual dimension of the human person.[1] Furthermore, my position is supported by the general structure of this work, namely that theology as an academic discipline possesses the resources to provide explanations for the various phenomena of human experience. Finally, scholars such as Hampson and Hoff have advocated for theology to inform psychology.[2] They note how, despite the fact that Cartesian anthropology has been roundly critiqued for its inability to capture essential elements of the human being, one still awaits a compelling alternative anthropology.[3] A dialogue between theology and psychology could address this lacuna.[4]

In this respect, it is useful to recall that one can plausibly consider Augustine the first psychologist[5] (if not Heraclitus, as Kahn suggests). As we have seen, his own introspective methods – especially that of confession – served a therapeutic function. In light of the fact that contemporary society has embraced therapy as a mode of introspection, Parsons argues that Augustine's thought can be fruitfully received and assist in the fundamentally human search for truth.[6] In addition to the search for truth, the *Conf.* addresses other shared aspects of the human condition,[7] which suggests that it could be a useful resource for self-enquiry. In his monograph on Augustine and Freud, Parsons endeavours to show how the *Conf.* can inform both contemporary psychoanalysis and spirituality.[8] He also believes that the content of Augustine's findings can speak to seminal insights in the history of psychology, such as the discovery of the profoundly uncertain nature of subjectivity revealed by Freud.[9] Indeed, we have already seen how in locations such as *Conf.* 10 Augustine grapples with the inner experience of otherness.[10]

As already suggested by the consideration of Komatsu's research, psychology largely assumes a conception of the self which is consistent with Cartesian philosophy. As Bendeck Sotillos argues, this is no coincidence. He quotes René Guénon, according to whom 'Cartesian duality ... has imposed itself on all modern Western thought.'[11] Bendeck Sotillos also references Ludwig Binswanger and Victor Danner, who have claimed that one of the results of modernity is a strict divide between subject and object, inner and outer, within the realm of psychology.[12] Such changes in thought patterns have implications which are realized at the level of lived experience. 'This bifurcation', Bendeck Sotillos writes, 'has created a *void* in the human psyche that has proven to be *profoundly traumatic*'.[13] Similarly, modern psychology seems to assume a deep division between the self and other, which is also informed by Cartesian metaphysics.[14] In general, the advent of Enlightenment involved a fundamental reconstruction of how one understands oneself and one's relationships to the world.[15] Unfortunately, the results of this philosophical paradigm shift have been largely negative for human life.[16]

While the premodern dispensation understood the person as integrally related with oneself, the world, others and especially God, the modern dispensation does not acknowledge the essentially multifaceted and interconnected nature of the human being, what I have called its dialectical constitution.[17] For the former, to be human was to possess both an inner and an outer dimension, as well as an orientation beyond oneself, both horizontally and vertically.[18] Concerning the human being in both interior and exterior terms, various spiritual traditions did not envision these in opposition to each other.[19] The task was to ensure a *harmonious* order between them, for which religious sources provided a variety of images.[20] Furthermore, both the inner and the outer aspects of the human being were both considered to be grounded in a profound unity with the cosmos.[21]

Besides sharing a commitment to the transcendent orientation of the human person, religious traditions seem to agree that the divine is somehow present within the person and vice versa.[22] 'The spiritual traditions', writes Bendeck Sotillos, 'teach that there is a part of us that is always firmly rooted in divine reality'.[23] Therefore, human interiority is never purely its own thing; it is 'in us but not of us'.[24] For Augustine, reflecting on this divine indwelling occasions a movement beyond binary categories. In the Hadith Qudsi, one finds a saying that could fit very easily within the *Conf.*: 'The heavens and the earth cannot contain Me, but the heart of my believing servant does contain me.'[25] In addition to the anthropological, ontological and epistemological, the significance of this intimate contact with the divine is also therapeutic and psychological, for the spiritual traditions hold that only the divine can ensure the integrity of a human being.[26] Various traditions speak of a divine inner teacher, who can also be described as an inner therapist or physician,[27] just as Augustine addresses God as the physician of his inner life (*medice meus intime*).[28]

This paradoxical interior presence relates to polarity insofar as many religious practises are means provided for the sake of recognizing the fundamental unity of being.[29] Bendeck Sotillos calls for a return to traditional, pre-Cartesian ways of thinking which are consistent with the dialectical picture of reality which we have discussed.[30] In his estimation, not only would such a reorientation reflect the true nature of being, it would also contribute to the overall well-being of humanity, both individually and collectively.[31]

NOTES

General Introduction

1   Lope Cilleruelo, '"Deum videre" en San Agustín', *Salmanticensis* 12, no. 1 (1965): 3–31.

2   Richard Dawkins, *The God Delusion*, new edn (Boston, MA: Mariner, 2008), 415–16; Tina Beattie, *The New Atheists* (England: Darton, Longman & Todd, 2007), 105.

3   Dawkins, *The God Delusion*, 415–16; Beattie, *The New Atheists*, 105.

4   Ibid.

5   Steven Grand, *Creation: Life and How to Make It* (London: Weidenfeld & Nicholson, 2000), 30, quoted in Dawkins, *The God Delusion*, 415–16; cf. Beattie, *The New Atheists*, 105.

6   Brian Stock, *The Integrated Self: Augustine, the Bible, and Ancient Thought* (Philadelphia, PA: University of Pennsylvania Press, 2017), 28.

7   'Bernard Williams on Descartes: Section 5', video, 07:47, *YouTube*, posted by Flame0430, 24 December 2008, accessed 3 October 2023, https://youtu.be/2z-obRljOXY. See 1:39 to 2:20.

8   Jeffrey C. Pugh, 'Searching for Myself', in *The Matrix of Faith: Reclaiming a Christian Vision* (New York, NY: Crossroad Pub., 2001), 28–9.

9   Ibid., 29.

10   Ibid.

11   Ingolf U. Dalferth, 'What Does It Mean to Be Human?', in *Kierkegaardian Essays: A Festschrift in Honour of George Pattison*, ed. Christopher B. Barnett and Clare Carlisle (Berlin: De Gruyter, 2022), 1.

12   I am grateful to Dr. Grant Gholson for this insight.

13   David W. Tracy, 'Augustine our Contemporary: The Overdetermined, Incomprehensible Self', in *Augustine Our Contemporary: Examining the Self in Past and Present*, ed. Willemien Otten and Susan E. Schreiner (Notre Dame, IN: University of Notre Dame Press, 2018), 68.

14   Beattie, *The New Atheists*, 105.

15   Ibid.

16   Steven Reidbord, MD, 'Dialectics in Psychotherapy: An Introduction to the Meaning and Central Role of Dialectics in Therapy', *Psychology Today*,

last modified 13 September 2019, accessed 3 October 2023, https://www.
psychologytoday.com/us/blog/sacramento-street-psychiatry/201909/dialectics-
in-psychotherapy#:~:text=Broadly%20speaking%2C%0a%20dialectic%20
is,arguments%2C%20is%20a%20classic%20example.

17 Julie E. Maybee, 'Hegel's Dialectics', *Stanford Encyclopedia of Philosophy*,
last modified 2 October 2020, accessed 3 October 2023, https://plato.
stanford.edu/entries/hegel-dialectics/.

18 Cf. Patrick Lee Miller, *Becoming God: Pure Reason in Ancient Greek
Philosophy* (London: Continuum, 2011), 33.

19 Wayne J. Hankey, '"Knowing as We Are Known" in *Confessions* 10 and Other
Philosophical, Augustinian and Christian Obedience to the Delphic *Gnothi
Seauton* from Socrates to Modernity', *Augustinian Studies* 34, no. 1 (2003):
23–48, here [11]: 'in principle, self-knowledge and interior dialogue with God
belong together'.

Chapter 1

1   Peter Adamson, *A History of Philosophy Without Any Gaps: Classical
Philosophy* (Oxford: Oxford University Press, 2016), 3, 30.

2   Aryeh Finkelberg, *Heraclitus and Thales' Conceptual Scheme* (Leiden: Brill,
2017), 21.

3   Krzysztof Narecki, 'The Image of the River in the Fragments of Heraclitus',
Philotheos 12 (2012): 66–77, here 66; Finkelberg, *Conceptual Scheme*, 21.

4   Finkelberg, *Conceptual Scheme*, 21; cf. Daniel W. Graham, *The Texts of Early
Greek Philosophy: The Complete Fragments and Selected Testimonies of the
Major Presocratics* (Cambridge: Cambridge University Press, 2010), 135.

5   Finkelberg, *Conceptual Scheme*, 22; Maria Michela Sassi and Michele Asuni,
The Beginnings of Philosophy in Greece (Princeton: Princeton University
Press, 2020), 103–4; cf. Charles H. Kahn, *The Art and Thought of Heraclitus:
An Edition of the Fragments with Translation and Commentary* (Cambridge:
Cambridge University Press, 1979), 285.

6   Finkelberg, *Conceptual Scheme*, 22.

7   Harold Cherniss, 'The Characteristics and Effects of Presocratic Philosophy',
Journal of the History of Ideas 12, no. 3 (1951): 319–45, here 330; A. V.
Halapsis, 'Man and *Logos*: Heraclitus' Secret', *Anthropological Measurements
of Philosophical Research* 17 (2020): 119–30, here 122; Miller, *Becoming
God*, 40; Sassi and Asuni, *Beginnings of Philosophy*, 103–4; cf. Finkelberg,
Conceptual Scheme, 93, 101.

8   Finkelberg, *Conceptual Scheme*, 23.

9   Ibid., 23, 30.

10 Ibid., 24.

11 Ibid., 24–5.

12 Ibid., 24–30.
13 Richard Neels, 'Elements and Opposites in Heraclitus', *Apeiron* 51, no. 4 (2018): 1–26.
14 Finkelberg, *Conceptual Scheme*, 27.
15 Cf. Narecki, 'The Image of the River', 66.
16 Finkelberg, *Conceptual Scheme*, 39.
17 Halapsis, 'Man and *Logos*', 120–1; Finkelberg, *Conceptual Scheme*, 39.
18 Finkelberg, *Conceptual Scheme*, 39.
19 Narecki, 'The Image of the River', 66.
20 Finkelberg, *Conceptual Scheme*, 36–8.
21 Ibid., 38.
22 Ibid. Cf. Kahn, *The Art and Thought of Heraclitus*, 136.
23 Cherniss, 'Presocratic Philosophy', 332; cf. Miller, *Becoming God*, 15.
24 Finkelberg, *Conceptual Scheme*, 38. Cf. Kahn, *The Art and Thought of Heraclitus*, 136.
25 Finkelberg, *Conceptual Scheme*, 39; cf. Halapsis, 'Man and *Logos*', 120; Narecki, 'The Image of the River', 66.
26 Finkelberg, *Conceptual Scheme*, 40.
27 Ibid.
28 Celso Vieira, 'Heraclitus' Bow Composition', *The Classical Quarterly* 63, no. 2 (2013): 473–90, here 474.
29 Finkelberg, *Conceptual Scheme*, 36.
30 Sassi and Asuni, *Beginnings of Philosophy*, 102.
31 Vieira, 'Heraclitus' Bow Composition', 474.
32 Sassi and Asuni, *Beginnings of Philosophy*, 103; Vieira, 'Heraclitus' Bow Composition', 476–7.
33 Finkelberg, *Conceptual Scheme*, 34.
34 Ibid., 35–6.
35 Ibid., 34.
36 Ibid.
37 Ibid., 36.
38 Miller, *Becoming God*, 19.
39 Ibid., 27.
40 Cf. Vieira, 'Heraclitus' Bow Composition', 473.
41 Sassi and Asuni, *Beginnings of Philosophy*, 101, 102, 104, 106.
42 Ibid., 104.
43 Ibid., 101.
44 Ibid., 101–2, 104, 106.
45 Ibid., 101–2, 104, 106.
46 Miller, *Becoming God*, 40. Stated yet another way, Heraclitus' work seems 'to hide the obvious using different linguistic strategies in order to extend

both the knowledge about the world and self-knowledge'. Mariana Gardella, 'Heráclito de Éfeso, Cleobulina de Lindos y la tradición de los enigmas', *Revista de Filosofía* 46, no. 1 (2021): 45–62, at 45 (abstract).

47 Miller, *Becoming God*, 21.
48 Ibid.
49 Ibid., 13, 19.
50 Graham, *Texts of Early Greek Philosophy*, 161.
51 Miller, *Becoming God*, 19–20.
52 Ibid., 40; cf. Halapsis, 'Man and *Logos*', 124. An additional reason for attributing to Heraclitus a deliberately obscure style is the widely held belief that he imitated the enigmatic pronouncements of the Delphic oracle. However, Finkelberg objects to this reading on two grounds. First, he argues that due to Heraclitus' genuine religious piety, it is doubtful that he would have so boldly embraced an oracular style. Secondly, recent scholarship has nuanced the traditional idea that oracles themselves were as mysterious as they have been assumed to be. See Finkelberg, *Conceptual Scheme*, 36–7, plus n. 75.
53 Miller, *Becoming God*, 40.
54 Ibid.
55 Ibid.
56 Glenn W. Most, 'Heraclitus Fragment B123 DK', in *What Reason Promises: Essays on Reason, Nature and History*, ed. Wendy Doniger, Peter Galison and Susan Neiman (Berlin and Boston: De Gruyter, 2016), 123.
57 Graham, *Texts of Early Greek Philosophy*, 149.
58 Miller, *Becoming God*, 39.
59 Ibid., 40.
60 Ibid.
61 Ibid., 39.
62 Ibid., 40.
63 Halapsis, 'Man and *Logos*', 125–6.
64 Vieira, 'Heraclitus' Bow Composition', 476.
65 Miller, *Becoming God*, 27; Vieira, 'Heraclitus' Bow Composition', 480.
66 Vieira, 'Heraclitus' Bow Composition', 473, 477, 482.
67 Ibid., 482.
68 Graham, *Texts of Early Greek Philosophy*, 161.
69 Miller, *Becoming God*, 20–1; cf. Vieira, 'Heraclitus' Bow Composition', 482.
70 Miller, *Becoming God*, 31.
71 Ibid.
72 Finkelberg, *Conceptual Scheme*, 34.
73 Ibid., 40.
74 Sassi and Asuni, *Beginnings of Philosophy*, 102.
75 Halapsis, 'Man and *Logos*', 119–20, 124; Sassi and Asuni, *Beginnings of Philosophy*, 101.

76   Sassi and Asuni, *Beginnings of Philosophy*, 106.

77   Ibid.

78   Most, 'Heraclitus Fragment B123 DK', 121–2.

79   Ibid., 122.

80   Graham, *Texts of Early Greek Philosophy*, 135–6.

81   Cherniss, 'Presocratic Philosophy', 336–7.

82   Adamson, *Classical Philosophy*, 33; Graham, *Texts of Early Greek Philosophy*, 135–6; cf. Narecki, 'The Image of the River', 68–9.

83   Adamson, *Classical Philosophy*, 33; Graham, *Texts of Early Greek Philosophy*, 135–6.

84   Kahn, *The Art and Thought of Heraclitus*, 285.

85   Narecki, 'The Image of the River', 66.

86   Graham, *Texts of Early Greek Philosophy*, 163.

87   Adamson, *Classical Philosophy*, 32.

88   Ibid., 32.

89   Kahn, *The Art and Thought of Heraclitus*, 186.

90   Ibid.

91   Ibid., 187–8.

92   Ibid., 188.

93   Ibid., 187.

94   Ibid., 187.

95   See Plato, *Theatetus*, trans. M. J. Levett, with an Introduction by Bernard Williams (Indianapolis/Cambridge: Hackett Publishing Company, 1992), here 152a, p. 14.

96   Kahn, *The Art and Thought of Heraclitus*, 187–9.

97   Ibid., 189.

98   Adamson, *Classical Philosophy*, 32.

99   Kahn, *The Art and Thought of Heraclitus*, 189.

100   Ibid., 199; Vieira, 'Heraclitus' Bow Composition', 473.

101   Ibid., 195. Graham (*Texts of Early Greek Philosophy*, 161) translates B51 as follows: 'They do not understand how being at variance with itself it agrees: back-turning structure as of a bow or lyre.'

102   Ibid., 198–9; cf. B67, B41.

103   Miller, *Becoming God*, 19.

104   Cf. ibid., 20.

105   Ibid., 20, 42.

106   Ibid., 42.

107   Kahn, *The Art and Thought of Heraclitus*, 199.

108   Ibid., 285.

109   Ibid., 199.

110   Miller, *Becoming God*, 20.

111 Ibid. Miller writes that this fragment can even accommodate the third aforementioned sense of 'harmony', for instance if the lyre were being played at a feast celebrating a treaty agreed between former enemies.

112 Kahn, *The Art and Thought of Heraclitus*, 199.

113 Ibid., 198.

114 Ibid., 198–9.

115 Ibid.

116 Ibid., 199.

117 Ibid.

118 Ibid., 196, 197; cf. 198, 199.

119 Ibid., 199.

120 Miller, *Becoming God*, 19.

121 Kahn, *The Art and Thought of Heraclitus*, 197; cf. ibid., 199: According to Kahn, 'The concept of *harmoniê* as a unity composed of conflicting parts is the model for an understanding of the world ordering as a unified whole.'

122 Cf. Miller, *Becoming God*, 19; Vieira, 'Heraclitus' Bow Composition', 473.

123 Kahn, *The Art and Thought of Heraclitus*, 199.

124 Miller, *Becoming God*, 19.

125 Vieira, 'Heraclitus' Bow Composition', 478 n. 16, citing W. K. C. Guthrie, *History of Greek Philosophy I: The Earlier Presocratics and the Pythagoreans* (Cambridge, UK: Cambridge University Press, 1962), 437.

126 Vieira, 'Heraclitus' Bow Composition', 478.

127 Miller, *Becoming God*, 21.

128 Kahn, *The Art and Thought of Heraclitus*, 197–8.

129 Ibid., 197; Mark A. Johnstone, 'On "*Logos*" in Heraclitus', *Oxford Studies in Ancient Philosophy* 47 (2014): 1–29, here 24. Augustine too has a notion of reason as shared among minds, a point he openly expresses in works such as *De Magistro* and *De Libero Arbitrio*.

130 Kahn, *The Art and Thought of Heraclitus*, 197.

131 Miller, *Becoming God*, 29, 31, 32.

132 Ibid., 29.

133 Ibid.

134 Graham, *Texts of Early Greek Philosophy*, 159.

135 Kahn, *The Art and Thought of Heraclitus*, 281.

136 Miller, *Becoming God*, 31.

137 Kahn, *The Art and Thought of Heraclitus*, 286.

138 Ibid., 282.

139 Ibid., 282. As indicated *supra*, Sassi and Asuni speak of the 'irreducible duplicity' of being. Sassi and Asuni, *Beginnings of Philosophy*, 101.

140 Kahn, *The Art and Thought of Heraclitus*, 282.

141 Ibid., 283; cf. Miller, *Becoming God*, 29.

142 Ibid., 286; cf. Miller, *Becoming God*, 29.

143 Cf. ibid., 130; Miller, *Becoming God*, 37.

144 Ibid., 283.

145 Ibid., 284.

146 Graham, *Texts of Early Greek Philosophy*, 159.

147 Kahn, *The Art and Thought of Heraclitus*, 286.

148 Miller, *Becoming God*, 37.

149 Most, 'Heraclitus Fragment B123 DK', 121.

150 Kahn, *The Art and Thought of Heraclitus*, 282.

151 Ibid.

152 Miller, *Becoming God*, 30; emphases added.

153 Ibid.

154 Ibid., 31–2.

155 Ibid., 30.

156 Ibid.

157 Ibid.

158 Ibid.

159 Ibid., 30–1.

160 Ibid., 30.

161 Ibid.

162 Ibid., 31.

163 Graham, *Texts of Early Greek Philosophy*, 159.

164 Narecki, 'The Image of the River', 68 (n. 9).

165 Cf. Kahn, *The Art and Thought of Heraclitus*, 166–8; Narecki, 'The Image of the River', 68.

166 Miller, *Becoming God*, 13.

167 Kahn, *The Art and Thought of Heraclitus*, 167; Narecki, 'The Image of the River', 71.

168 Miller, *Becoming God*, 13.

169 Ibid.

170 Kahn, *The Art and Thought of Heraclitus*, 167; Narecki, 'The Image of the River', 71.

171 Kahn, *The Art and Thought of Heraclitus*, 167.

172 Ibid., 167–8.

173 Ibid., 167.

174 Ibid.; cf. Narecki, 'The Image of the River', 71–2. Plato seems to endorse this idea at *Symposium* 207D.

175 Kahn, *The Art and Thought of Heraclitus*, 168.

176 Miller, *Becoming God*, 13; emphasis added.

177 Narecki, 'The Image of the River', 66; Johnstone, 'On "*Logos*"', 21; Miller, *Becoming God*, 15; Neels, 'Elements and Opposites', 5; cf. Vieira, 'Heraclitus' Bow Composition', 482.

178 Miller, *Becoming God*, 39.
179 Kahn, *The Art and Thought of Heraclitus*, 126.
180 Ibid., 126–7.
181 Ibid., 126.
182 Ibid., 127.
183 Richard D. McKirahan, *Philosophy Before Socrates: An Introduction with Texts and Commentary*, 2nd edn (Indianapolis, IN: Hackett, 2011), 141; Kahn, *The Art and Thought of Heraclitus*, 127.
184 Halapsis, 'Man and *Logos*', 127; Kahn, *The Art and Thought of Heraclitus*, 127.
185 Finkelberg, *Conceptual Scheme*, 187; Halapsis, 'Man and *Logos*', 126.
186 James I. Porter, 'Time for Foucault? Reflections on the Roman Self from Seneca to Augustine', *Foucault Studies* (6 January 2017): 113–33, here 113–14.
187 Graham, *Texts of Early Greek Philosophy*, 149.
188 Kahn, *The Art and Thought of Heraclitus*, 116.
189 Ibid., 116.
190 Graham, *Texts of Early Greek Philosophy*, 167.
191 McKirahan, *Philosophy Before Socrates*, 140–1.
192 Kahn, *The Art and Thought of Heraclitus*, 128, 130; Finkelberg, *Conceptual Scheme*, 188; Halapsis, 'Man and *Logos*', 126.
193 Halapsis, 'Man and *Logos*', 125.
194 Ibid., 119, 127; Kahn, *The Art and Thought of Heraclitus*, 130; Miller, *Becoming God*, 28.
195 Finkelberg, *Conceptual Scheme*, 182–3.
196 Ibid., 188.
197 Miller, *Becoming God*, 32.
198 Ibid.
199 Ibid., 33, 38.
200 Ibid., 33.
201 Ibid., 33, 38.
202 Ibid., 33, 37.
203 Halapsis, 'Man and *Logos*', 125.
204 Ibid., 124.
205 Dalferth, 'What Does It Mean to Be Human?', 1.
206 Halapsis, 'Man and *Logos*', 124.
207 Ibid., 126.
208 Ibid., 125.
209 Cherniss, 'Presocratic Philosophy', 334.
210 Miller, *Becoming God*, 23.
211 Ibid.

212 Graham, *Texts of Early Greek Philosophy*, 177.
213 Miller, *Becoming God*, 23–5.
214 Graham, *Texts of Early Greek Philosophy*, 177.
215 Miller, *Becoming God*, 23.
216 Ibid.
217 Ibid.

Chapter 2

1 James I. Porter, 'Time for Foucault? Reflections on the Roman Self from Seneca to Augustine', *Foucault Studies* (6 January 2017): 121.
2 Ibid., 114.
3 Miller, *Becoming God*, 27.
4 Finkelberg, *Conceptual Scheme*, 24.
5 Porter, 'Time for Foucault?', 121.
6 Cf. ibid., 130.
7 Ibid., 113, 114.
8 Ibid., 133.
9 Ibid., 113–14.
10 Ibid., 124, 130.
11 Ibid., 113.
12 Ibid., 114, 115, 119.
13 Ibid., 114, 115.
14 Ibid., 115.
15 Ibid., 113, 115, 116.
16 Ibid., 116.
17 Ibid., 116.
18 Ibid., 117.
19 Cf. Alain Michel, 'Dialogue philosophique et vie intérieure: Cicéron, Sénèque, Saint Augustin', *Helmantica* 28 (1977): 353–76, here 371.
20 John M. Rist, *What Is a Person?: Realities, Constructs, Illusions* (Cambridge; New York; Port Melbourne; New Delhi; Singapore: Cambridge University Press, 2020), 47; Jérôme Lagouanère, 'Agustín lector de Séneca: el caso de la *bona uoluntas*', *Augustinus* 64, no. 252–3 (2019): 193–202, here 193. However, Stock denies this connection. See Stock, *The Integrated Self*, n. 21 to the Introduction.
21 Michel, 'Dialogue philosophique', 371–2.
22 Ibid., 370.
23 Ibid., 371.
24 Porter, 'Time for Foucault?', 127 (n. 60).

25 Michel, 'Dialogue philosophique', 370.

26 Ibid.

27 Ibid.

28 Porter, 'Time for Foucault?', 122.

29 Ibid.

30 Ibid., 122, 123.

31 Ibid., 124.

32 Ibid.

33 Ibid., 122.

34 Lucius Annaeus Seneca, *Natural Questions*, trans. Harry Hine (Chicago: University of Chicago Press, 2010), 6.1.1, p. 87. (Hereafter cited as *Quaest. Nat.* with localization and page numbers from the Hine translation.)

35 Seneca, *Quaest. Nat.* 6.1.6–7, p. 88.

36 Seneca, *Quaest. Nat.* 6.1.10, p. 89.

37 Seneca, *Quaest. Nat.* 6.1.1, p. 87.

38 Seneca, *Quaest. Nat.* 6.1.14, p. 89.

39 Seneca, *Quaest. Nat.* 6.1.15, p. 89.

40 Seneca, *Quaest. Nat.* 6.1.11; transl. Hine, p. 89.

41 Porter, 'Time for Foucault?', 123–4.

42 Cf. ibid., 122.

43 Seneca, *Quaest. Nat.* 6.2.1–2, pp. 89–90.

44 Seneca, *Quaest. Nat.* 6.2.3, p. 90.

45 Seneca, *Quaest. Nat.* 6.2.3–5, p. 90.

46 Seneca, *Quaest. Nat.* 6.2.5, transl. Hine, p. 90.

47 Seneca, *Quaest. Nat.* 6.2.6, p. 90.

48 Seneca, *Quaest. Nat.* 6.2.6, transl. Hine, p. 90.

49 Seneca, *Quaest. Nat.* 6.2.7, p. 90.

50 Seneca, *Quaest. Nat.* 6.2.3, p. 90.

51 Seneca, *Quaest. Nat.* 6.3.2, p. 91.

52 Michel, 'Dialogue philosophique', 368.

53 Lucius Annaeus Seneca, *Letters on Ethics: To Lucilius*, trans. Margaret Graver and A. A. Long (Chicago: University of Chicago Press, 2015), *Ep.* 104.11, p. 414.

54 Seneca, *Ep.* 104.12, trans. Graver and Long, p. 414.

55 Seneca, *Ep.* 104.12, p. 414.

56 Michel, 'Dialogue philosophique', 369.

57 Seneca, *Ep.* 104.11, p. 414.

58 Cf. Porter, 'Time for Foucault?', 127; Marcus Aurelius, *Med.* 4.3.

59 Porter, 'Time for Foucault?', 129.

60 Ibid., 126.

61 Ibid., 127. Cf. Jacques-Alain Miller, 'Extimité', *Prose Studies* 11, no. 3 (1988): 121–31.

62 Ibid., 125.

63 Ibid., 127.

64 Ibid., 125.

65 Ibid., 127.

66 Ibid., 129.

67 Ibid., 125.

68 Ibid., 129.

69 Ibid., 125.

70 Ibid., 125.

71 Catherine Conybeare, '*Quotquot haec legerint meminerint*: All Who Read This Will Remember', *MLN* 127, no. 5 (2012): S23–33, here S28.

72 Porter, 'Time for Foucault?', 124–5.

73 Ibid., 126.

74 Ibid., 130.

75 Ibid., 133.

76 Ibid.

77 Ibid., 132.

78 Ibid.

79 Richard Shusterman, *Thinking Through the Body: Essays in Somaesthetics* (Cambridge: Cambridge University Press, 2012), 68.

80 Christian Lotz, 'Responsive Life and Speaking to the Other', *Augustinian Studies* 37, no. 1 (2006): 89–109, here [19]. I have referenced a version of the article available on the author's Academia.edu page, hence the pagination is in brackets. See https://www.academia.edu/28743190/_Responsive_Life_and_Speaking_To_the_Other_A_Phenomenological_Interpretation_of_Book_One_of_Augustine_s_Confessions_in_Augustinian_Studies_2006_37_1_2006_89_109.

81 Shusterman, *Thinking Through the Body*, 68.

82 Ibid., 68–9.

83 Wayne J. Hankey, '"Knowing as We Are Known" in *Confessions* 10 and Other Philosophical, Augustinian and Christian Obedience to the Delphic *Gnothi Seauton* from Socrates to Modernity', *Augustinian Studies* 34, no. 1 (2003): 23–48, here [15]. Pauliina Remes, 'Inwardness and Infinity of Selfhood: From Plotinus to Augustine', in *Ancient Philosophy of the Self*, ed. Pauliina Remes and Juha Sihvola (Dordrecht: Springer, 2008), 155. A version of Hankey's article is available on his Academia.edu profile. I have used the pagination of this text. See https://www.academia.edu/11708435/_Knowing_as_we_are_Known_in_Confessions_10_and_Other_Philosophical_Augustinian_and_Christian_Obedience_to_the_Delphic_Gnothi_Seauton_from_Socrates_to_Modernity_.

84 Hankey, '"Knowing"', [6]. Hankey cites both Chadwick and Courcelle in support of this claim.

85 Johnstone, 'On "*Logos*"', 21.

86 Ibid.

87 Ibid., 21.
88 Ibid., 21, 23, 24.
89 Ibid., 21, 24.
90 Vieira, 'Heraclitus' Bow Composition', 476.
91 Ibid.
92 Johnstone, 'On "*Logos*"', 21, 22, 24.
93 Ibid., 22.
94 Ibid., 23.
95 Augustine, *Confessions, Volume II Books 9–13*, Loeb Classical Library 27 (Cambridge, MA: Harvard University Press, 2016), 10.6.8.
96 *Conf.* 10.6.8; Loeb 27, trans. Hammond.
97 Cf. Eun Young Hwang, 'The Paradoxical Place of the Self: Augustine and Zhi Yi on the Question of the Self and World Experience and the Revelatory Power of Self-Inspection', *Buddhist-Christian Studies* 37 (2017): 173–90, here 185–6.
98 *Conf.* 10.6.8; Loeb 27, trans. Hammond.
99 *Conf.* 10.6.10; Loeb 27, trans. Hammond.
100 Ibid.
101 *Conf.* 10.26.37; Loeb 27, trans. Hammond.

Chapter 3

1 Guy G. Stroumsa, 'The New Self and Reading Practices in Late Antique Christianity', *Church History and Religious Culture* 95, no. 1 (2015): 1–18, here 5.
2 Stroumsa, 'The New Self', 5.
3 Ibid.
4 Ibid.
5 Ibid., 5–6.
6 Rist, *What Is a Person?*
7 Ibid., 45.
8 Cf. ibid., 45, 53–5. Concerning the first of these, see *infra* on Husserl's distinction between *Leib* and *Körper*.
9 Cf. ibid., 49–50.
10 Ibid., 45; cf. Samuel Bendeck Sotillos, 'The Inner and Outer Human Being', *The Mountain Path* 60, no. 2 (2023): 9–26, here 10.
11 Rist, *What Is a Person?*, 49.
12 Andreas Nordlander, 'The Emergence of Soul: Retrieving Augustine's Potentialism for Contemporary Theological Anthropology', *Modern Theology* 35, no. 1 (2018): 122–37, here 132–5.

13 Augustinus, *S. Aurelii Augustini Opera Omnia*, ed. J.-P. Migne, Patrologia Latina 38 (Paris: 1841–6), here *Io. eu. tr.* 19.15, PL 35. Available at http://www.augustinus.it/latino/discorsi/index2.htm.

14 *Io. eu. tr.* 19.15, PL 35: 'Sicut anima habens corpus, non facit duas personas, sed unum hominem; sic Verbum habens hominem, non facit duas personas, sed unum Christum'.

15 Rist, *What Is a Person?*, 47.

16 Cf. ibid.

17 Ibid., 48. See also ibid., 49: 'The *persona*, as a whole, both transcends its "parts" [...] and is also fully represented by each of them'.

18 Ibid., 48.

19 Sophie-Jan Arrien, 'Penser sans Dieu, vivre avec Dieu: Heidegger lecteur d'Augustin', *Esprit* Janvier, no. 1 (2013): 68–80, here [4]. John C. Cavadini, *Visioning Augustine* (Hoboken: Wiley/Blackwell, 2019), 141–2. For Arrien's article, I located the full text online at https://www.cairn.info/revue-esprit-2013-1-page-68.htm?contenu=article and copied and pasted the text into a word processing document. Hence my idiosyncratic pagination, which I reference in brackets.

20 Brian Stock, *Augustine's Inner Dialogue: The Philosophical Soliloquy in Late Antiquity* (New York: Cambridge University Press, 2010), 10.

21 Rist, *What Is a Person?*, 53; see also Cavadini, *Visioning Augustine*, 141–2.

22 Ibid.

23 Maren Wehrle, 'Being a Body and Having a Body: The Twofold Temporality of Embodied Intentionality', *Phenomenology and the Cognitive Sciences* 19, no. 3 (2019): 499–521, here 508.

24 Rist, *What Is a Person?*, 55: '[Augustine] knew that (in modern language) human beings – persons – are both objective realities and subjective historical structures'. Cf. Wehrle, 'Being a Body and Having a Body', 508.

25 Cf. Rist, *What Is a Person?*, 53.

26 Ibid.

27 Gerard J. P. O'Daly, 'Two Kinds of Subjectivity in Augustine's *Confessions*: Memory and Identity, and the Integrated Self' *Ancient Philosophy of the Self* (2008): 195–203, here 197.

28 Rist, *What Is a Person?*, 54. See also O'Daly, 'Two Kinds of Subjectivity', 203.

29 See Porter, 'Time for Foucault?', 119; Michel, 'Dialogue philosophique', 365; O'Daly, 'Two Kinds of Subjectivity', 199–200, plus n. 16 on 199.

30 Charles Mathewes, 'Pluralism, Otherness, and the Augustinian Tradition', *Modern Theology* 14, no. 1 (1998): 83–112, here 99–100, emphases added.

31 Tracy, 'The Overdetermined, Incomprehensible Self', 28; cf. Mathewes, 'Pluralism', 99.

32 Tracy, 'The Overdetermined, Incomprehensible Self', 28.

33 Christine Mohrmann, 'Saint Augustin écrivain', *Revue d'Études Augustiniennes et Patristiques* 50, no. 1 (2004): 43–66, here 43.

34 Conybeare, '*Quotquot haec legerint*', S24.

35   Ibid., S28.
36   Ibid.
37   Mathewes, 'Pluralism', 84.
38   Stock, *The Integrated Self*, 10.
39   *Gn. litt.* 3.19.29, PL 34.
40   Ibid.
41   Carmela Bianco, 'Insegnare agli ignoranti. Attualità della tradizione sul Maestro interiore', *Asprenas: Rivista di Teologia* 62, no. 3 (2015): 171–86, here 175.
42   *Mag.* 11.38, PL 32: 'De uniuersis autem quae intellegimus non loquentem qui personat foris, sed intus ipsi menti praesidentem consulimus ueritatem, uerbis fortasse ut consulamus admoniti'. See Bianco, 'Insegnare agli ignoranti', 174 (n. 9).
43   Cf. Bianco, 'Insegnare agli ignoranti', 181, 184.
44   Cf. ibid., 181. The inner presence of the divine is, in Mathewes's words, 'a transcendental fact of our constitution'. Mathewes, 'Pluralism', 94.
45   Bianco, 'Insegnare agli ignoranti', 181.
46   Ibid.
47   Ibid., 183.
48   Therese Fuhrer, 'Conversationalist and Consultant: Augustine in Dialogue', in *A Companion to Augustine*, ed. Mark Vessey, *Blackwell Companions to the Ancient World* (Malden, MA/Oxford/Chichester: Wiley-Blackwell, 2012), 278.
49   Augustine, *On the Free Choice of the Will: On Grace and Free Choice; and Other Writings*, trans. Peter King, 2010 edn (Cambridge: Cambridge University Press, 2010), 2.6.14, p. 43. References to *De Libero Arbitrio* (*Lib. Arb.*) are taken from King's translation.
50   Erik Kenyon, 'Platonic Pedagogy in Augustine's Dialogues', *Ancient Philosophy* 34, no. 1 (2014): 151–68, here 161.
51   Ibid., 162.
52   *Lib. Arb.* 2.7.15; trans. King, p. 43.
53   *Lib. Arb.* 2.7.16; trans. King, p. 44.
54   *Lib. Arb.* 2.7.19; trans. King, p. 45.
55   *Lib. Arb.* 2.7.17; trans. King, p. 44.
56   *Lib. Arb.* 2.7.17; trans. King, p. 45.
57   *Lib. Arb.* 2.7.19; trans. King, p. 46.
58   Cf. *Lib. Arb.* 2.14.38; trans. King, p. 60.
59   *Lib. Arb.* 2.8.22; trans. King, p. 47.
60   Here I am invoking – anachronistically – the principle of *discerptibility*, which is essential to Anselm's so-called Ontological Argument. He argues that God alone is not discerptible, that is, divisible, *even* conceptually, whereas other realities could at least be *conceived* to be separable, even if in reality they cannot be divided. See Desmond Paul Henry, *The Logic of Saint Anselm* (Oxford: Clarendon, 1967), 146–8. See also *Lib. Arb.* 2.6.14; trans. King, p. 43.

61 *Lib. Arb.* 2.8.22; trans. King, p. 47.

62 *Lib. Arb.* 2.8.22; trans. King, p. 48.

63 *Lib. Arb.* 2.8.22; trans. King, p. 47.

64 Ibid.

65 Ibid.

66 *Lib. Arb.* 2.8.22; trans. King, p. 48.

67 *Lib. Arb.* 2.7.19; 2.8.21; trans. King, p. 46.

68 *Lib. Arb.* 2.9.25; trans. King, p. 48. The certitudes present to the mind as identified in *Lib. Arb.* 2 are similar to those of *Acad.* 3.23–9. See Kenyon, 'Platonic Pedagogy', 162.

69 Cf. *Lib. Arb.* 2.9.25; trans. King, p. 48.

70 *Lib. Arb.* 2.10.28; trans. King, p. 52; cf. ibid. 2.9.26.

71 *Lib. Arb.* 2.9.25; trans. King, p. 48.

72 *Lib. Arb.* 2.9.26.

73 *Lib. Arb.* 2.10.28; trans. King, p. 52; cf. ibid. 2.9.26.

74 *Lib. Arb.* 2.8.21; King, p. 47. To be sure, Augustine is wading into metaphysically controversial waters concerning the objective and eternal existence of number and mathematical relationships. Within his own context, however, this position would not have raised the doubts it does today. Furthermore, this position is not completely rejected today. Roger Penrose, for example, holds that mathematics exists independently of the human intellect in an abstract way. Roger Penrose and Robert Lawrence Kuhn, 'Is Mathematics Invented or Discovered?', video, 04:14, Closer to Truth, accessed 6 October 2023, https://closertotruth.com/video/penro-003/?referrer=7983.

75 *Lib. Arb.* 2.8.23; trans. King, p. 48.

76 *Lib. Arb.* 2.9.26; cf. 2.10.28.

77 *Lib. Arb.* 2.10.29; trans. King, p. 53.

78 *Lib. Arb.* 2.12.34; trans. King, p. 57.

79 Ibid.

80 Ibid.

81 *Conf.* 10.40.65; Loeb 27, trans. Hammond.

82 Kenyon, 'Platonic Pedagogy', 163.

83 Augustine, *De Genesi ad litteram Libri Duodecim*, ed. I. Zycha, Corpus Scriptorum Ecclesiasticorum Latinorum 28,1 (Vindobonae: Tempsky, 1894), here 3.20.31, p. 86.

84 Jules Chaix-Ruy, 'Note: La création du monde d'après Augustin', *Revue des Études Augustiniennes* 11, no. 1–2 (1965): 85–8, here 87.

85 Chaix-Ruy, 'La création du monde', 85.

86 Matthew Drever, 'Redeeming Creation: *Creatio ex nihilo* and the *Imago Dei* in Augustine', *International Journal of Systematic Theology* 15, no. 2 (2013): 135–53, here 143.

87 Nordlander, 'The Emergence of Soul', 132.

88   *Gn. litt.* 1.4.9–5.10, CSEL 28,1, pp. 7–9; ibid. 1.9.17, p. 13; 3.20.32, p. 87.

89   Chaix-Ruy, 'La création du monde', 86. Cf. Werner Beierwaltes, 'Augustins Interpretation von Sapientia 11, 21', *Revue des Études Augustiniennes* 15, no. 1–2 (1969): 51–61, here 52.

90   Manfred Svensson, '*Scientia* y *sapientia* en *De Trinitate* XII: San Agustín y las formas de la racionalidad', *Teolgía y Vida* 51 (2010): 79–103, here 99; *Trin.* 11.12.16.

91   Svensson, '*Scientia* y *sapientia*', 100.

92   Ibid., 101.

93   Drever, 'Redeeming Creation', 146.

94   Ibid., emphasis added.

95   Lope Cilleruelo, 'Pro memoria Dei', *Revue d'Études Augustiniennes et Patristiques* 12 (1966): 65–84, here 81.

96   Lope Cilleruelo, '¿Por qué "memoria Dei"?', *Revue des Études Augustiniennes* 10, no. 4 (1964): 289–94, here 292.

97   Cilleruelo, 'Pro memoria Dei', 77.

98   'Dios grabó, imprimió, estampó en el alma humana la memoría "sapientia" [...]'. Cilleruelo, 'Pro memoria Dei', 74, my translation. Cf. Christoph Horn, 'Augustins Philosophie der Zahlen', *Revue des Études Augustiniennes* 40 (1994): 389–415, here 396–7.

99   Gaëlle Jeanmart, *Herméneutique et Subjectivité dans les* Confessions *d'Augustin*, Monothéismes et Philosophie 8 (Turnhout: Brepols, 2006), 36.

100 Stephen Menn, 'The Desire for God and the Aporetic Method in Augustine's *Confessions*', in *Augustine's* Confessions: *Philosophy in Autobiography*, ed. W. Mann (New York: Oxford University Press, 2014), 81, 84; *Trin.* 8.6.

101 Cilleruelo, 'Pro memoria Dei', 71–2, 74.

102 Lope Cilleruelo, 'Pro memoria Dei', 81. However, one should also consider Madec's critique of Cilleruelo and Moran on this issue. See Goulven Madec, 'Note: Pour et contre la "memoria Dei": Réponse à L. Cilleruelo et J. Moran', *Revue des Études Augustiniennes* 11, no. 1–2 (1965): 89–92.

103 'El alma tiene de si misma un conocimiento ontológico o preontológico, prereflexivo, prelógico, [...], que se llama simplemente "presencia del alma ante si misma"'. My translation. Cilleruelo, 'Pro memoria Dei', 79; *Trin.* 9.3.3.

104 Cilleruelo, 'Pro memoria Dei', 79.

105 Cf. ibid., 71.

106 Augustine, *De Trinitate libri XV*, ed. W. Mountain, Corpus Christianorum Series Latina, 50–50A (Turnholti: Brepols, 1968), here 8.3.5, p. 274.

107 Cilleruelo, '¿Por qué "memoria Dei"?', 290.

108 *Trin.* 8.6.9, p. 280: 'aliqua regula notitiae'.

109 *Trin.* 8.9.13, CCL 50, p. 290: 'non tamquam omnino incogniti, aut omnino non dilecti'.

110 Drever, 'Redeeming Creation', 148.

111 Ibid.

112 Charles Mathewes, 'Augustinian Anthropology: *Interior intimo meo*', *The Journal of Religious Ethics* 27, no. 2 (Summer 1999): 195–221, here 198.

113 Ibid., 195.

114 Kim Sang Ong-Van-Cung, 'Le moi et l'interiorité chez Augustin et Descartes', *Chora: Journal of Ancient and Medieval Studies* 9/10 (2011–12): 321–38, here 335.

115 Mathewes, 'Augustinian Anthropology', 196.

116 Jean-Louis Chrétien, *L'espace intérieur* (Paris: Minuit, 2014), 66; Mathewes, 'Augustinian Anthropology', 196.

117 Ong-Van-Cung, 'Le moi et l'interiorité', 335.

118 Ibid., 337.

119 Evocations of Platonic and Aristotelian categories of form are inevitable here, although unhelpful. See Jean-Luc Marion, 'Resting, Moving, Loving: The Access to the Self according to Saint Augustine', *Journal of Religion* 91, no. 1 (2011): 24–42, here 27–8.

120 Marion, 'Resting, Moving, Loving', 25–6. See also Gerald Boersma, *Augustine's Early Theology of Image: A Study in the Development of Pro-Nicene Theology*, Oxford Studies in Historical Theology (New York: Oxford University Press, 2016) and R. A. Markus, '"Imago" and "Similitudo" in Augustine', *Revue des Études Augustiniennes* 10, no. 2–3 (1964): 125–43.

121 *Conf.* 13.22.32; Loeb 27, trans. Hammond, p. 389. Cf. Marion, 'Resting, Moving, Loving', 25–6.

122 Marion, 'Resting, Moving, Loving', 26.

123 Ibid. 28.

124 Beattie, *The New Atheists*, 174–5. Mick Gordon, *On Religion* (London: Oberon Books, 2006), 75–6.

125 Beattie, *The New Atheists*, 174–5.

126 Ibid.

127 Ibid.

128 Ibid.

129 Ibid.

130 William Desmond, 'Augustine's *Confessions*: On Desire, Conversion and Reflection', *Irish Theological Quarterly* 47, no. 1 (March 1980): 24–33, here 31–2.

131 Desmond, 'On Desire, Conversion and Reflection', 31–2.

132 Marion, 'Resting, Moving, Loving', 32.

133 Ibid., 28.

134 Ibid.

135 Ibid., 41.

136 Ibid., 31.

137 Desmond, 'On Desire, Conversion and Reflection', 26, 27.

138 Ibid.

139 For more on this theme, see, for example, Arrien, 'Penser sans Dieu'.

140 Marion, 'Resting, Moving, Loving', 32.
141 Ong-Van-Cung, 'Le moi et l'interiorité', 321.
142 Desmond, 'On Desire, Conversion and Reflection', 31.
143 Ibid., 31–2.
144 Ibid., 31.
145 Ibid., 25.
146 Ibid.
147 Cilleruelo, 'Pro memoria Dei', 81–2.
148 Marion, 'Resting, Moving, Loving', 27–8.
149 Drever, 'Redeeming Creation', 144–5; *Gn. litt.* 1.5.10.
150 *Trin.* 8.3.5, CCL 50, p. 274.
151 Ong-Van-Cung, 'Le moi et l'interiorité', 328.
152 Cilleruelo, 'Pro memoria Dei', 74, 77; Cilleruelo, '¿Por qué "memoria Dei"?', 292.
153 Drever, 'Redeeming Creation,' 135, 147.
154 *Trin.* 8.3.4, CCL 50, p. 272.
155 Mathewes, 'Augustinian Anthropology', 201.
156 *Trin.* 8.9.13, CCL 50, p. 290.
157 *Trin.* 8.8.12, CCL 50, p. 287.
158 *S.* 76.1.1–2.2, PL 38.
159 *S.* 76.3.4, PL 38.
160 *S.* 76.2.3, PL 38.
161 *S.* 76.3.4, PL 38: '[In Petro] utrumque genus significandum fuit, id est, firmi et infirmi: quia sine utroque non est Ecclesia'.
162 *S.* 76.3.4, PL 38.
163 *S.* 76.4.6, PL 38.
164 Ibid.
165 Ibid.
166 *S.* 76.3.5, PL 38.
167 *S.* 76.4.6, PL 38: 'Hi sunt firmi Ecclesiae'.
168 *S.* 76.3.5, PL 38.
169 *S.* 76.5.8, PL 38.
170 *S.* 75.2.2, PL 38.
171 *S.* 75.9.10, PL 38.
172 *S.* 75.2.2, PL 38.
173 Ibid.
174 *S.* 76.6.9, PL 38.
175 Ibid.
176 This section originated as a paper given for Villanova University's Patristic, Medieval and Renaissance Studies conference in 2021.
177 Stock, *The Integrated Self*, 27.

178 Johan Bouman and Sven Gross, *Augustinus – Die Theologie Seiner Predigten Über Die Psalmen* (Paderborn: Ferdinand Schöningh, 2019), 111 n. 38.

179 Stock, *The Integrated Self*, 27.

180 Hankey, '"Knowing"', [7]; emphases added.

181 Ibid., emphases added.

182 Chrétien, *L'espace intérieur*, ch. 4.

183 *En Ps.* 4.6.

184 The heart 'désigne le lieu en nous où Dieu parle et où il faut revenir pour trouver la vérité'. Ong-Van-Cung, 'Le moi et l'interiorité', 330.

185 Cavadini, *Visioning Augustine*, 145–7.

186 *Conf.* 10.3.4; Loeb 27, trans. Hammond, p. 72: 'cor meum, ubi ego sum quicumque sum'.

187 Georgiana Huian, 'The Mystery of the Human Being in Augustine: In Quest of the Foundations of an Apophatic Anthropology', *New Europe College Ştefan Odobleja Program Yearbook 2015–2016* (2017): 51–92, here 66; *En Ps. 7.9.*

188 Ibid., 64.

189 Chrétien, *L'espace intérieur*, ch. 3.

190 Huian, 'The Mystery of the Human Being', 71.

191 Ibid.

192 Cf. ibid., 61.

193 Chrétien, *L'espace intérieur*, ch. 4; *En Ps.* 17.7.

194 Chrétien, *L'espace intérieur*, ch. 4.

195 Ibid.

196 Huian, 'The Mystery of the Human Being', 62.

197 Ibid., 65.

198 Chrétien, *L'espace intérieur*.

199 Bouman and Gross, *Augustinus – Die Theologie*, 112.

200 Ibid., 113.

201 *En. Ps.* 75.8, in Bouman and Gross, *Augustinus – Die Theologie*, 114.

202 *En Ps.* 33.2.9, PL 36.

203 Chrétien, *L'espace intérieur*, ch. 4.

204 *En Ps.* 12.6, PL 36.

205 *En Ps.* 17.11.

206 Chrétien, *L'espace intérieur*, ch. 4.

207 *En Ps.* 33.2.9, PL 36.

208 Chrétien, *L'espace intérieur*, ch. 4.

209 *En Ps.* 17.8.

210 *En Ps.* 12.1.

211 Chrétien, *L'espace intérieur*, ch. 4.

212 Ibid.

213 *En Ps.* 12.2.

214 Chrétien, *L'espace intérieur*, ch. 4.

215 *En Ps*. 4.5, PL 36: 'hic nos admoneri credo, ut magna intentione cordis, id est, interno et incorporeo clamore auxilium imploremus Dei'.

216 Samuel Bellafiore, '*Musica Sanans*: Individual and Communal Reintegration in Augustine's *Expositions of the Psalms*', *Sacred Music* 146, no. 2 (2019): 28–34, here 32.

217 Bellafiore, '*Musica Sanans*', 28, 29.

218 Ibid., 30.

219 Ibid., 31.

220 Ibid., 32.

221 Chrétien, *L'espace intérieur*, ch. 4.

222 Ibid.

223 Ibid.

224 Anne-Claire Favry, 'Monter vers Dieu dans les larmes et la consolation – L'interprétation augustinienne de Mt 5, 5', *Revista Agustiniana* (2019).

225 Favry, 'Monter vers Dieu', 8.

226 Ibid., 1.

227 Bouman and Gross, *Augustinus – Die Theologie*, 113.

228 Ibid., 116.

229 Ibid., 117.

230 Ibid., 109.

231 *En Ps*. 4.9.

232 *En Ps*. 33.2.8.

233 *En Ps*. 12.2.

234 Bouman and Gross, *Augustinus – Die Theologie*, 109.

235 Ibid., 108.

236 Ibid.

237 Ibid., 115.

238 Favry, 'Monter vers Dieu', 2.

239 Ibid., 5.

240 Ibid., 8.

241 Ibid., 9.

242 Ibid., 2.

243 Ibid., 5.

244 Ibid., 2.

245 Ibid., 3.

246 Ibid., 3.

247 Ibid., 3.

248 Ibid., 3.

249 Ibid., 4.

250 Ibid.

251 Ibid.
252 Ibid.
253 Ibid., 5.
254 Ibid., 8.
255 Ibid., 9.
256 *En Ps.* 4.2; cf. Huian, 'The Mystery of the Human Being', 68.

Chapter 4

1 Rainer Thiel, 'Zum philosophischen und philosophisch-theologischen Dialog in der paganen und christlichen Spätantike', in *Der Dialog in der Antike: Formen und Funktionen einer literarischen Gattung zwischen Philosophie, Wissensvermittlung und dramatischer Inszenierung*, ed. Sabine Föllinger and Gernot Michael Müller (Berlin, Boston: De Gruyter, 2013), 141.

2 Thiel, 'Dialog in der paganen und christlichen Spätantike', 142.

3 Ibid., 141.

4 Ibid., 142. Thiel describes the former as 'hyphegetischen Dialogen (Lehrgesprächen)' and the latter as 'zetetischen (untersuchenden) Dialogen'. Throughout his chapter, Thiel considers four particular dialogues, two which (generally) correspond to the former category, and the other two to the latter: Porphyry's *Commentary in question and answer*; Dexippos' *Commentary*, which is situated within the 'problem and solution' tradition; Aineias' *Theophrastus*; and the *Ammonios* of Zacharias Scholastikos. See also Kenyon, 'Platonic Pedagogy', 160–1.

5 Thiel, 'Dialog in der paganen und christlichen Spätantike', 142 n. 4, 143. Here he disagrees with Hirzel (1895).

6 Cf. Gillian Clark, 'Can We Talk? Augustine and the Possibility of Dialogue', in *The End of Dialogue in Antiquity*, ed. Simon Goldhill (Cambridge, UK/New York: Cambridge University Press, 2008), 123. Mathewes, 'Pluralism', 84.

7 Averil Cameron, *Dialoguing in Late Antiquity* (Washington, DC: Center for Hellenic Studies, 2014), 8. See also Clark, 'Can We Talk?', 118.

8 Cameron, *Dialoguing in Late Antiquity*, 7, 20, 50–1, 54.

9 Ibid., 4. However, Fuhrer seems to offer a differing opinion. Therese Fuhrer, 'Augustine in Dialogue', 278.

10 Therese Fuhrer, 'Augustine on Rhetoric and Dialectic in Theory and Practice', *Classica – Revista Brasileira de Estudos Clássicos* 19, no. 1 (2006): 99–114, here 100–1.

11 Cameron, *Dialoguing in Late Antiquity*, 4.

12 Michel, 'Dialogue philosophique', 376.

13 Cameron, *Dialoguing in Late Antiquity*, 1, 5.

14 Michel, 'Dialogue philosophique', 365–7.

15 Cameron, *Dialoguing in Late Antiquity*, 20.

16 Ibid., 9.

17 Ibid., 10.

18 Ibid., 20.

19 Richard Miles, '"Let's (Not) Talk about It". Augustine and the Control of Epistolary Dialogue', in *The End of Dialogue in Antiquity*, ed. Simon Goldhill (Cambridge, UK/New York: Cambridge University Press, 2008), 138.

20 Miles, '"Let's (Not) Talk about It"', 141.

21 Cameron, *Dialoguing in Late Antiquity*, 9–10.

22 Ibid., 10.

23 Ibid.

24 See Fuhrer, 'Augustine in Dialogue', 279.

25 Catherine Conybeare, *The Irrational Augustine* (Oxford: Oxford University Press, 2009), 41, quoted in Fuhrer, 'Augustine in Dialogue', 275.

26 Clark, 'Can We Talk?', 133–4.

27 Antonio Patativa de Sales, 'Hermenêutica e estile literário no "primeiro" e "segundo Agostinho"', *Civitas Augustiniana* 5 (2016): 9–29, here 11–12.

28 Mohrmann, 'Saint Augustin écrivain', 44: 'Il s'agit d'une différence essentielle entre les œuvres de Cassiciacum et toutes les autres œuvres augustiniennes [...]'.

29 Conybeare, *The Irrational Augustine*, 41, quoted in Fuhrer, 'Augustine in Dialogue', 275.

30 Cf. Clark, 'Can We Talk?', 132–3.

31 Ibid., 124.

32 Ibid., 126, 133, 134.

33 Ibid., 134.

34 Fuhrer, 'Augustine in Dialogue', 270, 279.

35 Ibid., 270.

36 Mickaël Ribreau, 'Une écoute individuelle en contexte collectif. Étude de la deuxième personne dans quelques sermons d'Augustin', *Revue d'histoire des religions* 233, no. 4 (2016): 505–31.

37 Fuhrer, 'Augustine in Dialogue', 270; Miles, '"Let's (Not) Talk about It"', 139.

38 Stock, *The Integrated Self*, 27.

39 See also Clark, 'Can We Talk?', 124–5.

40 Fuhrer, 'Augustine in Dialogue', 270.

41 Miles, '"Let's (Not) Talk about It"', 139.

42 Ibid.

43 Ibid.

44 Ibid.

45 Fuhrer, 'Augustine in Dialogue', 277.

46 Ibid., 275.

47 Charlotte Köckert, 'Augustine and Nebridius (Augustine, epp. 3–14): Two Christian Intellectuals and Their Project of a Philosophical Life', *Revue d'Études Augustiniennes et Patristiques* 62 (2016): 235–62, here 235–6.

48 Köckert, 'Augustine and Nebridius', 258–9.

49 Ibid., 238.

50 Ibid., 238, 253, 256.

51 See Josef Lössl, 'The One (unum) – A Guiding Concept in "De vera religione": An Outline of the Text and the History of Its Interpretation', *Revue des Études Augustiniennes* 40 (1994): 79–103.

52 Christof Müller and Guntram Förster, *Dialog und Dialoge bei Augustinus: Vermehrte Beiträge Des 14. Würzburger Augustinus-Studientages vom 17. Juni 2016* (Würzburg: Augustinus bei Echter, 2019). Critical treatments of all of the Cassiciacum works have been completed in the last quarter-century (Fuhrer, Doignon, Trelenberg, Schlapbach). In the recent years, a complete translation and critical treatment of these works by Foley has appeared with Yale University Press, and Milusheva's commentary on *De beata uita* has recently appeared from Echter.

53 Kenyon, 'Platonic Pedagogy', 151.

54 Erik Kenyon, *Augustine and the Dialogue* (Cambridge, UK/New York: Cambridge University Press, 2018).

55 Kenyon, 'Platonic Pedagogy', 166.

56 Stock, *Augustine's Inner Dialogue*, 6.

57 Kenyon, 'Platonic Pedagogy', 158.

58 Nordlander, 'The Emergence of Soul', 133, 134.

59 Mathewes, 'Pluralism', *passim*.

60 See Mathewes, 'Pluralism', 86–7, 100–3.

61 See ibid.

62 Cf. Mathewes, 'Pluralism', 94.

63 Mathewes, 'Pluralism', 84, 93–4.

64 Ibid., 105. The Catholic Church seems to endorse a view of dialogue consistent with that which Mathewes propounds. *Dialogue and Proclamation* (1984) indicates that both forms of discourse are essential and mutually reinforcing elements of the Christian life.

65 See Mathewes, 'Pluralism', 102.

66 Ibid., 103.

67 Ibid., 89.

68 Ibid., 88.

69 Michel, 'Dialogue philosophique', 372.

70 Ibid.

71 Cf. Mathewes, 'Pluralism', 89, *inter alia*.

72 Mathewes, 'Liberation', 557.

73 Ibid., 550, 557.

74   Ibid., 540.

75   Ibid.

76   Ibid.

77   Ibid., 556.

78   Ibid., 542.

79   Ibid., 547.

80   Ibid., 557.

81   Cf. ibid., 555.

82   Ibid., 539.

83   Ibid., 542.

84   Ibid., 552.

85   Ibid.

86   Ibid., 545–6.

87   Ibid., 542, 544, 545.

88   Ibid., 551.

89   Ibid.

90   Michael P. Foley, trans., *Soliloquies* (New Haven: Yale University Press, 2020).
      For my quotations from the *Soliloquia*, I use Foley's translation throughout.

91   Brian Stock, 'Self, Soliloquy, and Spiritual Exercises in Augustine and Some Later
      Authors', *The Journal of Religion* 91, no. 1 (2011): 5–23, here 6. *Sol.* 2.8.14.

92   Stock, *Augustine's Inner Dialogue*, 1.

93   Jérôme Lagouanère, 'Le *De Quantitate Animae* d'Augustin, un dialogue
      philosophique?', *Zeitschrift für Antikes Christentum/Journal of Ancient
      Christianity* 23, no. 2 (2019): 252–87, here 256.

94   Augustine himself seems to endorse this conclusion in the *Retr.* 1.4.1, in
      which he states that in the *Sol.*, he was speaking alone, and only speaking
      with his own reason as 'as if' (*tamquam*) they were two. See Stock,
      'Self, Soliloquy, and Spiritual Exercises', 6; Tobias Uhle, 'Philosophisches
      Argument und literarische Form in Augustins *Soliloquia*', in *Argument
      und literarische Form in antiker Philosophie: Akten des 3. Kongresses
      der Gesellschaft für antike Philosophie 2010*, ed. Michael Erler and Jan
      Erik Heßler (Berlin and Boston: De Gruyter, 2013), 550; Michael Foley,
      'A Spectacle to the World: The Theatrical Meaning of St. Augustine's
      Soliloquies', *Journal of Early Christian Studies* 22, no. 2 (2014): 243–60,
      here 254.

95   Uhle, 'Philosophisches Argument', 549.

96   Ibid.

97   Willemien Otten, 'Does the Canon Need Converting? A Meditation on
      Augustine's *Soliloquies*, Eriugena's *Periphyseon*, and the Dialogue with the
      Religious Past', in *How the West Was Won: Essays on Literary Imagination,
      the Canon and the Christian Middle Ages for Burcht Pranger*, ed. Willemien
      Otten, Arjo J. Vanderjagt and Hent De Vries, Brill's Studies in Intellectual
      History 188 (Leiden: Brill, 2010), 209.

98   Iglika Milusheva, 'Das Bild des *inmanissimus mons* in Augustins Frühschrift *De Beata Vita*', *Acta Antiqua Academiae Scientiarum Hungaricae* 56, no. 1 (2016): 119–26, here 120; Lagouanère, 'Le *De quantitate animae* d'Augustin', 255. Milusheva, who is informed by B. Voss, employs the term 'szenisch' in the German. However, one should note that, as Lagouanère observes, Fuhrer does not endorse Voss's distinction.

99   Uhle, 'Philosophisches Argument', 549.

100   Ibid.

101   Stock, 'Self, Soliloquy, and Spiritual Exercises', 6.

102   Fuhrer, 'Augustine in Dialogue', 274.

103   Stock, 'Self, Soliloquy, and Spiritual Exercises', 6.

104   Lagouanère, 'Le *De quantitate animae* d'Augustin', 256.

105   Foley, 'Spectacle', 244.

106   Stock, 'Self, Soliloquy, and Spiritual Exercises', 6.

107   Stock, *The Integrated Self*, 23; see also Uhle, 'Philosophisches Argument', 560.

108   Foley, 'Spectacle', 259.

109   Ibid., 256.

110   Ibid., 260.

111   Ibid.

112   Ibid.

113   Ibid., 253.

114   Norbert Fischer, 'Vom Berühren der ewigen Wahrheit: Zu Augustins christlicher Umdeutung der neuplatonischen Mystik', *Acta Universitatis Carolinae Theologica* 3, no. 1 (2013): 37–64, here 39–40.

115   Fischer, 'Vom Berühren der ewigen Wahrheit', 41.

116   Michel, 'Dialogue philosophique', 375.

117   Ibid.

118   Fischer, 'Vom Berühren der ewigen Wahrheit', 40.

119   Otten, 'Canon', 214.

120   Ibid.

121   Ibid.

122   Uhle, 'Philosophisches Argument', 541.

123   Ibid., 550. In an interview with the BBC, the renowned Descartes scholar Bernard Williams noted how, despite the former's emphasis on the difference between subject and object, it seems that this distinction seems unavoidable.

124   Uhle, 'Philosophisches Argument', 560.

125   Ibid., 551.

126   Ibid.

127   Ibid., 552.

128   Foley, 'Spectacle', 250. See *Sol.* 2.7.14. See also Tobias Uhle, *Augustin und die Dialektik: Eine Untersuchung der Argumentationsstruktur in den Cassiciacum-Dialogen* (Tübingen: Mohr Siebeck, 2012), 10 (n. 37).

129 Foley, 'Spectacle', 250–1.

130 Ibid., 250.

131 Ibid.

132 *Sol.* 1.14.25; *Retr.* 1.4.1; Uhle, 'Philosophisches Argument', 549–50; Foley, 'Spectacle', 254.

133 See Kenyon, *Augustine and the Dialogue*, 152–3.

134 Foley, 'Spectacle', 254.

135 Ibid.

136 Ibid., 251.

137 Ibid.

138 Ibid.

139 Ibid., 252.

140 Ibid.

141 Ibid.

142 Ibid.

143 Ibid., 253.

144 Ibid., 255.

145 Ibid.

146 Ibid., 254, 256.

147 Ibid., 255.

148 Ibid., 256.

149 Ibid.

150 Ibid.

151 Ibid., 257.

152 Ibid., 259.

153 See Fischer, 'Vom Berühren der ewigen Wahrheit', 42.

154 Cf. Michel, 'Dialogue philosophique', 375.

155 Cf. Mathewes, 'Pluralism', 95.

156 Fischer, 'Vom Berühren der ewigen Wahrheit', 42.

157 Foley, 'Spectacle', 257.

158 Otten, 'Canon', 213.

159 Ibid., 209.

160 Kenyon, 'Platonic Pedagogy', 160.

161 Otten, 'Canon', 215.

162 Ibid., 214.

163 Michel, 'Dialogue philosophique', 373.

164 Stock, *The Integrated Self*, 7.

165 William Barclay Parsons, *Freud and Augustine in Dialogue: Psychoanalysis, Mysticism, and the Culture of Modern Spirituality* (Charlottesville: University of Virginia Press, 2013), 20 (n. 51).

166 Stock, *The Integrated Self*, 23.
167 Porter, 'Time for Foucault?', 131.
168 Stock, *The Integrated Self*, 23.
169 Michel, 'Dialogue philosophique', 367.
170 Remes, 'Inwardness and Infinity of Selfhood', 169.
171 Ibid., 171.
172 Stock, *The Integrated Self*, 26.
173 Ibid., 6, 25–6; Mathewes, 'Liberation', 551–2.
174 Stock, *The Integrated Self*, 25.
175 See *Ep*. 80.3, PL 33.
176 Stock, *The Integrated Self*, 26.
177 Stock, *Augustine's Inner Dialogue*, 14.
178 Ibid., 10; emphases added.
179 Parsons, *Freud and Augustine in Dialogue*, 20 (n. 51).
180 Stock, *Augustine's Inner Dialogue*, 9.
181 Uhle, *Augustin und die Dialektik*, 7.
182 Parsons, *Freud and Augustine in Dialogue*, 20 (n. 49).
183 Charles Mathewes, 'The Liberation of Questioning in Augustine's "Confessions"', *Journal of the American Academy of Religion* 70, no. 3 (2002): 539–60, here 555.
184 Mathewes, 'Liberation', 552.
185 Ibid.
186 Stock, *The Integrated Self*, 25.
187 Mathewes, 'Liberation', 552.
188 Stroumsa, 'The New Self', 4.
189 Religions and Ethics Newsweekly, 'Looking Back: Rituals', video, 05:12, PBS.org, 24 February 2017, accessed 7 October 2023, https://www.pbs.org/video/religion-and-ethics-newsweekly-looking-back-rituals/. 'Ancient Jewish Meditation Literature', video, 04:30, *YouTube*, posted by BibleProject, 3 August 2017, accessed 7 October 2023, https://youtu.be/VhmlJBUIoLk.
190 Stock, *The Integrated Self*, 25. See *Conf*. 11.27.35–8; for more on spiritual exercises, see Pierre Hadot and Michael Chase, *Philosophy as a Way of Life: Spiritual Exercises from Socrates to Foucault*, ed. Arnold Ira Davidson (Malden, MA: Blackwell Publishing, 2017).
191 William L. Porter, *Tradition and Incarnation: Foundations of Christian Theology* (New York and Mahwah, NJ: Paulist Press, 1994), 61–6.
192 Portier, *Tradition and Incarnation*, 54–61.
193 Reinhart Herzog, 'Non in sua voce: Augustins Gespräch mit Gott in den Confessiones – Voraussetzungen und Folgen', in *Spätantike: Studien zur romischen und lateinisch-christlichen Literatur*, with an Introduction by Manfred Fuhrmann, ed. Peter Habermehl (Göttingen: Vandenhoeck & Ruprecht, 2002), 214.

194 *Conf.* 9.4.4; Loeb 27, trans. Hammond: 'nec sic ea dicerem, si me ab eis audiri viderique sentirem, nec, si dicerem, sic acciperent quomodo mecum et mihi coram te de familiari affectu animi mei'. The context is how the Manichees would not have understood how and what Augustine was saying had they heard him.

195 *Conf.* 12.10.10; Loeb 27, trans. Hammond.

196 Herzog, 'Non in sua voce', 213.

197 Ibid., 213–14.

198 Anne-Isabelle Bouton-Touboulic, 'Les Confessions d'Augustin: une métamorphose de la *parrhesia*?', *Chôra* 11 (2013): 59–75, here 59.

199 Laurie Douglass, 'Voice Re-Cast: Augustine's Use of Conversation in *De ordine* and the *Confessions*', *Augustinian Studies* 27, no. 1 (1996): 39–54, here 43; Bouton-Touboulic, 'Une métamorphose', 60.

200 Bouton-Touboulic, 'Une métamorphose', 60.

201 Ibid., emphasis added. See also Douglass, 'Voice Re-Cast', 43.

202 Ibid., 59.

203 *Conf.* 10.1.1; Loeb 27, trans. Hammond.

204 *Conf.* 10.4.6; Loeb 27, trans. Hammond.

205 *Conf.* 10.3.4; Loeb 27, trans. Hammond.

206 *Conf.* 10.3.5; Loeb 27, trans. Hammond.

207 *Conf.* 10.3.3, 10.3.4; Loeb 27, trans. Hammond.

208 Ibid.

209 Mathewes, 'Liberation', 541.

210 Ibid., 547.

211 Ibid., 542.

212 Ibid., 539.

213 Ibid., 543.

214 Ibid.

215 Ibid.

216 Ibid., 555.

217 Ibid.

218 Ibid., 556.

219 Ibid., 555–6.

220 Lotz, 'Responsive Life', [4–5].

221 Cf. Huian, 'The Mystery of the Human Being', 73.

222 Porter, 'Time for Foucault?', 130.

223 Lotz, 'Responsive Life', [7–8].

224 Ibid., [8].

225 Ibid., [8–9].

226 Ibid., [23].

227 Ibid., [19].

228 Ibid.

229 Cf. ibid., [12].

230 Ibid.

231 Ibid., [10].

232 Martijn Boven, 'The Subtle Art of Plagiarizing God: Augustine's Dialogue with Divine Otherness', in *Non Laborat Qui Amat*, ed. A. P. DeBattista, J. Farrugia and H. Scerri (Valletta, Malta: Maltese Augustinian Province, 2020), 62–3.

233 Hwang, 'The Paradoxical Place of the Self', 175; *Conf.* 10.40.65.

234 Lotz, 'Responsive Life', [17–18, 20].

235 Ibid., [16].

236 Ibid., [17–18].

237 Boven, 'Plagiarizing God', 53, 64.

238 Ibid., 65.

239 Ibid., 53.

240 Ibid., 58.

241 Augustine, *Confessions, Volume I: Books 1–8*, trans. Carolyn J.-B. Hammond, Loeb Classical Library 26 (Cambridge, MA: Harvard University Press, 2014), 1.1.1; cf. Lotz, 'Responsive Life', [19]; O'Donnell, at *Conf.* 1.1.1.

242 Lotz, 'Responsive Life', [20].

243 Ibid.

244 Ibid.

245 Ibid.

246 *Conf.* 3.6.11; Loeb 26, trans. Hammond.

247 Cf. e.g. Herzog, 'Non in sua voce', 215.

248 *Conf.* 1.2.2; Loeb 26, trans. Hammond.

249 James J. O'Donnell, *Confessions: Introduction and Text* (Oxford: Clarendon, 2000), at 1.2.2.

250 *Conf.* 1.2.2; Loeb 26, trans. Hammond.

251 Ibid.

252 Ibid.

253 O'Donnell, at *Conf.* 1.2.2 and 1.3.3.

254 See O'Donnell, at *Conf.* 1.3.3: The phrase *ubique totus*, according to du Roy, indicates a Plotinian influence and only appears after Augustine's brief time in Rome in 388. (O'Connell concurs.)

255 Herzog, 'Non in sua voce', 219.

256 Ibid.

257 *Conf.* 10.5.7; Loeb 27, trans. Hammond: 'quia etsi nemo scit hominum quae sunt hominis, nisi spiritus hominis qui in ipso est, tamen est aliquid hominis quod nec ipse scit spiritus hominis qui in ipso est'.

258 Herzog, 'Non in sua voce', 219.

259   *Conf.* 10.5.7; Loeb 27, trans. Hammond.

260   Herzog, 'Non in sua voce', 219; *Conf.* 10.5.7; Loeb 27, trans. Hammond: 'tamen aliquid de te scio quod de me nescio'.

261   Graham, *Texts of Early Greek Philosophy*, 167.

262   'Among human beings, who knows what pertains to a person except the spirit of the person that is within? Similarly, no one knows what pertains to God except the Spirit of God' (NABRE).

263   O'Donnell, at *Conf.* 10.5.7.

264   Ibid.

265   O'Donnell, at *Conf.* 1.4.4.

266   *Conf.* 1.4.4; Loeb 26, trans. Hammond.

267   Cf. O'Donnell, at *Conf.* 1.4.4.

268   *Conf.* 1.4.4; Loeb 26, trans. Hammond.

269   Cf. ibid.

270   O'Donnell, at *Conf.* 1.3.3.

271   O'Donnell, at *Conf.* 1.4.4.

272   Ibid.

273   See Lotz, 'Responsive Life', [13].

274   Cf. Mohrmann, 'Saint Augustin écrivain', 49–50.

275   *Conf.* 1.1.1; Loeb 26, trans. Hammond.

276   O'Donnell, at *Conf.* 1.1.1.

277   Ibid.

278   *Conf.* 1.4.4; Loeb 26, trans. Hammond.

279   *En. Ps.* 102.8: 'ergo si non possumus dicere, et prae gaudio non permittitur tacere, nec loquamur, nec taceamus. Quid ergo faciamus, non loquentes et non tacentes'. See O'Donnell, at *Conf.* 1.4.4.

280   *Conf.* 1.1.1; Loeb 26, trans. Hammond.

281   O'Donnell, at *Conf.* 1.1.1.

282   *Conf.* 1.1.1; Loeb 26, trans. Hammond.

283   Kenyon, 'Platonic Pedagogy', 166.

284   Lotz, 'Responsive Life', [18].

285   O'Daly, 'Two Kinds of Subjectivity', 198. See Oliver O'Donovan, *The Problem of Self-Love in St. Augustine* (New Haven, CT: Yale University Press, 1980), 70–2.

286   Hwang, 'The Paradoxical Place of the Self', 174–5.

287   *Conf.* 10.4.6; Loeb 27, trans. Hammond.

288   Hwang, 'The Paradoxical Place of the Self', 174–5.

289   Ibid., 175.

290   Ibid., 174.

291   *Conf.* 10.40.65; Loeb 27, trans. Hammond.

292   Ibid.

293   *Conf.* 10.1.1; 10.5.7; Loeb 27, trans. Hammond.
294   *Conf.* 10.3.3; Loeb 27, trans. Hammond.
295   Boven, 'Plagiarizing God', 53.
296   Ibid., 58.
297   O'Daly, 'Two Kinds of Subjectivity', 199.
298   Ibid.
299   *Conf.* 10.1.1; Loeb 27, trans. Hammond.
300   *Conf.* 10.16.25; Loeb 27, trans. Hammond; cf. 10.8.15.
301   *Conf.* 10.8.15; Loeb 27, trans. Hammond, p. 93.
302   *Conf.* 10.17.26; Loeb 27, trans. Hammond, p. 113.
303   *Conf.* 10.17.26; Loeb 27, trans. Hammond, p. 112 n. 54.
304   *Conf.* 10.41.66; Loeb 27, trans. Hammond.
305   *Conf.* 10.40.65; Loeb 27, trans. Hammond.
306   Ibid.
307   Hwang, 'The Paradoxical Place of the Self', 176.
308   Ibid., 186.
309   Ibid., 176.
310   Cf. *Conf.* 10.2.2; Loeb 27, trans. Hammond.

Chapter 5

1   Hwang, 'The Paradoxical Place of the Self', 173.
2   *Conf.* 6.3.4; Loeb 26, trans. Hammond, p. 245.
3   Denys Turner, 'The Darkness of God and the Light of Christ: Negative
      Theology and Eucharistic Presence', *Modern Theology* 15, no. 2 (1999):
      143–58, here 146–7.
4   Turner, 'The Darkness of God', 146.
5   Ibid., 147.
6   Achim Schütz, 'Die mehrdimensionale Theo-Logik der Polarität:
      Anmerkungen zum Denken von E. Przywara', *Lateranum* 81, no. 1 (2015):
      69–99, here 70.
7   Schütz, 'Theo-Logik der Polarität', 78.
8   Ibid., 78–9.
9   *Conf.* 6.3.4; Loeb 26, trans. Hammond, p. 245.
10   Schütz, 'Theo-Logik der Polarität', 79.
11   Ibid., 77–8.
12   Ibid., 77.
13   Ibid., 94.
14   Cf. ibid.

15   Ibid., 70.
16   Ibid.
17   Ibid.
18   Ibid.
19   Ibid.
20   Ibid., 70, 92.
21   Ibid., 84.
22   Ibid., 82–3, 96–7.
23   Ibid., 96–7.
24   Ibid., 76, 94.
25   Ibid., 72, 76, 96.
26   Ibid., 72.
27   Ibid., 94.
28   Ibid., 96.
29   Ibid., 90.
30   Ibid.
31   Wehrle, 'Being a Body and Having a Body', 502.
32   Ibid., 500.
33   Ibid., 502.
34   Ibid., 508–9.
35   Ibid., 509.
36   Ibid., 514.
37   Ibid.
38   Ibid.
39   Ibid., 514, 516.
40   Ibid., 514.
41   Ibid., 500.
42   Ibid., 500. Przywara presents a similar distinction between being (*Wesen*) and
     personal existence (*Existenz*). Schütz, 'Theo-Logik der Polarität', 82.
43   Wehrle, 'Being a Body and Having a Body', 500.
44   Ibid., 501 (n. 1).
45   Ibid., 500.
46   Ibid., 500, 503.
47   Ibid., 500.
48   Ibid., 503.
49   Ibid., 500.
50   Ibid., 500–1.
51   Ibid., 518.
52   Koji Komatsu, 'Temporal Reticence of the Self: Who Can Know My Self?',
     Integrative Psychological and Behavioral Science 46, no. 3 (2012): 357–72, here
     357–60, 371. Koji Komatsu, 'On the Dialectic Nature of Human Mind: The

Dynamic Tension between Sameness and Non-Sameness', *Integrative Psychological and Behavioral Science* 50, no. 1 (2015): 174–83, here 174.

53 Komatsu, 'Temporal Reticence of the Self', 360.
54 Ibid.
55 Ibid.
56 Ibid., 358–61.
57 Ibid., 361; cf. 358.
58 Ibid., 360–1.
59 Ibid., 363.
60 Ibid., 360.
61 Ibid., 360–1.
62 Cf. Cavadini, *Visioning Augustine*, 141.
63 Komatsu, 'On the Dialectic Nature of the Human Mind', 175.
64 Ibid., 176.
65 Ibid.
66 Ibid., 175.
67 Ibid.
68 Ibid., 176.
69 Ibid.
70 Ibid., 177, 179.
71 Ibid., 177.
72 Ibid.
73 Komatsu, 'Temporal Reticence of the Self', 357, 371.
74 Komatsu, 'On the Dialectic Nature of the Human Mind', 179.
75 Ibid., 176.
76 Ibid., 179.
77 Ibid., 177.
78 Cf. ibid.
79 Komatsu, 'Temporal Reticence of the Self', 359.
80 Ibid., 370.
81 Ibid.
82 Ibid., 361; Komatsu, 'On the Dialectic Nature of the Human Mind', 177.
83 Komatsu, 'Temporal Reticence of the Self', 361.
84 Ibid., 370.
85 Ibid., 358.
86 Ibid.
87 Ibid., 359.
88 Komatsu, 'On the Dialectic Nature of the Human Mind', 179.
89 Komatsu, 'Temporal Reticence of the Self', 358.
90 Komatsu, 'On the Dialectic Nature of the Human Mind', 180.
91 Ibid., 178.

92   Ibid., 179.
93   Ibid.
94   Ibid., 178.
95   Ibid.
96   An Yountae, 'The Dialectical Abyss', in *The Decolonial Abyss: Mysticism and Cosmopolitics from the Ruins* (New York: Fordham University Press, 2017), 48, 55–6.
97   Yountae, 'The Dialectical Abyss', 49.
98   Ibid., 49, 57–8.
99   Ibid., 55.
100 Ibid., 49.
101 Ibid., 55.
102 Ibid., 49; emphases added.
103 Ibid., 55; cf. 48.
104 Ibid., 48, 54, 56.
105 Ibid., 47, 51.
106 Ibid., 50.
107 Ibid., 51.
108 Ibid., 50–1.
109 Ibid., 50.
110 Ibid., 47–8.
111 Ibid., 56.
112 Ibid., 48.
113 Ibid.
114 Ibid., 54.
115 Ibid.
116 Ibid., 48.
117 Schütz, 'Theo-Logik der Polarität', 94.
118 Huian, 'The Mystery of the Human Being', 62; Tracy, 'The Overdetermined, Incomprehensible Self', 28.
119 Cavadini, *Visioning Augustine*, 138.
120 Ibid., 138–9.
121 Ibid., 139.
122 Ibid., 138.
123 Cf. ibid., 139.
124 Ibid.
125 Ibid., 139 (cf. n. 5).
126 Ibid., 140, 142.
127 Ibid., 141; emphasis added.
128 Ibid., 142.
129 Cf. ibid., 141.

130   Ibid., 141.

131   Cf. Huian, 'The Mystery of the Human Being', 61, 73, 76.

132   Cavadini, *Visioning Augustine*, 143–4.

133   Dany Praet, 'Augustine of Hippo and Michel Foucault's History of Sexuality', in *Nos sumus tempora: Studies on Augustine and His Reception Offered to Mathijs Lamberigts*, ed. A. Dupont, W. François and J. Leemans, Bibliotheca Ephemeridum Theologicarum Lovaniensium 316, 213–35 (Leuven, Paris and Bristol: Peeters, 2020), 225. See also Winrich Löhr, 'Christianity as Philosophy: Problems and Perspectives of an Ancient Intellectual Project', *Vigiliae Christianae* 64, no. 2 (2010): 160–88.

134   Robert Cushman, *Therapeia: Plato's Conception of Philosophy* (New Brunswick, NJ and London, UK: Transaction Books, 2002).

135   Cushman, *Therapeia*, 71, 144, 150, 298.

136   Ibid., 298.

137   Ibid., 300.

138   Ibid., 147.

139   Ibid., xxi.

140   Ibid., 236.

141   Ibid., 71, 147, 233, 235, 236, 298, 299.

142   Ibid., 147.

143   Praet, 'History of Sexuality', 225.

144   Michael Foley, 'Cicero, Augustine, and the Philosophical Roots of the Cassiciacum Dialogues', *Revue des Études Augustiniennes* 43 (1999): 51–77, here 53.

145   Johannes Brachtendorf, 'Cicero and Augustine on the Passions', *Revue des Études Augustiniennes* 43 (1997): 289–308, here 289–90, 295.

146   Michel, 'Dialogue philosophique', 365.

147   Christopher Star, *Seneca* (London, England: I.B. Tauris & Co., 2016), 33.

148   Rist, *What Is a Person?*, 47.

149   Lagouanère, 'Agustín lector de Séneca', 193. However, Stock denies this connection. See Stock, *The Integrated Self*, n. 21 to the Introduction.

150   Star, *Seneca*, 32, 33, 56.

151   Ibid., 32.

152   Ibid., 33; emphasis mine.

153   Köckert, 'Augustine and Nebridius', 239–40.

154   Cushman, *Therapeia*, 52–4.

155   Parsons, *Freud and Augustine in Dialogue*, 15.

156   Philip Woollcott, 'Some Considerations of Creativity and Religious Experience in St. Augustine of Hippo', *Journal for the Scientific Study of Religion* 5, no. 2 (1966): 273–83, here 283.

157   Woollcott, 'Some Considerations', 283.

158   Parsons, *Freud and Augustine in Dialogue*, 4–5, 25.

159   Porter, 'Time for Foucault?', 130.

160 O'Donnell, at 4.9.9.

161 Augustine, *Confessions*, 2nd edn, trans. F. J. Sheed, ed. Michael P. Foley (Indianapolis, IN: Hackett, 2007), 4.4.8.

162 *Conf.* 4.4.8.

163 *Conf.* 4.4.9.

164 *Conf.* 4.4.9. The translation 'tremendous pain' is mine.

165 O'Daly, 'Two Kinds of Subjectivity', 201.

166 *Conf.* 4.4.9.

167 Ibid.

168 Ibid.

169 O'Daly, 'Two Kinds of Subjectivity', 200.

170 *Conf.* 4.5.10.

171 Ibid.

172 Ibid.

173 O'Daly, 'Two Kinds of Subjectivity', 201.

174 *Confessions* 4.6.11. However, Augustine suggests in his *Retr.* 2.6.2 that even this reference is more sentimental than expressive of Christian love.

175 *Conf.* 4.6.11.

176 Cushman, *Therapeia*, 71, 147, 233, 235, 236, 298.

177 *Conf.* 4.7.12.

178 Ibid.

179 Ibid.

180 *Conf.* 4.7.12: 'ego mihi remanseram infelix locus, ubi nec esse possem nec inde recedere. quo enim cor meum fugeret a corde meo? quo a me ipso fugerem? quo non me sequerer?'

181 *Conf.* 4.7.12.

182 Ibid.

183 Ibid.

184 Ibid.

185 *Conf.* 4.6.11.

186 *Conf.* 4.7.12.

187 *Conf.* 4.4.9; emphasis mine.

188 *Conf.* 4.6.11.

189 *Conf.* 4.4.9.

190 Marie-Anne Vannier, 'Aversion and Conversion', in *The Cambridge Companion to Augustine's 'Confessions'*, ed. Tarmo Toom (Cambridge: Cambridge University Press, 2020), 64.

191 *Conf.* 4.4.9.

192 *Conf.* 4.7.12.

193 *Conf.* 4.4.9.

194 Cf. *Conf.* 4.7.12.

195 Vannier, 'Aversion and Conversion', 66.

196 Ibid., 63, 65.

197 Ibid., 64.

198 Christian Tornau, '*Ratio in subiecto?* The Sources of Augustine's Proof for the Immortality of the Soul in the *Soliloquia* and Its Defense in *De immortalitate animae*', *Phronesis* 62 (2017): 319–54, here 344.

199 Vannier, 'Aversion and Conversion', 65.

200 Ibid., 73.

201 Ibid., 64.

202 Cushman, *Therapeia*, 150, 301.

203 Ibid., 301.

204 Ibid.

205 Vannier, 'Aversion and Conversion', 63, 68.

206 Ibid., p. 70.

207 Cushman, *Therapeia*, 301. See also Stroumsa, 'The New Self', 6.

208 Vannier, 'Aversion and Conversion', 63–4.

209 Ibid., 70.

210 Ibid., 66.

211 *Conf.* 4.4.9.

212 Fischer, 'Vom Beruhren der ewigen Wahrheit', 60.

213 Ibid., 61.

214 Parsons, *Freud and Augustine in Dialogue*, 4.

215 Ibid., 25; emphasis added.

216 Ibid., 4–5.

217 Vannier, 'Aversion and Conversion', 64.

218 Ibid.

219 Fischer, 'Vom Beruhren der ewigen Wahrheit', 63; Huian, 'The Mystery of the Human Being', 55, 60.

220 Huian, 'The Mystery of the Human Being', 54. For more on this topic in Augustine, see Susannah Ticciati, *A New Apophaticism: Augustine and the Redemption of Signs*, Studies in Systematic Theology 14 (Leiden: Brill, 2013).

221 Huian, 'The Mystery of the Human Being', 77.

222 Ibid.

223 Ibid., 73.

224 Ibid., 60.

225 Vannier, 'Aversion and Conversion', 65, 73.

226 Miller, *Becoming God*, 33.

227 Ibid., 34.

228 Ibid., 36.

229 Ibid.

230 Ibid., 33–4.

231 Ibid., 36.

232 Ibid.

233 Ibid., 34.

234 Ibid., 36.

235 Ibid., 34.

236 Ibid., 34, 35.

237 Ibid., 36.

238 Ibid.

239 Ibid., 35.

240 Ibid.

241 Ibid.

242 Ibid., 34.

243 Ryan Coyne, *Heidegger's Confessions: The Remains of Saint Augustine in 'Being and Time' and Beyond* (Chicago: University of Chicago Press, 2015), 54.

244 Coyne, *Heidegger's Confessions*, 56.

245 Cf. Coyne, *Heidegger's Confessions*, *passim*; Arrien, 'Penser sans Dieu, vivre avec Dieu', [1].

246 Coyne, *Heidegger's Confessions*, 90.

247 Ibid., 91, 92.

248 Ibid., 92, 93.

249 See ibid., 91, 93, 94.

250 Ibid., 56.

251 See ibid., 77.

252 Ibid., 57.

253 Cf. ibid., 75.

254 Ibid., 55.

255 Ibid., 56.

256 Ibid., 53.

257 Ibid., 77.

258 Arrien, 'Penser sans Dieu', [2]; Coyne, *Heidegger's Confessions*, 60.

259 Cf. Coyne, *Heidegger's Confessions*, 77.

260 Cf. Arrien, 'Penser sans Dieu', [5].

261 Ibid.

262 Ibid., [2]; Coyne, *Heidegger's Confessions*, 54.

263 Coyne, *Heidegger's Confessions*, 55.

264 Arrien, 'Penser sans Dieu', [6].

265 Coyne, *Heidegger's Confessions*, 60.

266 Ibid., 94.

267 Arrien, 'Penser sans Dieu', [2].

268 Ibid.

269 Ibid.

270 Coyne, *Heidegger's Confessions*, 63–4.
271 Ibid., 61.
272 Ibid., 78–9.
273 Ibid., 60.
274 Arrien, 'Penser sans Dieu', [3].
275 Coyne, *Heidegger's Confessions*, 57.
276 Ibid., 81.
277 Arrien, 'Penser sans Dieu', [3].
278 Ibid.
279 Coyne, *Heidegger's Confessions*, 78–9.
280 Ibid., 77.
281 Ibid., 76.
282 Arrien, 'Penser sans Dieu', [6].
283 Coyne, *Heidegger's Confessions*, 94.
284 Ibid., 80.
285 Ibid., 85.
286 Arrien, 'Penser sans Dieu', [5].
287 Coyne, *Heidegger's Confessions*, 80.
288 Ibid., 84, 85.
289 Arrien, 'Penser sans Dieu', [5].
290 Coyne, *Heidegger's Confessions*, 83.
291 Martin Heidegger, *Being and Time*, trans. John Macquarrie and Edward Robinson (Oxford, UK and Cambridge, USA: Blackwell, 2001), §30, 180.
292 Heidegger, *Being and Time*, trans. Macquarrie and Robinson, §30, 182.
293 Arrien, 'Penser sans Dieu', [4].
294 Heidegger, *Being and Time*, trans. Macquarrie and Robinson, §30, 181: 'Fear discloses Dasein predominantly in a privative way'.
295 Heidegger, *Being and Time*, trans. Macquarrie and Robinson, §30, 180–1.
296 Ibid., 181.
297 Ibid.
298 Heidegger, *Being and Time*, trans. Macquarrie and Robinson, §30, 179–80.
299 Ibid.
300 Ibid., 180.
301 Arrien, 'Penser sans Dieu', [4]; Coyne, *Heidegger's Confessions*, 80–1.
302 Arrien, 'Penser sans Dieu', [5].
303 Coyne, *Heidegger's Confessions*, 84.
304 Arrien, 'Penser sans Dieu', [2].
305 Sean Hannan, 'To See Coming: Augustine and Heidegger on the Arising and Passing Away of Things', *Medieval Mystical Theology* 21, no. 1 (2012): 75–91, here 84.
306 Porter, 'Time for Foucault?', 129.

Concluding Thoughts

1 See Margaret Clark, *Understanding Religion and Spirituality in Clinical Practice* (London: Karnac Books, 2012), especially the Introduction.

2 Peter J. Hampson and Johannes Hoff, 'Whose Self? Which Unification? Augustine's Anthropology and the Psychology-theology Debate', *New Blackfriars* 91, no. 1035 (2010): 546–66, here 564.

3 Hampson and Hoff, 'Whose Self? Which Unification?', 565.

4 Ibid.

5 Ibid., 549.

6 Parsons, *Freud and Augustine in Dialogue*, 2, 10.

7 Ibid., 3; emphasis added.

8 Ibid., 11.

9 Ibid., 2.

10 Ibid., 3.

11 Bendeck Sotillos, 'The Inner and Outer Human Being', 12.

12 Ibid., 13–14.

13 Ibid., 26; emphases added.

14 Ibid., 11–12.

15 Ibid., 9–10.

16 Ibid., 10–11.

17 Cf. ibid., 11–12, 14.

18 Ibid., 12, 14, 20.

19 Ibid., 12.

20 Ibid., 16, 18–19.

21 Ibid., 12.

22 Ibid., 15.

23 Ibid., 19.

24 Ibid., 16; cf. Hampson and Hoff, 'Whose Self? Which Unification?', 551. See also Terence Sweeney, 'God and the Soul: Augustine on the Journey to True Selfhood', *The Heythrop Journal* 57, no. 4 (2014): 678–91, 685.

25 Bendeck Sotillos, 'The Inner and Outer Human Being', 15.

26 Ibid., 21.

27 Ibid., 25.

28 *Conf.* 10.3.4; Loeb 27, trans. Hammond.

29 Bendeck Sotillos, 'The Inner and Outer Human Being', 24.

30 Ibid., 23.

31 Ibid., 26; cf. 10.

BIBLIOGRAPHY

Primary sources, commentaries and translations

Augustine

Foley, Michael P., trans. *Soliloquies*. New Haven, CT: Yale University Press, 2020.

Hammond, Carolyn J.-B., trans. *Confessions, Volume I: Books 1–8*. Loeb Classical Library 26. Cambridge, MA: Harvard University Press, 2014.

Hammond, Carolyn J.-B., *Confessions, Volume II: Books 9–13*. Loeb Classical Library 27. Cambridge, MA: Harvard University Press, 2016.

King, Peter, trans. *On the Free Choice of the Will: On Grace and Free Choice; and Other Writings*. 2010 edn. Cambridge: Cambridge University Press, 2010.

Migne, Jacques-Paul, ed. *S. Aurelii Augustini Opera Omnia*. Patrologia Latina 32–45. Paris: 1841–6. http://www.augustinus.it/latino/discorsi/index2.htm.

Mountain, William J. Mountain and François Glorie, ed. *De Trinitate*. Corpus Christianorum Series Latina 50–50A. Turnholti: Brepols, 1968.

O'Donnell, James J. *Confessions: Introduction and Text*. Oxford: Clarendon, 2000. https://faculty.georgetown.edu/jod/conf/.

Sheed, Frank J., trans., Michael P. Foley, ed. *Confessions*. 2nd edn. Indianapolis, IN: Hackett, 2007.

Zycha, Iosephus, ed. *De Genesi ad litteram*. Corpus Scriptorum Ecclesiasticorum Latinorum 28, vol. 1. Vindobonae: Tempsky, 1894.

Heraclitus

Graham, Daniel W. *The Texts of Early Greek Philosophy: The Complete Fragments and Selected Testimonies of the Major Presocratics*. Cambridge: Cambridge University Press, 2010.

Kahn, Charles H. *The Art and Thought of Heraclitus: An Edition of the Fragments with Translation and Commentary*. Cambridge: Cambridge University Press, 1979.

McKirahan, Richard D. *Philosophy Before Socrates: An Introduction with Texts and Commentary*. 2nd edn. Indianapolis, IN: Hackett, 2011.

Seneca

Letters on Ethics: To Lucilius. Translated by Margaret Graver and Anthony A. Long. Chicago: University of Chicago Press, 2015.

Natural Questions. Translated by Harry Hine. Chicago: University of Chicago Press, 2010.

Secondary literature

Adamson, Peter. *A History of Philosophy Without Any Gaps: Classical Philosophy*. Oxford: Oxford University Press, 2016.

'Ancient Jewish Meditation Literature'. Video, 04:30. *YouTube*. Posted by BibleProject, 3 August 2017. Accessed 7 October 2023. https://youtu.be/VhmlJBUIoLk.

Arrien, Sophie-Jan. 'Penser sans Dieu, vivre avec Dieu: Heidegger lecteur d'Augustin'. *Esprit* Janvier, no. 1 (2013): 68–80. https://doi.org/10.3917/espri.1301.0068. See https://www.cairn.info/revue-esprit-2013-1-page-68.htm?contenu=article.

Beattie, Tina. *The New Atheists*. England: Darton, Longman & Todd, 2007.

Beierwaltes, Werner. 'Augustins Interpretation von Sapientia 11, 21'. *Revue des Études Augustiniennes* 15, no. 1–2 (1969): 51–61.

Bellafiore, Samuel. '*Musica Sanans*: Individual and Communal Reintegration in Augustine's *Expositions of the Psalms*'. *Sacred Music* 146, no. 2 (2019): 28–34.

Bendeck Sotillos, Samuel. 'The Inner and Outer Human Being'. *The Mountain Path* 60, no. 2 (2023): 9–26.

'Bernard Williams on Descartes: Section 5'. Video, 07:47. *YouTube*. Posted by Flame0430, 24 December 2008. Accessed 3 October 2023. https://youtu.be/2z-obRljOXY.

Bianco, Carmela. 'Insegnare agli ignoranti: Attualità della tradizione sul Maestro interiore'. *Asprenas: Rivista di Teologia* 62, no. 3 (2015): 171–86.

Boersma, Gerald P. *Augustine's Early Theology of Image: A Study in the Development of Pro-Nicene Theology*. New York: Oxford University Press, 2016.

Bouman, Johan, and Sven Gross. *Augustinus – Die Theologie seiner Predigten über die Psalmen.* Paderborn: Ferdinand Schöningh, 2019.

Bouton-Touboulic, Anne-Isabelle. 'Les Confessions d'Augustin: une métamorphose de la *parrhesia?*'. *Chôra* 11 (2013): 59–75. https://doi.org/10.5840/chora2013115.

Boven, Martijn. 'The Subtle Art of Plagiarizing God: Augustine's Dialogue with Divine Otherness'. In *Non Laborat Qui Amat,* edited by André P. DeBattista, Jonathan Farrugia, and Hector Scerri, 51–68. Valletta, Malta: Maltese Augustinian Province, 2020.

Brachtendorf, Johannes. 'Cicero and Augustine on the Passions'. *Revue des Études Augustiniennes* 43 (1997): 289–308.

Cameron, Averil. *Dialoguing in Late Antiquity.* Washington, DC: Center for Hellenic Studies, 2014.

Cavadini, John C. *Visioning Augustine.* Hoboken: Wiley/Blackwell, 2019.

Chaix-Ruy, Jules. 'Note: La création du monde d'après Augustin'. *Revue des Études Augustiniennes* 11, no. 1–2 (1965): 85–8.

Cherniss, Harold. 'The Characteristics and Effects of Presocratic Philosophy'. *Journal of the History of Ideas* 12, no. 3 (1951): 319–45. https://doi.org/10.2307/2707750.

Chrétien, Jean-Louis. *L'espace intérieur.* Paris: Éditions de Minuit, 2013.

Cilleruelo, Lope. '"Deum videre" en San Agustín'. *Salmanticensis* 12, no. 1 (1965): 3–31. https://doi.org/10.36576/summa.6565.

Cilleruelo, Lope. '¿Por qué "memoria Dei"?'. *Revue des Études Augustiniennes* 10, no. 4 (1964): 289–94.

Cilleruelo, Lope. 'Pro memoria Dei'. *Revue d'Études Augustiniennes et Patristiques* 12 (1966): 65–84.

Clark, Gillian. 'Can We Talk? Augustine and the Possibility of Dialogue'. In *The End of Dialogue in Antiquity,* edited by Simon Goldhill, 117–34. Cambridge, UK/New York: Cambridge University Press, 2008.

Clark, Margaret. *Understanding Religion and Spirituality in Clinical Practice.* London: Karnac Books, 2012.

Conybeare, Catherine. *The Irrational Augustine.* Oxford: Oxford University Press, 2009.

Conybeare, Catherine. '*Quotquot haec legerint meminerint*: All Who Read This Will Remember'. *MLN* 127, no. 5 (2012): S23–33. http://www.jstor.org/stable/41810220.

Coyne, Ryan. *Heidegger's Confessions: The Remains of Saint Augustine in 'Being and Time' and Beyond.* Chicago: University of Chicago Press, 2015.

Cushman, Robert Earl. *Therapeia: Plato's Conception of Philosophy.* New Brunswick, NJ/London: Transaction Books, 2002.

Dalferth, Ingolf U. 'What Does It Mean to Be Human?'. In *Kierkegaardian Essays: A Festschrift in Honour of George Pattison,* edited by

Christopher B. Barnett and Clare Carlisle, 1–14. Berlin: De Gruyter, 2022.

Dawkins, Richard. *The God Delusion*. New edn. Boston, MA: Mariner, 2008.

Desmond, William. 'Augustine's *Confessions*: On Desire, Conversion and Reflection'. *Irish Theological Quarterly* 47, no. 1 (1980): 24–33. https://doi.org/10.1177/002114008004700102.

Douglass, Laurie. 'Voice Re-Cast: Augustine's Use of Conversation in *De ordine* and the *Confessions*'. *Augustinian Studies* 27, no. 1 (1996): 39–54. https://doi.org/10.5840/augstudies19962712.

Drever, Matthew. 'Redeeming Creation: *Creatio ex nihilo* and the *Imago Dei* in Augustine'. *International Journal of Systematic Theology* 15, no. 2 (2013): 135–53. https://doi.org/10.1111/j.1468-2400.2012.00655.x.

Favry, Anne-Claire. 'Monter vers Dieu dans les larmes et la consolation – L'interprétation augustinienne de Mt 5, 5'. *Revista Agustiniana* 60, no. 181–2 (2019): 95–116. https://dialnet.unirioja.es/servlet/articulo?codigo=6945544.

Finkelberg, Aryeh. *Heraclitus and Thales' Conceptual Scheme*. Leiden: Brill, 2017.

Fischer, Norbert. 'Vom Berühren der ewigen Wahrheit. Zu Augustins christlicher Umdeutung der neuplatonischen Mystik'. *Acta Universitatis Carolinae Theologica* 3, no. 1 (2013): 37–64. https://doi.org/10.14712/23363398.2015.32.

Foley, Michael. 'Cicero, Augustine, and the Philosophical Roots of the Cassiciacum Dialogues'. *Revue des Études Augustiniennes* 45 (1999): 51–77.

Foley, Michael. 'A Spectacle to the World: The Theatrical Meaning of St. Augustine's *Soliloquies*'. *Journal of Early Christian Studies* 22, no. 2 (2014): 243–60. https://doi.org/10.1353/earl.2014.0024.

Fuhrer, Therese. 'Augustine on Rhetoric and Dialectic in Theory and Practice'. *Classica – Revista Brasileira de Estudos Clássicos* 19, no. 1 (2006): 99–114. https://doi.org/10.24277/classica.v19i1.107.

Fuhrer, Therese. 'Conversationalist and Consultant: Augustine in Dialogue'. In *A Companion to Augustine*, edited by Mark Vessey, 270–83. Blackwell Companions to the Ancient World. Malden, MA/Oxford/Chichester: Wiley Blackwell, 2012.

Gardella, Mariana. 'Heráclito de Éfeso, Cleobulina de Lindos y la tradición de los enigmas'. *Revista de Filosofía* 46, no. 1 (2021): 45–62.

Gordon, Mick. *On Religion*. London: Oberon Books, 2006.

Grand, Steven. *Creation: Life and How to Make It*. London: Weidenfeld & Nicholson, 2000.

Guthrie, William K. C. *History of Greek Philosophy I: The Earlier Presocratics and the Pythagoreans*. Cambridge: Cambridge University Press, 1962.

Hadot, Pierre, and Michael Chase. *Philosophy as a Way of Life: Spiritual Exercises from Socrates to Foucault*. Edited by Arnold Ira Davidson. Malden, MA: Blackwell Publishing, 2017.

Halapsis, Alex V. 'Man and *Logos*: Heraclitus' Secret'. *Anthropological Measurements of Philosophical Research* 17 (2020): 119–30.

Hampson, Peter J., and Johannes Hoff. 'Whose Self? Which Unification? Augustine's Anthropology and the Psychology-theology Debate'. *New Blackfriars* 91, no. 1035 (2010): 546–66. https://doi.org/10.1111/j.1741-2005.2009.01340.x.

Hankey, Wayne J. '"Knowing as We Are Known" in *Confessions* 10 and Other Philosophical, Augustinian and Christian Obedience to the Delphic *Gnothi Seauton* from Socrates to Modernity'. *Augustinian Studies* 34, no. 1 (2003): 23–48. https://doi.org/10.5840/augstudies20033413. Available at https://www.academia.edu/11708435/_Knowing_as_we_are_Known_in_Confessions_10_and_Other_Philosophical_Augustinian_and_Christian_Obedience_to_the_Delphic_Gnothi_Seauton_from_Socrates_to_Modernity_.

Hannan, Sean. 'To See Coming: Augustine and Heidegger on the Arising and Passing Away of Things'. *Medieval Mystical Theology* 21, no. 1 (2012): 75–91.

Heidegger, Martin. *Being and Time*. Translated by John Macquarrie and Edward Robinson. Oxford, UK/Cambridge, MA: Blackwell, 2001.

Henry, Desmond Paul. *The Logic of Saint Anselm*. Oxford: Clarendon, 1967.

Herzog, Reinhart. 'Non in sua voce: Augustins Gespräch mit Gott in den Confessiones – Voraussetzungen und Folgen'. In *Spätantike: Studien zur romischen und lateinisch-christlichen Literatur*, with an Introduction by Manfred Fuhrmann, edited by Peter Habermehl, 213–50. Göttingen: Vandenhoeck & Ruprecht, 2002. https://doi.org/10.13109/9783666252709.235.

Horn, Christoph. 'Augustins Philosophie der Zahlen'. *Revue des Études Augustiniennes* 40 (1994): 389–415.

Huian, Georgiana. 'The Mystery of the Human Being in Augustine: In Quest of the Foundations of an Apophatic Anthropology'. *New Europe College Ştefan Odobleja Program Yearbook 2015–2016* (2017): 51–92. https://www.academia.edu/37420611/The_Mystery_of_the_Human_Being_in_Augustine_In_Quest_of_the_Foundations_of_an_Apophatic_Anthropology.

Hwang, Eun Young. 'The Paradoxical Place of the Self: Augustine and Zhi Yi on the Question of the Self and World Experience and the Revelatory Power of Self-Inspection'. *Buddhist-Christian Studies* 37 (2017): 173–90. http://www.jstor.org/stable/44632365.

Jeanmart, Gaëlle. *Herméneutique et Subjectivité dans les* Confessions *d'Augustin*. Turnhout: Brepols, 2006.

Johnstone, Mark A. 'On "*Logos*" in Heraclitus'. *Oxford Studies in Ancient Philosophy* 47 (2014): 1–29.

Kenyon, Erik. *Augustine and the Dialogue*. Cambridge: Cambridge University Press, 2018.

Kenyon, Erik. 'Platonic Pedagogy in Augustine's Dialogues'. *Ancient Philosophy* 34, no. 1 (2014): 151–68. https://doi.org/10.5840/ancientphil20143419.

Köckert, Charlotte. 'Augustine and Nebridius (Augustine, epp. 3–14): Two Christian Intellectuals and Their Project of a Philosophical Life'. *Revue d'Études Augustiniennes et Patristiques* 62 (2016): 235–62.

Komatsu, Koji. 'On the Dialectic Nature of Human Mind: The Dynamic Tension between Sameness and Non-Sameness'. *Integrative Psychological and Behavioral Science* 50, no. 1 (2015): 174–83. https://doi.org/10.1007/s12124-015-9325-3.

Komatsu, Koji. 'Temporal Reticence of the Self: Who Can Know My Self?'. *Integrative Psychological and Behavioral Science* 46, no. 3 (2012): 357–72. https://doi.org/10.1007/s12124-012-9199-6.

Lagouanère, Jérôme. 'Agustín lector de Séneca: el caso de la *bona uoluntas*'. *Augustinus* 64, no. 252–3 (2019): 193–202.

Lagouanère, Jérôme. 'Le *De Quantitate Animae* d'Augustin, un dialogue philosophique?'. *Zeitschrift für Antikes Christentum/Journal of Ancient Christianity* 23, no. 2 (2019): 252–87. https://doi.org/10.1515/zac-2019-0014.

Löhr, Winrich. 'Christianity as Philosophy: Problems and Perspectives of an Ancient Intellectual Project'. *Vigiliae Christianae* 64, no. 2 (2010): 160–88.

Lössl, Josef. 'The One (unum) – A Guiding Concept in "De vera religione". An Outline of the Text and the History of Its Interpretation'. *Revue des Études Augustiniennes* 40 (1994): 79–103.

Lotz, Christian. 'Responsive Life and Speaking to the Other'. *Augustinian Studies* 37, no. 1 (2006): 89–109. https://doi.org/10.5840/augstudies20063714. Available at https://www.academia.edu/28743190/_Responsive_Life_and_Speaking_To_the_Other_A_Phenomenological_Interpretation_of_Book_One_of_Augustine_s_Confessions_in_Augustinian_Studies_2006_37_1_2006_89_109.

Madec, Goulven. 'Note: Pour et contre la "memoria Dei": Réponse à L. Cilleruelo et J. Moran'. *Revue d'Études Augustiniennes et Patristiques* 11, no. 1–2 (1965): 89–92.

Marion, Jean-Luc. 'Resting, Moving, Loving: The Access to the Self According to Saint Augustine'. *The Journal of Religion* 91, no. 1 (2011): 24–42. https://doi.org/10.1086/656605.

Markus, Robert A. '"Imago" and "Similitudo" in Augustine'. *Revue des Études Augustiniennes* 10, no. 2–3 (1964): 125–43.

Mathewes, Charles. 'Augustinian Anthropology: *Interior intimo meo*'. *The Journal of Religious Ethics* 27, no. 2 (Summer 1999): 195–221.

Mathewes, Charles. 'The Liberation of Questioning in Augustine's "Confessions"'. *Journal of the American Academy of Religion* 70, no. 3 (2002): 539–60. http://www.jstor.org/stable/1466523.

Mathewes, Charles. 'Pluralism, Otherness, and the Augustinian Tradition'. *Modern Theology* 14, no. 1 (1998): 83–112. https://doi.org/10.1111/1468-0025.00057.

Maybee, Julie E. 'Hegel's Dialectics'. *Stanford Encyclopedia of Philosophy*. Last modified 2 October 2020. Accessed 3 October 2023. https://plato.stanford.edu/entries/hegel-dialectics/.

Michel, Alain. 'Dialogue philosophique et vie intérieure: Cicéron, Sénèque, Saint Augustin'. *Helmantica* 28 (1977): 353–76.

Miles, Richard. '"Let's (Not) Talk about It": Augustine and the Control of Epistolary Dialogue'. In *The End of Dialogue in Antiquity*, edited by Simon Goldhill, 134–48. Cambridge, UK/New York: Cambridge University Press, 2008.

Miller, Jacques-Alain. 'Extimité'. *Prose Studies* 11, no. 3 (1988): 121–31.

Miller, Patrick Lee. *Becoming God: Pure Reason in Ancient Greek Philosophy*. London: Continuum, 2011.

Milusheva, Iglika. 'Das Bild des *inmanissimus mons* in Augustins Frühschrift *De Beata Vita*'. *Acta Antiqua Academiae Scientiarum Hungaricae* 56, no. 1 (2016): 119–26. https://doi.org/10.1556/068.2016.56.1.7.

Mohrmann, Christine. 'Saint Augustin écrivain'. *Revue d'Études Augustiniennes et Patristiques* 50, no. 1 (2004): 123–46.

Most, Glenn W. 'Heraclitus Fragment B123 DK'. In *What Reason Promises Essays on Reason, Nature and History*, edited by Wendy Doniger, Peter Galison, and Susan Neiman, 117–23. Berlin/Boston, 2016. https://doi.org/10.1515/9783110455113-016.

Müller, Christof, and Guntram Förster. *Dialog und Dialoge bei Augustinus: Vermehrte Beiträge des 14. Würzburger Augustinus-Studientages vom 17. Juni 2016*. Würzburg: Augustinus bei Echter, 2019.

Narecki, Krzysztof. 'The Image of the River in the Fragments of Heraclitus'. *Philotheos* 12 (2012): 66–77. https://doi.org/10.5840/philotheos2012126.

Neels, Richard. 'Elements and Opposites in Heraclitus'. *Apeiron* 51, no. 4 (2018): 1–26. https://doi.org/10.1515/apeiron-2017-0029.

New American Bible Revised Edition. New American Bible. Accessed 7 October 2023. https://www.biblegateway.com/.

Nordlander, Andreas. 'The Emergence of Soul: Retrieving Augustine's Potentialism for Contemporary Theological Anthropology'. *Modern*

Theology 35, no. 1 (2018): 122–37. https://doi.org/10.1111/
moth.12443.

O'Daly, Gerard J. P. 'Two Kinds of Subjectivity in Augustine's
Confessions: Memory and Identity, and the Integrated Self'. In *Ancient
Philosophy of the Self*, edited by Pauliina Remes and Juha Sihvola,
195–203. The New Synthese Historical Library 64. Dordrecht:
Springer, 2008. https://doi.org/10.1007/978-1-4020-8596-3_10.

O'Donovan, Oliver. *The Problem of Self-Love in St. Augustine*. New
Haven, CT: Yale University Press, 1980.

Ong-Van-Cung, Kim Sang. 'Le moi et l'intériorité chez Augustin et
Descartes'. *Chôra* 9 (2011): 321–38. https://doi.org/10.5840/
chora2011/20129/1016.

Otten, Willemien. 'Does the Canon Need Converting? A Meditation on
Augustine's *Soliloquies*, Eriugena's *Periphyseon*, and the Dialogue with
the Religious Past'. In *How the West Was Won: Essays on Literary
Imagination, the Canon and the Christian Middle Ages for Burcht
Pranger*, edited by Willemien Otten, Arjo J. Vanderjagt, and Hent De
Vries, 195–223. Brill's Studies in Intellectual History 188. Leiden: Brill,
2010. https://doi.org/10.1163/ej.9789004184961.i-422.72.

Parsons, William Barclay. *Freud and Augustine in Dialogue:
Psychoanalysis, Mysticism, and the Culture of Modern Spirituality*.
Charlottesville: University of Virginia Press, 2013.

Patativa de Sales, Antonio. 'Hermenêutica e estile literário no "primeiro" e
"segundo Agostinho"'. *Civitas Augustiniana* 5 (2016): 9–29.

Penrose, Roger, and Robert Lawrence Kuhn. 'Is Mathematics Invented or
Discovered?'. Video, 04:14. *Closer to Truth*. Accessed 6 October 2023.
https://closertotruth.com/video/penro-003/?referrer=7983.

Plato. *Thaetetus*. Translated by Mary Jane Levett with an Introduction
by Bernard Williams. Indianapolis/Cambridge: Hackett Publishing
Company, 1992.

Porter, James I. 'Time for Foucault? Reflections on the Roman Self from
Seneca to Augustine'. *Foucault Studies*, 6 January 2017, 113–33.
https://doi.org/10.22439/fs.v0i0.5247.

Portier, William L. *Tradition and Incarnation: Foundations of Christian
Theology*. New York/Mahwah, NJ: Paulist Press, 1994.

Praet, Dany. 'Augustine of Hippo and Michel Foucault's History of
Sexuality'. In *Nos sumus tempora: Studies on Augustine and His
Reception Offered to Mathijs Lamberigts*, edited by Anthony Dupont,
Wim François and Johan Leemans, 213–35. Bibliotheca Ephemeridum
Theologicarum Lovaniensium 316. Leuven, Paris and Bristol:
Peeters, 2020.

Pugh, Jeffrey C. 'Searching for Myself'. In *The Matrix of Faith: Reclaiming
a Christian Vision*, 28–39. New York: Crossroad Pub., 2001.

Reidbord, Steven, MD. 'Dialectics in Psychotherapy an Introduction to the Meaning and Central Role of Dialectics in Therapy'. *Psychology Today*. Last modified 13 September 2019. Accessed 3 October 2023. https://www.psychologytoday.com/us/blog/sacramento-street-psychiatry/201909/dialectics-inpsychotherapy#:~:text=Broadly%20speaking%2C%20a%20dialectic%20is,arguments%2C%20is%20a%20classic%20example.

Religions and Ethics Newsweekly. 'Looking Back: Rituals'. Video, 05:12. *PBS.org*. 24 February 2017. Accessed 7 October 2023. https://www.pbs.org/video/religion-and-ethics-newsweekly-looking-back-rituals/.

Remes, Pauliina. 'Inwardness and Infinity of Selfhood: From Plotinus to Augustine'. In *Ancient Philosophy of the Self*, edited by Pauliina Remes, and Juha Sihvola, 155–76. Dordrecht: Springer, 2008.

Ribreau, Mickaël. 'Une écoute individuelle en contexte collectif. Étude de la deuxième personne dans quelques sermons d'Augustin'. *Revue d'histoire des religions* 233, no. 4 (2016): 505–31.

Rist, John M. *What Is a Person?: Realities, Constructs, Illusions*. Cambridge/New York/Port Melbourne/New Delhi/Singapore: Cambridge University Press, 2020.

Sassi, Maria Michela, and Michele Asuni. *The Beginnings of Philosophy in Greece*. Princeton: Princeton University Press, 2020.

Schütz, Achim. 'Die mehrdimensionale Theo-Logik der Polarität: Anmerkungen zum Denken von E. Przywara'. *Lateranum* 81, no. 1 (2015): 69–99.

Shusterman, Richard. *Thinking Through the Body: Essays in Somaesthetics*. Cambridge: Cambridge University Press, 2012.

Star, Christopher. *Seneca*. London: I.B. Tauris & Co., 2016.

Stock, Brian. *Augustine's Inner Dialogue: The Philosophical Soliloquy in Late Antiquity*. New York: Cambridge University Press, 2010.

Stock, Brian. *The Integrated Self: Augustine, the Bible, and Ancient Thought*. Philadelphia, PA: University of Pennsylvania Press, 2017.

Stock, Brian. 'Self, Soliloquy, and Spiritual Exercises in Augustine and Some Later Authors'. *The Journal of Religion* 91, no. 1 (2011): 5–23. https://doi.org/10.1086/656604.

Stroumsa, Guy G. 'The New Self and Reading Practices in Late Antique Christianity'. *Church History and Religious Culture* 95, no. 1 (2015): 1–18. http://www.jstor.org/stable/43946197.

Svensson, Manfred. '*Scientia y sapientia* en *De Trinitate* XII: San Agustín y las formas de la racionalidad'. *Teolgía y Vida* 51 (2010): 79–103.

Sweeney, Terence. 'God and the Soul: Augustine on the Journey to True Selfhood'. *The Heythrop Journal* 57, no. 4 (2014): 678–91. https://doi.org/10.1111/heyj.12166.

Thiel, Rainer. 'Zum philosophischen und philosophisch-theologischen Dialog in der paganen und christlichen Spätantike'. In *Der Dialog in der Antike: Formen und Funktionen einer literarischen Gattung zwischen Philosophie, Wissensvermittlung und dramatischer Inszenierung*, edited by Sabine Föllinger and Gernot Michael Müller, 141–52. Berlin/Boston: De Gruyter, 2013. https://doi. org/10.1515/9783110311945.141.

Ticciati, Susannah. *A New Apophaticism: Augustine and the Redemption of Signs*. Studies in Systematic Theology 14. Leiden: Brill, 2013.

Tornau, Christian. 'Ratio in subiecto? The Sources of Augustine's Proof for the Immortality of the Soul in the *Soliloquia* and Its Defense in *De immortalitate animae*'. *Phronesis* 62 (2017): 319–54.

Tracy, David W. 'Augustine Our Contemporary: The Overdetermined, Incomprehensible Self'. In *Augustine Our Contemporary: Examining the Self in Past and Present*, edited by Willemien Otten and Susan E. Schreiner, 27–73. Notre Dame, IN: University of Notre Dame Press, 2018. https://doi.org/10.2307/j.ctvpj7567.4.

Turner, Denys. 'The Darkness of God and the Light of Christ: Negative Theology and Eucharistic Presence'. *Modern Theology* 15, no. 2 (1999): 143–58. https://doi.org/10.1111/1468-0025.00091.

Uhle, Tobias. *Augustin und die Dialektik: Eine Untersuchung der Argumentationsstruktur in den Cassiciacum-Dialogen*. Tübingen: Mohr Siebeck, 2012.

Uhle, Tobias. 'Philosophisches Argument und literarische Form in Augustins *Soliloquia*'. In *Argument und literarische Form in antiker Philosophie: Akten des 3. Kongresses der Gesellschaft für antike Philosophie 2010*, edited by Michael Erler and Jan Erik Heßler, 541–64. Berlin/Boston: De Gruyter, 2013.

Vannier, Marie-Anne. 'Aversion and Conversion'. In *The Cambridge Companion to Augustine's 'Confessions'*, edited by Tarmo Toom, 63–74. Cambridge: Cambridge University Press, 2020. https://doi. org/10.1017/9781108672405.007.

Vieira, Celso. 'Heraclitus' Bow Composition'. *The Classical Quarterly* 63, no. 2 (2013): 473–90. https://doi.org/10.1017/s0009838813000037.

Wehrle, Maren. 'Being a Body and Having a Body: The Twofold Temporality of Embodied Intentionality'. *Phenomenology and the Cognitive Sciences* 19, no. 3 (2019): 499–521. https://doi.org/10.1007/s11097-019-09610-z.

Woollcott, Philip. 'Some Considerations of Creativity and Religious Experience in St. Augustine of Hippo'. *Journal for the Scientific Study of Religion* 5, no. 2 (1966): 273–83.

Yountae, An. 'The Dialectical Abyss'. In *The Decolonial Abyss: Mysticism and Cosmopolitics from the Ruins*, 47–82. New York: Fordham University Press, 2017.

INDEX